DATE DUE

Demco, Inc. 38-293

ERZSÉBET HEGYI

SOLFEGE ACCORDING
TO THE
KODÁLY-CONCEPT
II

ERZSÉBET HEGYI

SOLFEGE ACCORDING TO THE KODÁLY-CONCEPT II

INTERMEDIATE LEVEL

CHAPTERS VI TO IX

EDITIO MUSICA BUDAPEST 1979

Edited in co-operation with the ZOLTÁN KODÁLY PEDAGOGICAL INSTITUTE OF MUSIC
(Kecskemét, Hungary)

Translated by KATA ITTZÉS

Revised by Alexander Farkas

ISBN 963 330 273 0 Complete Works
ISBN 963 010 118 1 Volume I
ISBN 963 330 274 9 Volume II

CONTENTS

Introduction 17

CHAPTER VI

(Material in staff notation uses E flat and E as "d".)

Kodály material 21

Unison pentatonic melodies
  Material in staff notation: 333 Reading Exercises *21*.
  Material in solfa notation: Pentatonic Music I—IV; 333 Reading Exercises
            Familiar elements (♪♫; ¢ ; $\frac{5}{4}$) *22*. New elements (Minor seventh down-
            wards; Major ninth upwards; Augmentation and diminution; Alterna-
            tion of $\frac{5}{8}$ and $\frac{6}{8}$; Tonal and real fifth-change; Five-line melody; Two-line
            melody as a period; Heteropody; Organically built melody) *22*. Easy
            melodies for practising note name singing *26*.
Two-part material
  Preparatory exercises: "Let Us Sing Correctly" *27*.
  Two-part works
    Pentatonic range of notes *27*.
            Bicinia Hungarica IV/126,124,137,146 *28*. Suggested further exercises *29*.
    Diatonic range of notes
            Bicinia Hungarica I/44,37,39 *30*. Bicinia Hungarica III/114 *32*.
    Range including altered notes
            Bicinia Hungarica I/60 *32*. 66 Two-Part Exercises 51,23,45 *32*. 44 Two-
            Part Exercises 29 *35*. Suggested further exercise *35*.
    Modulating musical material
            77 Two-Part Exercises 69 *36*. Fifteen Two-Part Exercises 14 *37*.
    Bitonality in the two-part material
            Bicinia Hungarica II/66 *39*.

Theoretical information and technical exercises 41

Range of notes, hand-signs

> Pentatony (Note name singing to hand-signs) *41*. Diatony (Note name singing to hand-signs) *41*. Diatony + alteration (Solfa singing from staff notation; Solfa-note name singing in answering form; Practising change of key from hand-signs) *42*.

Keys and modes

> The pentatonic modes (With E♭ and E as "d"; From the same key-note) *44*. Major and minor keys with three flats or four sharps (Forms of practising the minor) *45*. Note finding exercises in major and harmonic minor (In E♭ and E major; In C and C♯ minor) *46*. Church modes (New method of practising the comparative names; Singing to note names) *46*. Summary of the note groups within pentatony, diatony and the harmonic minor system *47*. Transformed singing *50*.

Intervals

> Intervals within the pentatonic modes *56*. Practice of fourths and fifths *56*. The intervals of the harmonic minor pentachords *58*. New forms of practising the sixths *59*. The intervals of the first and second inversion triads in major *60*.

Chords

> Triadic functions *61*. Singing exercises for practising chord functions *62*. Other forms of practising the triads *63*. Seventh chords (In the major and harmonic minor keys; The types of seventh chords; Inversions of the seventh chords) *64*. Singing exercises with the seventh chords *65*. Harmonic analysis *67*.

Sight-singing 77

Unison extracts from the musical literature
  Material in staff notation

> Melodies in pentatonic and church modes *77*. Major and minor melodies (Remaining in the same key signature; With "d" change; Suggested further material) *80*.

  Extracts in solfa notation *85*.
Material in several parts *88*.

Development of musical memory 107

Memorizing and transposing a unison melody *107*.
Memorizing and transposing two-part material *108*.
Memorizing three-part material *111*.
Memorizing chord progressions *115*.

Ear training **117**

Recognition of intervals

       Interval progressions within the major and minor tonality *117*. Intervals in the diatonic hexachords *117*. Intervals within the pentatonic modes *118*. Interval recognition from "Let Us Sing Correctly" *118*.

Chord recognition

       Root position triad, 6 chord and $\frac{6}{4}$ chord from a given scale degree *118*. Seventh chords (Type recognition; Seventh chords placed within tonality) *119*. First inversion seventh chords (Type recognition; $\frac{6}{5}$ chords placed within tonality) *120*. Chord progressions *121*.

Rhythm dictation *121*.

Kodály: 24 Little Canons *122*.

Melody dictation

       One-part dictation *122*. Two-part dictation *123*.

Bach chorale extracts *125*.

Planning suggestion **126**

CHAPTER VII

(Material in staff notation uses A and A flat as "d".)

Kodály material **129**

Unison pentatonic melodies

  Material in solfa notation: Pentatonic Music I—IV; 333 Reading Exercises

       New elements (Alternation of $\frac{5}{4}$ and $\frac{4}{4}$; Major tenth upwards; Alternation of $\frac{3}{8}$ and $\frac{4}{8}$; Alternation of metres with different metrical units) *129*. Easy melodies for practising note name singing *131*.

Two-part material

  Preparatory exercises: "Let Us Sing Correctly" *132*.

  Two-part works

    Pentatonic range of notes *132*.

    Diatonic range of notes

       44 Two-Part Exercises 22, Var.11 *133*. Bicinia Hungarica III/110 *133*. 55 Two-Part Exercises 27 *134*.

    Range including altered notes

       55 Two-Part Exercises 5,20 *134*. 66 Two-Part Exercises 40 *136*. Suggested further exercises *137*.

    Modulating musical material

       66 Two-Part Exercises 27 *137*. 33 Two-Part Exercises 2 *139*. 44 Two-Part Exercises 18 *140*. 33 Two-Part Exercises 3 *142*. 66 Two-Part Exercises 44 *142*. Suggested further exercises *146*.

Three-part material
        Tricinia 3 *147.*
Melody with piano accompaniment
        Epigrams 4,1 *150.*

Theoretical information and technical exercises 153

Range of notes, hand-signs
        Pentatony (Note name singing to hand-signs) *153.* Diatony (Note name singing to hand-signs) *153.* Diatony + alteration (Solfa singing from staff notation; Solfa-note name singing in answering form; Note name singing to hand-signs with change of key) *153.*
Keys and modes
        The pentatonic modes (With A and A♭ as "d"; From the same key-note) *155.* Major and minor keys with three sharps or four flats (Forms of practising the minor) *155.* Note finding exercises in major and harmonic minor *156.* Church modes (The characteristic intervals of the modes; Forms of practising the intervals; Note name singing of the modes) *156.* Transformed singing *159.*
Intervals
        New forms of practising fifths and sixths *163.* The intervals of the first and second inversion triads in harmonic minor *164.* The intervals of the harmonic minor hexachords *165.* Practice of sevenths *165.* General revision exercises with the interval types of pentatony *166.*
Chords
        Triads *167.* Seventh chords *167.* Harmonic analysis *169.*

Sight-singing 187

Unison extracts from the musical literature
  Material in staff notation
        Melodies in pentatonic and church modes *187.* Major and minor melodies (Remaining in the same key signature; With "d" change; Suggested further material) *190.*
  Extracts in solfa notation *196.*
Material in several parts *198.*

Development of musical memory 215

Memorizing and transposing a unison melody *215.*
Memorizing and transposing two-part material *215.*
Memorizing three-part material *217.*
Memorizing and transposing chord progressions *220.*

Ear training 223

Recognition of intervals
> Interval progressions within the major and minor tonality *223*. The intervals of the harmonic minor pentachords *223*. The intervals of the first and second inversion triads *224*. Interval recognition from "Let Us Sing Correctly" *225*. The characteristic intervals of the modes *225*.

Chord recognition
> Second inversion seventh chords (Type recognition; $\frac{4}{3}$ chords placed within tonality) *226*. Third inversion seventh chords (Type recognition; $\frac{4}{2}$ chords placed within tonality) *226*. Seventh chord and its inversions from a given note of the major key *226*. Chord progressions (Recognition with the help of singing; Recognition with the help of inner hearing) *227*.

Rhythm dictation *227*.
Melody dictation *228*.
> One-part dictation *228*. Two-part dictation *228*.

Bach chorale extracts *229*.

Planning suggestion 230

CHAPTER VIII
(Material in staff notation uses D and D flat as "d".)

Kodály material 233

Unison pentatonic melodies
> Material in staff notation: 333 Reading Exercises *233*.
>> New elements ($\frac{7}{4}$ metre; $4+\frac{4}{}$ melodic beginning) *233*. Familiar elements (Tripody; Isorhythm; Descending fifth-change with pentatonic sixth) *234*.
> Material in solfa notation: Pentatonic Music I—IV; 333 Reading Exercises
>> New elements ($\frac{7}{4}$ metre) *234*. Familiar elements (Alternation of metres with constant metrical units; Alternation of metres with different metrical units) *235*. Easy melodies for practising note name singing *238*.

Two-part material
> Preparatory exercises: "Let Us Sing Correctly" *239*.
> Two-part works
>> Pentatonic range of notes: One-system pentatonic themes *239*.
>>> Bicinia Hungarica IV/150 *240*. Suggested further exercises *241*.
>> Pentatonic range of notes: Two-system pentatonic themes
>>> Bicinia Hungarica IV/158, 130, 160, 170 *241*. Suggested further exercise *246*.

Diatonic range of notes
      Bicinia Hungarica II/89 *246*. Suggested further exercises *246*.
Range including altered notes
      55 Two-Part Exercises 21, 38 *247*. Suggested further exercise *249*.
Modulating musical material
      66 Two-Part Exercises 59 *249*. 44 Two-Part Exercises 19 *251*. 66 Two-Part Exercises 61 *253*. 44 Two-Part Exercises 39 *254*. Suggested further exercises *256*.
Three-part material
      Tricinia 4.17 *257*.

Theoretical information and technical exercises 261

Range of notes, hand-signs
      Pentatony (Note name singing to hand-signs) *261*. Diatony (Note name singing to hand-signs) *261*. Diatony + alteration (Solfa singing from staff notation; Solfa-note name singing in answering form; Practising change of key from hand-signs) *261*.
Keys and modes
      The pentatonic modes with D and D♭ as "d" *264*. Two-system pentatony (Practising two-system pentatonic modes) *264*. Major and minor keys with two sharps or five flats (Forms of practising the minor) *266*. Note finding exercises in major and harmonic minor *267*. Church modes *268*. Transformed singing *268*.
Intervals
      New forms of practising sixths and sevenths *271*. Singing augmented and diminished intervals (Augmented 2nd; Diminished 3rd; Augmented 4th; Diminished 5th) *272*. Combined sequences of fourths and fifths *274*.
Metre *276*.
Chords
      Revision exercises *276*. Altered chords within functional harmony *276*. Secondary dominants (The type of secondary dominants; Secondary dominants in the major and minor keys; Singing exercises with secondary dominants) *277*. Secondary dominants in chain-like succession *282*. Harmonic analysis *283*.

Sight-singing 301

Unison extracts from the musical literature
   Material in staff notation
      Melodies in pentatonic and church modes *301*. Major and minor melodies (Remaining in the same key signature; With "d" change; Suggested further material) *305*.
   Extracts in solfa notation *310*.
Material in several parts *313*.

Development of musical memory 329

Memorizing and transposing two-part material *329.*
Memorizing and transposing three-part material *331.*
Memorizing and transposing chord progressions *333.*
Memorizing choral extracts *335.*

Ear training 339

Recognition of intervals
      Interval progressions within the major and minor tonality *339.* The intervals of the harmonic minor hexachords *339.* The interval types of pentatony from a given note *339.* Pairs of intervals not derived from the triads *340.* Interval successions independent of tonality *341.*
Chord recognition
      Seventh chord and its inversions from a given tone of the harmonic minor key *341.* Secondary dominants in major and minor tonality *342.* Chord progressions (Recognition with the help of singing; Recognition with the help of inner hearing) *342.* Chord analysis of quotations taken from musical literature by ear *343.*
Rhythm dictation *343.*
Kodály: 24 Little Canons *343.*
Melody dictation
      One-part dictation *344.* Two-part dictation *344.* Two- and three-part canons *344.*
Bach chorale extracts *345.*

Planning suggestion 346

CHAPTER IX

(Material in staff notation uses G and G flat as "d".)

Kodály material 349

Unison pentatonic melodies
  Material in staff notation: 333 Reading Exercises *349.*
  Material in solfa notation: Pentatonic Music I,IV; 333 Reading Exercises
      Melodies for practising more difficult musical elements ($\frac{5}{8}$; Alternation of $\frac{2}{4}$ and $\frac{6}{8}$) *349.* Melodies for practising note name singing *350.*

Two-part material
  Preparatory exercises: "Let Us Sing Correctly" *350.*
  Two-part works
    Pentatonic range of notes: Two-system pentatonic theme
      77 Two-Part Exercises 54 *350.*
    Pentatonic range of notes: Bitonality in the two-part material
      Bicinia Hungarica II/72 *352.*
    Range including altered notes
      Bicinia Hungarica III/113 *353.* Suggested further exercise *353.*
    Modulating musical material
      Fifteen Two-Part Exercises 7 *354.* Bicinia Hungarica I/59 *355.* 55 Two-Part Exercises 34 *356.* Fifteen Two-Part Exercises 12 *358.* 66 Two-Part Exercises 49 *359.* 33 Two-Part Exercises 1 *361.* 44 Two-Part Exercises 13 *361.* 33 Two-Part Exercises 27 *364.* 22 Two-Part Exercises 4 *365.* Suggested further exercises *368.*
Three-part material
    Tricinia 7,24,25 *369.* Suggested further works *373.*
Melody with piano accompanimet
    Epigrams 6 *373.* Suggested further work *374.*

Theoretical information and technical exercises 375

Range of notes, hand-signs
    Pentatony (Note name singing to hand-signs) *375.* Diatony (Note name singing to hand-signs) *375.* Diatony + alteration (Solfa singing from staff notation; Solfa-note name singing in answering form; Singing to hand-signs with change of key) *375.*
Keys and modes
    The pentatonic modes (With G and G♭ as "d"; Combined singing exercises) *377.* Major and minor keys with one sharp or six flats (Forms of practising the minor) *378.* Note finding exercises in major and harmonic minor *379.* Church modes *379.* Transformed singing (Themes changing mode; Themes sounding in the harmonic and melodic minor system; Diatonic themes remaining in the same tonality) *380.*
Intervals
    New diminished and augmented intervals (Diminished 4th; Augmented 5th; Augmented 6th; Diminished 7th) *383.* General revision exercises with the interval types of diatony *384.* Practising pairs of intervals changing direction *385.*
Chords
    Parallel chords in major *387.* Neapolitan sixth-chord *388.* Chords with augmented sixth *389.* Ninth chords (In major and minor) *389.* Enharmonic re-interpretations (Re-interpretation of the diminished seventh chord; Re-interpretation of the augmented $\frac{6}{5}$ chord and the dominant seventh chord) *392.* Harmonic analysis *393.*

Sight-singing 415

Unison extracts from the musical literature
   Material in staff notation
         Melodies in pentatonic and church modes *415*. Major and minor melodies
         (Remaining in the same key signature; With "d" change; Suggested
         further material) *418*.
   Extracts in solfe notation *423*.
Material in several parts *425*.

Development of musical memory 445

Memorizing and transposing two-part material *445*.
Memorizing and transposing three-part material *447*.
Memorizing and transposing chord progressions *451*.
Memorizing chorale extracts *454*.

Ear training 457

Recognition of intervals
         Pairs of intervals not derived from the triads *457*. Interval successions
         independent of tonality *457*. The interval types of diatony from a given
         note *457*. Diminished and augmented intervals *458*.
Chord recognition
         Seventh chord and its inversions from a given tone of the minor key *459*.
         Ninth chords within the major and minor tonality *459*. Characteristic
         altered subdominant chords *460*. Chord progressions (Recognition with
         the help of singing; Recognition with the help of inner hearing) *461*.
         Chord analysis of quotations taken from the musical literature by ear *461*.
Rhythm dictation *461*.
Melody dictation
         One-part dictation *462*. Two-part dictation *462*. Two- and three-part
         canons *463*.
Bach chorale extracts *463*.

Planning suggestion 464

SUPPLEMENT

Musical material for ear-training exercises

Chapter VI 467

Rhythm dictation 467
Melody dictation 471
  One-part dictation
       Melodies in pentatonic and church modes *471*. Major and minor melo-
       dies *474*.
  Two-part dictation
       Concentration on the vertical sounding *477*. Concentration on the hori-
       zontal melodic movement *479*.
Bach chorale extracts 481
  Two-part continuous writing *481*.
  Memorizing and writing down the bass *484*.

Chapter VII 485

Rhythm dictation 485
Melody dictation 489
  One-part dictation
       Melodies in pentatonic and church modes *489*. Major and minor melo-
       dies *492*.
  Two-part dictation
       Concentration on the vertical sounding *495*. Concentration on the hori-
       zontal melodic movement *497*.
Bach chorale extracts 500
  Two-part continuous writing *500*.
  Memorizing and writing down the bass of modulating musical material *503*.

Chapter VIII 505

Rhythm dictation 505
Melody dictation 509
  One-part dictation
       Melodies in pentatonic and church modes *509*. Major and minor melo-
       dies *512*.
  Two-part dictation
       Concentration on the vertical sounding *515*. Concentration on the hori-
       zontal melodic movement *517*.
  Two- and three-part canons *521*.

Bach chorale extracts 523
  Two-part continuous writing completed by figured bass notation *523.*
  Two-part continuous writing of modulating musical material *526.*

Chapter IX 529

Rhythm dictation 529
Melody dictation 533
  One-part dictation
        Melodies in pentatonic and church modes *533.* Major and minor melo-
        dies *536.*
  Two-part dictation
        Concentration on the vertical sounding *539.* Concentration on the hori-
        zontal melodic movement *542.*
  Two- and three-part canons *546.*
Bach chorale extracts 548
  Two-part continuous writing of modulating musical material completed by figured
  bass notation *548.*
  Two-part continuous writing of modulating musical material *551.*

Acknowledgments 555

INTRODUCTION

The present volume, a sequel to the earlier book of the same title (containing Chapters I to V), is intended for intermediate level students. Presupposing the knowledge of the previous chapters, this second volume specifies and explains only the new musical elements and the manner in which they are to be practised.

Each chapter follows, in its order of presentation, the plan of those contained in the earlier volume: Kodály materials, theoretical information, sight-singing examples, and material for training the ear and the musical memory. These four areas form an organic unity within each chapter and are presented each time with new "d" positions. (Chapter VI: "d" on E, E flat; Chapter VII: "d" on A, A flat; Chapter VIII: "d" on D, D flat; Chapter IX: "d" on G, G flat.)

As in the earlier volume, the musical materials presented for sight-singing, ear training, and development of musical memory once again consist of quotations chosen from Renaissance, Baroque, and Viennese classical periods and are closely tied to studies of harmony and form. Similarly, the stylistic framework has also been extended to permit examples in the church modes and the pentatonic system.

The ear training exercises can be found in the Supplement at the end of the volume.

References to examples taken from the 333 Elementary Exercises are now made to the revised edition new title 333 Reading Exercises (Boosey and Hawkes, 1972), whereas in the previous volume reference was made to an earlier edition of the same work in which staff notation was employed exclusively.

Since this volume is intended for the more advanced students, materials of an appropriately more difficult nature have been drawn from the volumes of the Kodály Choral Method.

October 1976

Erzsébet Hegyi

CHAPTER VI

(Material in staff notation uses E flat and E as "d".)

KODÁLY MATERIAL
Unison Pentatonic Melodies
MATERIAL IN STAFF NOTATION
(333 Reading Exercises)

The set of notes used for note-finding exercises in staff notation:

The following melodies from the 333 Reading Exercises are to be practised in several ways:

272 and 273

a/ With a three-bar ostinato. (For example ♩♩ | ♩♩ |)

or ♩♩)

b/ In answering form. (In the case of tripodic motifs, one group sings the outer bars, the other group sings the middle bar.)

c/ Alternating inner singing and singing aloud.

d/ Accompanied by the left hand marking the metrical unit beat (tapping), the right hand beating time.

274

a/ In rhythmic canon to the melody.

b/ With a two-bar ostinato. (E.g.: ♩♩ | ♩♩ |)

or ♩♩. | ♩)

c/ In answering form.

d/ Alternating inner singing and singing aloud.

e/ Accompanied by metrical unit beat (left hand) while beating time (right hand).

MATERIAL IN SOLFA NOTATION

(Pentatonic Music I–IV; 333 Reading Exercises)

Familiar elements

♫₃ : *IV/33*

Practise the following two-bar units before singing the melody:

♩ (²⁄₂): *II/35, 42*

These exercises are to be sung first in a slow tempo with the following two-part rhythmic accompaniment: ♩

⁵⁄₄ : *IV/56*

Practise a/ with beating time (in 2+3 inner division; see Chapter IV, page 265); b/ with the ostinato ⁵⁄₄ ♫♩ ♪♩ ♫♩ ♩♫♩.

New elements

Minor seventh downwards: III/41, IV/31

The downward s-l, interval of the minor seventh is easy to sing correctly if the "d" has a prominant position in the given melodic phrase. In these two melodies, however, the "d" occurs only once (or not at all) before the leap of the minor seventh. Therefore some preparatory practice is necessary. The following melodic sequences, to be sung from hand-signs or from solfa notation, are suggested:

d-l,-d-m-r-s-l,-d-r-s-l,-r-d-l,-s-m-d etc.

Major ninth upwards: I/34

The interval of the ninth is formed by the final note of the second line and the first note of the third line:

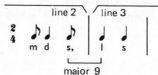

Since the musical material of the second and third lines is identical, the high "l" will not prove difficult to find as it has already been sung. The "s,", being the final note of a syncopa, is of insufficient duration to permit our hearing, now concentrated on the leap of the ninth, to place it accurately. This may explain the frequently uncertain intonation of "s," in an otherwise easy m–d–s, pattern.

In order to sing the "s," accurately, practise the following melodic line with a lengthened final note:

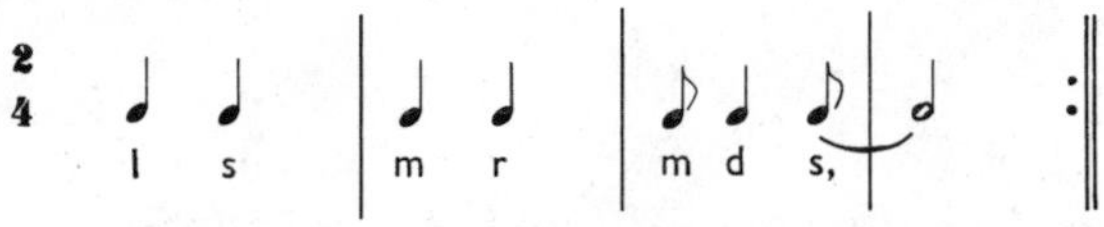

Augmentation and diminution: I/56, 60

The basic rhythmic structure of the eleven-syllable line:

However in the third line we find both an increase (augmentation) and a decrease (diminution) of rhythmic values:

a/ the original eleven-syllable phrase:

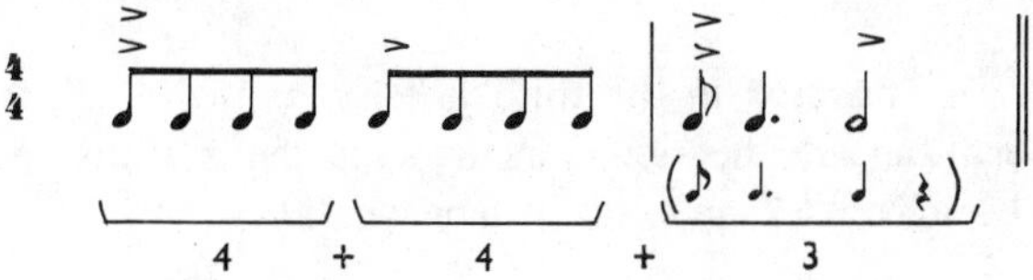

b/ the third line showing variants:

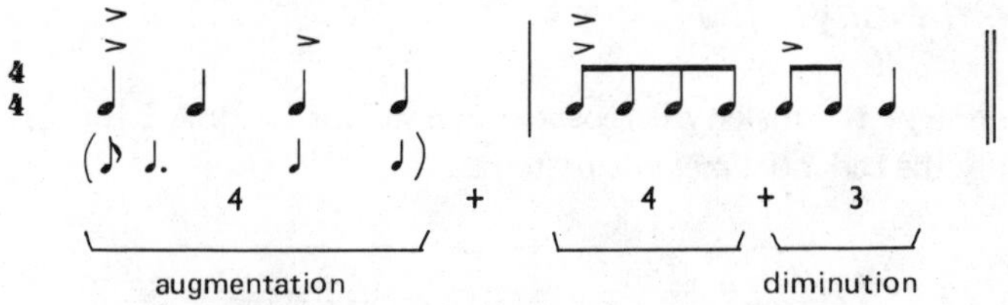

In the original eleven-syllable line, the first bar is spirited and quick-moving while the second bar slows down progressively. The third line on the contrary, begins in broad quarters and appears to quicken with the onset of eighth-note motion. We are consequently led into the fourth line in a more organic manner.

Alternation of $\frac{5}{8}$ and $\frac{6}{8}$:IV/59

The $\frac{5}{8}$ metre divides into $\frac{2}{8} + \frac{3}{8}$. Sing the melody

a/ while beating time (see Chapter IV, page 265 and Chapter II, page 138),

b/ with two types of ostinato (for example $\frac{5}{8}$ ♫ ♩ ♪ and $\frac{6}{8}$ ♩ ♪♫ ; or $\frac{5}{8}$ ♫ ♩ ♪ and $\frac{6}{8}$ ♩ ♪♫♫ ; or $\frac{5}{8}$ ♫ ♫ and $\frac{6}{8}$ ♫♩ ♪ ♫ ; etc.).

Fifth-change, tonal and real, within the same melody: I/77

If we examine the melodic structure of this tune, we find that the third line begins as a tonal fifth-change, while the fourth line begins as a real fifth-change:

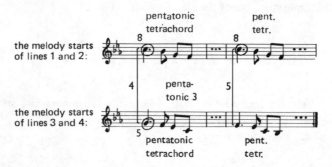

The keynote "l" is answered in the third line by its fifth "m", found here at the interval of a fourth below. This results in the appearance of the "pentatonic third". The fourth line begins on "r", an exact fifth below "l".

Five-line melody: I/53

The fourth line of the melody is repeated in a variant form: A B B C C,. The variant concerns only the cadential melodic patterns:

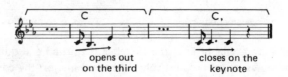

The five-line form is generated by the open cadence at the end of the fourth line, that is by an inner extension preceding the last and finally closed melodic ending.

Two-line melody as a period: IV/14

The tripodic (containing three metrical stresses) lines here show the form of the melody to be A A, . The two halves of the melody begin identically but end in a contrasting manner. The cadence of the first line is open, that of the second line closed.

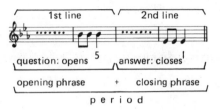

Heteropody (heteropodic melody): I/57

The rhythmic structure of the eleven-syllable line ⁴⁄₄ 𝅘𝅥𝅮𝅘𝅥𝅮𝅘𝅥𝅮𝅘𝅥𝅮 𝅘𝅥𝅮𝅘𝅥𝅮𝅘𝅥𝅮𝅘𝅥𝅮 | 𝅘𝅥𝅮𝅘𝅥. 𝅗𝅥 |
4   +   4   +   3
is already familiar (see Chapter VI, page 23). In the third line, the first four-syllable group is augmented while the rhythm of the subsequent 4+3 grouping remains unchanged. The resulting structure is a tripodic line:

augmentation

$$\begin{array}{c} ⁴⁄₄ \quad \overset{>}{\mathtt{♩}} \; \overset{>}{\mathtt{♩}} \; \mathtt{♩} \; \mathtt{♩} \; | \; \overset{>}{\mathtt{♪♪♪♪}} \; | \; \overset{>}{\mathtt{♪♪}}. \; \overset{>}{\mathtt{♩}} \; \| \\ 4 \quad + \quad 4 \quad + \quad 3 \end{array}$$

Due to the regular alternation of bipodic and tripodic lines, we shall designate this melody as being heteropodic and not isopodic. (A melody is isopodic if each line has the same number of bars, that is the same number of metrical stresses.)

Organically built melody: III/42

(A melody of few melodic patterns of small range built up as an organic unity.)
The entire melody is built upon one element:

pentatonic neighbouring
notes

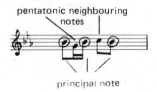

principal note

25

Based upon this five-note pattern, a continuous melodic line is constructed employing the lower and upper neighbouring notes of each descending pentatonic note:

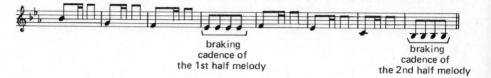

braking
cadence of
the 1st half melody

braking
cadence of
the 2nd half melody

Easy melodies for practising note name singing

(333/271, 282, 298, 312; I/1, 5, 55, 70, II/41, 47, III/39, 40, IV/8)

In this chapter all examples in staff notation use E♭ and E as "d". Thus for note name singing we shall use the following set of notes for the melodies in the s,–l range:

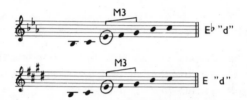

Begin by practising first in the E♭ "d" system and then change to note name singing in E "d".

We are already familiar with the type of melodic turns used in pentatonic melodies. After sufficient practice (see: Pentatony; Note name singing to hand-signs, Chapter VI, page 41).we may now attempt more difficult forms of note name singing.

Range of notes + melody note name singing

For example, melody II/47 of Pentatonic Music, using E♭ as "d":

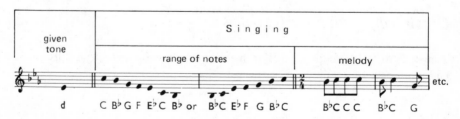

given tone	Singing	
	range of notes	melody

d   C B♭ G F E♭ C B♭ or   B♭C E♭ F G B♭C   B♭C C C   B♭C   G

Sight-singing to note names

Sing the melody after giving the "d" only.

Two-Part Material

PREPARATORY EXERCISES: "LET US SING CORRECTLY"

(Nos. 76, 77, 78, 79, 80, 81)

The singing of these exercises should be preceded by hand-sign practice and interval analysis, as in Chapters III—IV.

TWO-PART WORKS

Pentatonic range of notes

Pentatonic exercises based on E♭ "d" will here be found with a key signature of only two flats. Since the "f" (here A♭) is not used in the pentatonic system, the third flat is superfluous in the key signature.

To prepare for the additional Kodály examples in this chapter, as well as the sight-singing excerpts, practise staff notation singing not only in the E♭ "d" system, but also in the E "d" system in both treble and bass clefs from "m," to "d'".

a/ With E♭ as "d":

b/ With E as "d":

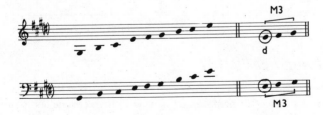

27

Bicinia Hungarica IV/126

1. The familiar pentatonic sixth ("m" in the second half of fifth-changing pentatonic melodies corresponding to "d'" in the first half) appears again in the fifth-changing "l" pentatonic theme.

2. Displacement of the metrical stress, due to the octave and fourth imitations beginning on unstressed beats, occurs in the accompanying voice (bars 1—8 in the alto, bars 9—16 in the soprano).

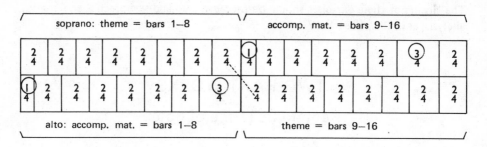

Bicinia Hungarica IV/124

1. The "s" in bars 2 and 4 of this "l" pentatonic melody may easily be uncertain in pitch after the prominent ♪♪ figure in bars 1 and 3. Care must therefore be taken to sing it accurately.

As preparation, practise singing the l—m and d'—s fourths both upwards and downwards using the following notes written on the blackboard:

E.g.: s—d'—l—m—d'—s—l—m—s—d'—m—l—d'—s—m—l etc.

2. Stress displacement is found here once again in the alto part:

Bicinia Hungarica IV/137

1. The exercise has a "l" pentatonic theme with fifth change and pentatonic sixth.

2. The displacement of the metric stress appears now again in the accompanying line in an unusually interesting manner:

a/ In the first half of the exercise, the alto (bars 2 and 3) makes up the two-beat displacement by narrowing its imitation of the soprano melody from $\frac{4}{4}$ to $\frac{3}{4}$, thereby enabling the two voices to end together in measure 4:

$$\frac{4}{4} \qquad \frac{3}{4} \qquad \frac{3}{4} \qquad \frac{4}{4}$$

b/ In the second half of the exercise, the accompanying part (soprano), in place of melodic imitation, introduces new melodic material while retaining rhythmic patterns taken from the theme (♩ ♩ ♩ ♩ , ♩ ♩ ♩ and ♩ ♩ ♩). These patterns then naturally determine the metric accentuation. The metric groups therefore take the following form in the second half of the exercise:

soprano: (accomp.)	$\frac{2}{4}$	$\frac{4}{4}$	$\frac{4}{4}$	$\frac{4}{4}$	$\frac{4}{4}$	$\frac{4}{4}$	$\frac{4}{4}$	
alto: (theme)	$\frac{4}{4}$	$\frac{4}{4}$	$\frac{4}{4}$	$\frac{4}{4}$	$\frac{4}{4}$	$\frac{2}{4}$	$\frac{4}{4}$	

Bicinia Hungarica IV/146

1. A "s" pentatonic theme with fifth change and pentatonic sixth.
2. Difficulties in intonation are found in those melodic phrases framed by the principal notes l—m—l, and d—s—d' in the second half of the accompanying part (bars 11—14, soprano). As preparation, sing the following sequence several times:

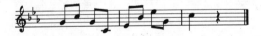

3. The accompanying part should be sung separately in a slow tempo with beating time, before performing the two parts together.
4. By all means, make sure that individual performances at the piano, singing one part while playing the other, are not omitted from the forms of practice.

Suggested further exercises: Bicinia Hungarica II/68, 69, 70; I/24.

Diatonic range of notes

Bicinia Hungarica I/44

1. This six-line theme, once again with fifth change and pentatonic sixth, remains within the pentatonic system except in bars 7 and 16. In these two bars, the pentatonic frame is filled out to include two non-pentatonic passing notes:

The full set of notes used in the theme:

Considering the final note of the melody, it would appear that the theme is in dorian mode with two flats. If, however, we look beyond the outer formal aspects and consider the function, frequency, and quality of each melodic note, we find, in fact, a "l" pentatonic melody with dorian pien notes. (The accompanying material includes no pien notes.)

2. We may explain the two pien notes as giving added colour to a pentatonic melody with a final note on "l":

(Cf.: The major or minor character of the church modes; Chapter IV, page 291.)

Bicinia Hungarica I/37

1. Each diatonic note plays an equal role in the "l" ending folksong theme which shows an A A⁵, A⁵, A,, form. It is therefore in aeolian mode.

2. Take notice of the "t" in line 4, bar 1: , as it can easily become flat.

Bicinia Hungarica I/39

1. Many pentatonic phrases can be found in this theme of A B B, A form. However, since the "t" is used so many times, often in a metrically stressed position, its function is more than that of a pien note. The mode here is therefore "l" pentatonic extended by "t".

2. The accompanying part (alto) presents each note of the diatonic system with equal importance. Its mode is therefore aeolian.

3. Here again we find displacement of the metric stress in the imitating alto line. The eleven-syllable unit of the theme:

$$4 \quad + \quad 4 \quad + \quad 3$$

appears now in this form: . In the first half

$$4 \quad + \quad 4 \quad + \quad 3$$

of the exercise, the metric stress assumes therefore the following form:

soprano: (theme)	$\frac{3}{4}$	$\frac{3}{4}$	$\frac{4}{4}$	$\frac{3}{4}$	$\frac{3}{4}$	$\frac{4}{4}$
alto: (accomp.)	$\frac{3}{4}$	$\frac{3}{4}$	$\frac{2}{4}$	$\frac{3}{4}$	$\frac{2}{4}$	$\frac{3}{4}$	$\frac{4}{4}$
	—	—	—				

narrowness
of rhythm

4. Difficulties in intonation appear in the final bars (10 and 12) of the alto part where the "t" falls on stressed beats.

a/ In bar 10, students often sing "d" instead of "t" since it is approached by leap and remains unresolved.

b/ In bar 12, the again unresolved "t" is often flat. We can insure correct intonation of the "t" in both instances if we temporarily practise singing a "d" in place of the "l" which follows.

If the students sing this melodic variant several times they will then hear the "t" even without the "d" and will be able to sing the original melody in tune.

Bicinia Hungarica III/114

1. The theme appears in the soprano.

a/ The notes of the theme:

final note = m

b/ Its key is G phrygian.

c/ The cadential pattern is a characteristic phrygian cadence of the Renaissance style:

f - m

(Cf.: Bicinia Hungarica I/59; Chapter IX, page 355)

2. If, because of the "t" (D), the intonation of bars 3—5 still remains uncertain, we may practise several times placing the "d" on B♭:

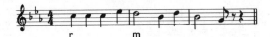

r   m

Range including altered notes

Bicinia Hungarica I/60

1. The alto line is in imitation of the soprano: in bars 1—9 it is a real imitation at the fourth below while from bar 10 it is a transformed imitation at the fifth within the diatonic system.

2. The altered notes "fi" in the soprano and "di" in the alto are ascending passing notes and are therefore not difficult to sing correctly.

66 Two-Part Exercises/51

1. This exercise is in the key of C minor. The soprano, with colouring altered notes, is in the harmonic minor, the alto in the natural minor.

2. The alto imitates the soprano in canon at the seventh. While the two parts correspond to each other in their intervallic movement, they differ in actual sound as a consequence of their respectively different minor modes.

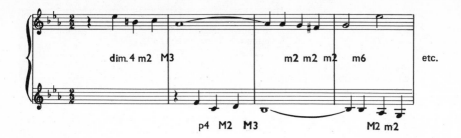

3. Difficult melodic intervals are the diminished fourth (bars 1, 9 and 14) and the diminished third (bars 12—13). The students have already sung the diminished fourth many times in their practice in harmonic minor, but this is the first time they have met the diminished third. Preparation must include note-finding exercises using the notes of the soprano line in staff notation:

altered notes:

diatonic notes:

66 Two-Part Exercises/23

1. In the course of this exercise, the four-bar theme undergoes interesting changes of form and tonality.

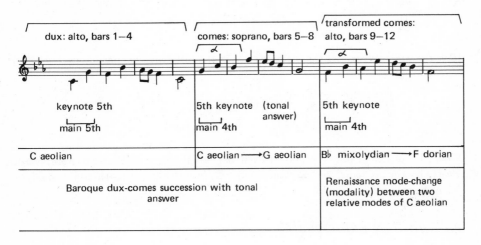

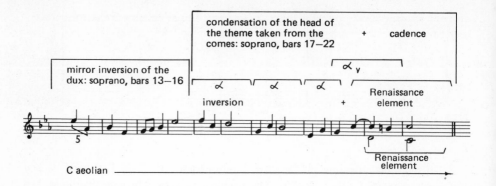

The final two bars present the most typical two-part cadence of the Palestrina style:

suspended leading tone

(Cf.: Chapter IV, page 284)

2. A serious problem arises concerning the intonation of the diminished intervals in bars 7—8 of the alto part:

dim. 5   dim. 4   dim. 5 + resolution

Have the students practise the melodic turns in the following manner:

dim. 5 + resolution   dim. 5 + resolution

When the principal notes beginning each sequential segment (C and B♭) are heard clearly by the students, we may remove the G, inserted as the resolution of the F♯, from the melody.

66 Two-Part Exercises/45

1. The final bars here sound essentially the same as the Renaissance-type cadence of the above mentioned exercise. The only difference is that the 2—1 cadential

element was previously sung by the alto (forming a final consonance at the octave), and is here sung by the soprano (forming a unison final consonance).

2. We must prepare the melodic turns of the alto part in bars 21 and 22. Practise the following melodic line several times:

44 Two-Part Exercises/29

This exercise demands great concentration. The only difficulty in intonation, however, is caused by the downward leap of the minor sixth in melodic minor (alto, bars 11—12).

The soprano part descends simultaneously in the natural minor causing even greater difficulty. Practise, first singing as a group, then individually, the following succession of motifs:

Suggested further exercise: 55 Two-Part Exercises/55.

Modulating musical material

77 Two-Part Exercises/69

1. The aeolian theme is followed by a real answer in the key of the dominant:

Dux: G aeolian   Comes: D aeolian

2. From bar 17 of the alto part, the theme is heard transformed to major (ionian) mode on B♭. The "t" is, however, replaced by a "ta", a frequent alteration in the Renaissance (modal) style, thereby avoiding the augmented fourth (t–f: A–E♭), and forming a consonant perfect fourth between the two prominent notes (A♭–E♭) in bars 17–18. (Cf.: Chapter VII, page 145 and Chapter IX, page 355).

3. The theme appears successively in the following keys:

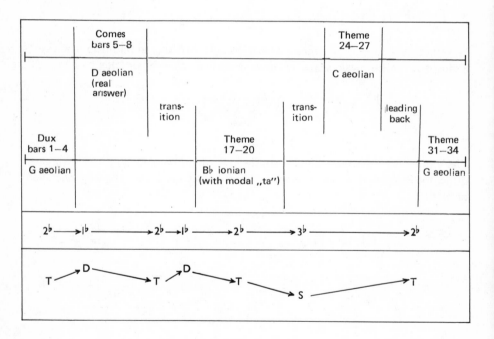

4. Suggested places for "d" change:

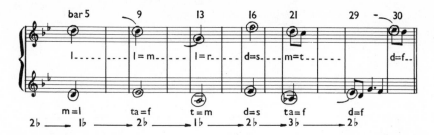

5. We find difficult melodic phrases in bars 7—8 of the alto and bars 11—12 of the soprano part. Both are typical melodic minor cadences, the first in D minor, the second in G minor. To prepare these cadences, practise the following melodic phrases, the students singing individually, as a group, and again individually:

a)

b)

Fifteen Two-Part Exercises/14

1. The theme, built on a minor hexachord, is followed by a tonal answer:
a/ Dux:

b/ Comes, as a tonal answer:

The comes becomes an exact answer at the fifth when the interval of the third replaces the corresponding thematic interval of the second:

2. The theme and its tonal answer are transformed to major in bars 17—24. The variant in major is first heard as the comes:

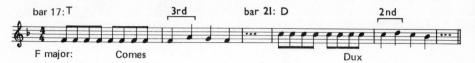

bar 17: T　　　　　3rd　　　　bar 21: D　　　　2nd

F major:　　　Comes　　　　　　　　　　Dux

3. The theme appears successively in the following keys:

	Comes 5—8			Dux 21—24		Dux 34—37		Dux 42—43	+ clos-ing sec-tion
	D→A minor hex. (tonal answer)		trans-ition	F major hex.	trans-ition	G minor hex.	lead-ing back	D minor head of theme	D minor
Dux bars 1—4		Comes 9—12		Comes 17—20		Dux 30—33		Dux 42—45	clos-ing
D minor hexa-chord		D→A minor hex. (tonal answer)		F→C major hex. (tonal answer)		C minor hex.		G minor hex.	sec-tion

transformation

$1^b \rightarrow 0 \rightarrow 1^b \rightarrow 0 \rightarrow 1^b \rightarrow (0) \rightarrow 1^b \rightarrow 2^b \rightarrow 3^b \rightarrow 2^b \rightarrow 1^b \rightarrow 2^b \rightarrow 1^b$

Since the theme occurs not only in the dominant and subdominant keys but also in the subdominant of the subdominant (C minor) we can demonstrate most clearly the key relations as a segment of the fifth pillar:

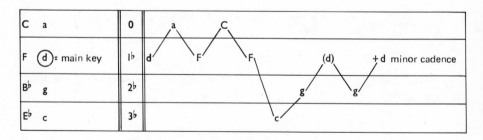

C a	0	
F (d) = main key	1^b	
B♭ g	2^b	
E♭ c	3^b	

Even more strongly than heretofore, the Baroque order of key relations
$$T \nearrow^{D} \searrow T \searrow_{S} \nearrow^{T}$$ is exemplified by the manner in which they follow
each other in the ascending progression leading to the final cadence:
C minor → G minor → D minor.
  (3♭)   (2♭)   (1♭)

4. Suggested places for "d" change:

Bitonality in the two-part material

Bicinia Hungarica II/66

1. The notes of the folksong theme:

final note = m

Only four pentatonic notes are used: m–r–d–l,–m,

$$\underbrace{1\ 2\ 3\ 4}\ =$$

The melody moves essentially within the minor-character m–r–d–l, pentatonic tetrachord. The final note repeats the highest (m) at the octave below. Rather than identify this melody as being in "m" pentatonic, which implies the full pentatonic scale, it is more accurately a "m"-ending pentatonic melody.

2. The notes of the accompanying part:

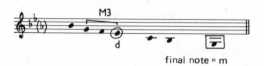

final note = m

Although all the pentatonic notes appear here, the major third occurs not on B♭–D, as in the theme, but on E♭–G, at the fifth below. Therefore, as indicated by the two different key signatures as well, the exercise is in two keys (bitonal). The soprano is a "m"-ending pentatonic with D as its final note, the alto is "m" pentatonic with G as its final note.

3. Practise singing the alto part alone before singing the two parts together. Sing the first bar of the theme as a lead-in to the alto part:

continuous singing

theme + accompanying part

etc.

40

THEORETICAL INFORMATION
AND TECHNICAL EXERCISES
Range of Notes, Hand-Signs

Pentatony

Note name singing to hand-signs

The students sing the pentatonic melody shown by the teacher's hand-signs using E or E$^\flat$ as "d".

For example, this series of notes on E$^\flat$ "d":

The teacher's hand-
sign melody: m r d m l, s, d m s r l d s l,
The students'
singing: G F E♭ G C B♭ E♭ G B♭ F C E♭ B♭ C

Actual pitch:

etc.

Diatony

Note name singing to hand-signs

The teacher presents a diatonic melody using hand-signs. The students sing back on letter names (note names) using the key signatures of 3 flats or 4 sharps:

The teacher's hand-
sign melody: d t, r f m t, l s r t d'
The students'
singing: E D♯ F♯ A G♯ D♯ C♯ B F♯ D♯ E

Actual pitch:

etc.

41

Diatony + alteration

Solfa singing from staff notation

The students should practise on the basis of the full set of notes including all the altered notes (fi, di, si, ri, li; ta, ma, lo, ra) as in Chapter IV:

a/ in the G clef:

b/ in the F clef:

Solfa – note name singing in answering form

Practise as in Chapters III and IV.
For example:

Practising change of key from hand-signs

With the appropriate re-interpretation of the notes "fi" and "ta" we can arrive at the dominant key and the subdominant key respectively:

(Cf.: Dual fifth pillar; Chapter III, page 198)

Although melodies containing modulations are at present practised only with solfa, it is very important that the students should name the notes corresponding to "fi" or "ta" at the point of key change and name the new key as well. We can use all the well-known "d" systems in practice (C, C#, C♭; F, F#; B♭, B; E♭, E).

For example, F major → B♭ major → F major in succession:

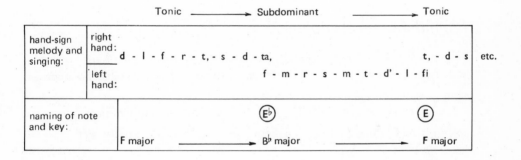

We can, of course, touch several keys in one exercise.

For example: C → F → B♭ → E♭; or E → B → F# → B → E, etc.

Keys and Modes
The pentatonic modes

With E♭ and E as "d"

The teacher writes on the blackboard a particular succession of modes, indicating ascending or descending direction for each, and giving the initial pitch of the "d" (in E♭ or in E). The students sing the modes right through with solfa + note names related to the given "d".

For example, the succession of d↑–l↓–r↑–s↓–m↑ pentatonic modes with E as "d":

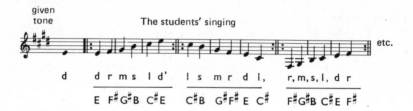

	d	d r m s l d'	l s m r d l,	r, m, s, l, d r
		E F#G#B C#E	C#B G#F#E C#	F#G#B C#E F#

From the same keynote

Sing the pentatonic modes according to a previously defined and fixed order with solfa names in the ⌢ direction, starting from the same pitch, accompanied with $\frac{5}{4}$ beating time and rhythm pattern.

For example, sing the "r", "l", "d", "m" and "s" pentatonic modes, from the starting note B, using the rhythm pattern $\frac{5}{4}$ ♩ ♩ ♩ ♩, with beating time divided into 3+2.

beating time:

singing:

r m s l d' r' d' l s m r | l, d r m s l s m

44

Major and minor keys with three flats or four sharps

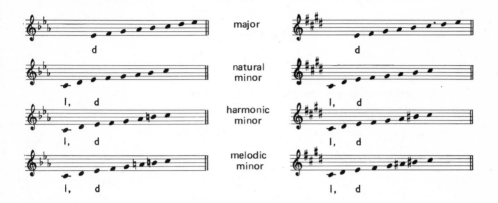

major

natural
minor

harmonic
minor

melodic
minor

Forms of practising the minor

(M)* Sing the natural, harmonic, and melodic minors on C and C♯ in a pattern of alternating 6-beat and 5-beat bars, while beating time, and in a rhythmic structure relating to the metric pulse.

For example, the various types of C♯ minor with the rhythmic patterns:

, alternating continuously:

Further variations may be jointly arrived at by the students and the teacher together.

---

* The letter M before a given exercise indicates that the students should perform the exercise from memory.

45

Note finding exercises in major and harmonic minor

In E♭ and E major

1. Note name singing from solfa letters in the range m,–d' (𝄞).

2. Solfa + note name singing from degree numbers within the range III–8 (𝄞).

3. Note name singing from the above degree numbers.

In C and C♯ minor

1. Note name singing from solfa letters in the range m,–d' (𝄞).

2. Solfa + note name singing from degree numbers in the range V–10 (𝄞).

3. Note name singing from the above degree numbers.

When singing always use the pitch appropriate to the given key signature (for detailed description, see pages 122–125 of Chapter II).

Church modes

New method of practising the comparative names

Sing the various modes in succession from the same keynote, 1 upwards and 1 downwards, alternating the diatonic and comparative names (see Chapter IV, page 291).

For example: dorian ↑ (diatonic) – lydian ↓ (comparative) – mixolydian ↑ (diat.) – phrygian ↓ (comp.) – lydian ↑ (diat.) – dorian ↓ (comp.) – phrygian ↑ (diat.) – mixolydian ↓ (comp.):

The teacher should devise similar sequences.

Singing to note names

1. (M) Practise the dorian mode with note names in various successions according to the fifth pillar: a/ 0 → 7♭; b/ 7♯ → 0; c/ 0 → 7♯; d/ 7♭ → 0.

Sing the chosen progression in the ⌢ direction, moving in even quarters, accompanied with beating $\frac{4}{4}$ time. In order to ensure continuity it is very useful —at least in the beginning—to name the successive keynotes in advance and to write them on the blackboard.

For example if we practise succession a/ we can put the following on the blackboard:

key signature:	0	1♭	2♭	3♭	4♭	5♭	6♭	7♭
keynote:	D	G	C	F	B♭	E♭	A♭	D♭

The exercise, accompanied by beating time, will thus sound:

 etc.

2. (M) Practise the phrygian mode in a similar way.

Summary of the note groups within pentatony, diatony and the harmonic minor system

(See the diagram on pages 48—49)

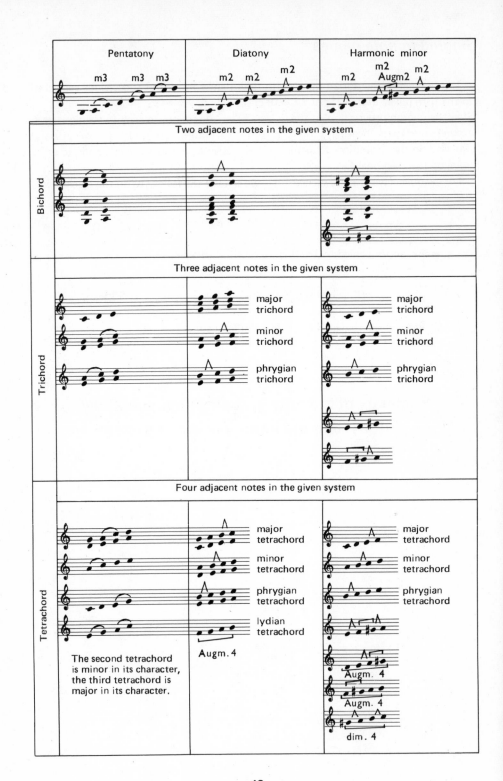

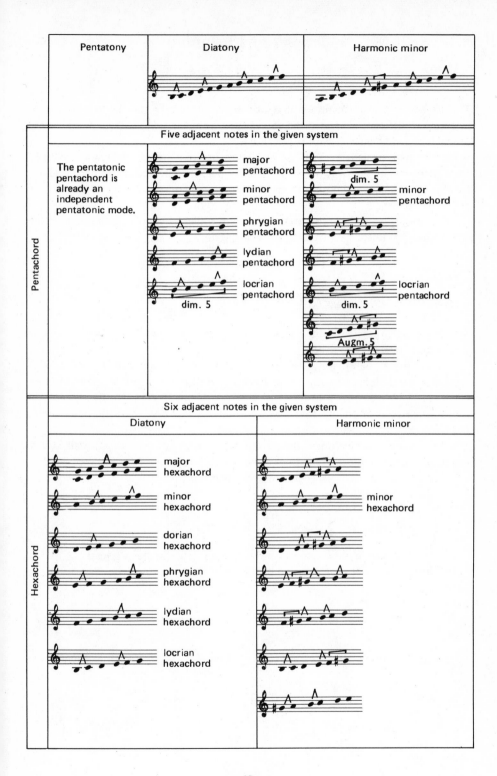

Transformed singing

The essence of transformation is that a theme, or motif, of a specific tonality is sung in a key of different character and sound type from the original (e.g. minor instead of major or lydian instead of phrygian, etc.).

Transformed singing is most useful if it is practised using well-known material from memory. In this way we can not only deepen our musical memory and our familiarity with keys and note systems but also develop our inner musical imagination and inner hearing.

Let us begin working with short, diatonic melodies of simple rhythmic structure and work out transformations using solfa names only.

Suggested method of practising

1. The students establish the key of the given excerpt. They then memorize the musical material with solfa.

2. When the students are all able to sing the melody accurately, with correct rhythm, they then list the other keys (sets of notes) possible within the framework of the same note system — in this case, diatony. If one exists with the same sound as the original, they should sing that one first. In this case the solfa alone needs to be changed, as the melody remains unchanged.

3. The students should then turn to other keys where the melody is really transformed as these keys are different not only in solfa but in sound type as well.

Let us attempt the above suggestions using the following motif:

a/ The notes used are those of the minor trichord (see Chapter VI, page 48);
b/ The most natural interpretation of the motif is:

$$\frac{2}{4} \quad \text{♩ ♩} \mid \text{♪♪♪♪} \mid \text{♩ ₹} \parallel$$

l, d   t, t, d t,   l,

c/ Within diatony the trichord starting from "r" is of the same sound type:

r f   m m f m   r

50

d/ The major and phrygian trichords are of a new type:

d m   r rm r d   or: f l   s s l s f   or: s t   l l t l s

and

m s   f f s f m   or: t, r   d d r d t,

Taking D as the lowest note the motif sounds like this:

original minor trichord	major trichord	phrygian trichord

l, d   t,t,d t, l,   d m r rm r d   m s   f f s f m
r   f   m m f m r   f l s s l s f   t, r d d r d t,
                            s t l l t l s

Musical quotations for transformed singing

As the number of the last extract in the first volume — containing Chapters I to V — was 559, the extracts from music literature found in this volume will start with number 560.

560. BARTÓK: MICROCOSM II. NO 62.

561. J.S.BACH: O HAUPT VOLL BLUT UND WUNDEN. CHORALE.

562. BARTÓK: 44 DUOS. NO 36.

563. BARTÓK: 44 DUOS. NO 12.

564. BARTÓK: MICROCOSM IV. NO 101.

565. BARTÓK: MICROCOSM I. NO 10.

566. J.S.BACH: KYRIE, GOTT VATER IN EWIGKEIT. CHORALE.

567. STRAVINSKY: THE RITE OF SPRING.

568. BARTÓK: MICROCOSM III. NO 87.

569. BARTÓK: MICROCOSM I. NO 15.

570. BARTÓK: MICROCOSM I. NO 17.

571. BARTÓK: MICROCOSM I. NO 2/b.

572. BARTÓK: 44 DUOS. NO 9.

573. BARTÓK: MICROCOSM II. NO 37.

574. MUSSORGSKY: BORIS GODUNOV I.

575. KODÁLY: WHITSUNTIDE.

576. BARTÓK: 44 DUOS. NO 14.

53

577. BARTÓK: MICROCOSM I. NO 24.

578. BARTÓK: 44 DUOS. NO 41.

579. BARTÓK: MICROCOSM I. NO 7.

580. KODÁLY: 66 TWO-PART EXERCISES. NO 28.

581. BARTÓK: THREE RONDOS I.

582. BARTÓK: 44 DUOS. NO 1.

583. BARTÓK: THREE RONDOS II.

584. BARTÓK: 44 DUOS. NO 29.

585. BARTÓK: MICROCOSM II. NO 55.

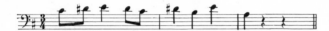

586. BARTÓK: MICROCOSM II. NO 43/a.

587. BARTÓK: MICROCOSM II. NO 50.

588. BARTÓK: MICROCOSM III. NO 90.

589. BARTÓK: MICROCOSM II. NO 55.

590. BARTÓK: MICROCOSM II. NO 63.

Intervals

Intervals within the pentatonic modes

(M) Practise singing in solfa + note names the intervals of the pentatonic modes within the octave in the previously known manner:

a/ Downwards, from smallest to largest interval;

b/ downwards, from largest to smallest interval;

c/ upwards, from smallest to largest interval;

d/ upwards, from largest to smallest interval.

For example, intervals within the "s" pentatonic, in downward direction, beginning with the largest from the given pitch A:

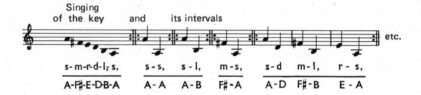

Practice of fourths and fifths

1. (M) Sing the sequences of combined fourths and fifths in E♭ major using solfa syllables.

a/ Perfect fourth downwards + perfect fifth upwards:

b/ Perfect fifth downwards + perfect fourth upwards.

c/ Perfect fifth upwards + perfect fourth downwards.

d/ Perfect fourth upwards + perfect fifth downwards.

2. (M) Sing the above exercises with solfa + note names.

For example, exercise 1.c/:

3. (M) Practise the sequences in 1. and 2. in E major as well.

4. (M) Sing the ascending and descending sequences of fifths in C and C# harmonic minor with solfa.

For example, the descending sequence in C# minor:

5. (M) Practise the sequences as described above (4.) with solfa + note name singing.

For example, the ascending sequence of fifths in C minor:

6. (M) Sing to solfa + note names all the different types of fifths, in C and C# harmonic minor, related to the given tonic.

a/ Perfect fifths upwards;   b/ perfect fifths downwards;
c/ diminished fifths upwards;   d/ diminished fifths downwards;
e/ augmented fifth upwards;   f/ augmented fifth downwards.

For example, diminished fifths downwards in C# minor:

(The summary of interval types can be found in Chapter II, page 130)

7. (M) Practise the sequential progressions of fourth-fifth and fifth-fourth at the pitch of E♭ and E major:

a/ Fourth–fifth interval pairs in ascending order;
b/ fourth–fifth interval pairs in descending order;
c/ fifth–fourth interval pairs in ascending order;
d/ fifth–fourth interval pairs in descending order.

For example, sequence a/ in E♭ major:

or sequence d/ in E major:

57

8. Have the students sing upward or downward fourths with solfa + note names from given scale degrees of the major and harmonic minor keys in 3 flats or 4 sharps.
For example, in E major upwards, from the given scale degrees 1 V 2 VI IV 3 VII V:

d - f - E - A   s,- d-B - E   r - s - F♯ B

or in C minor downwards, from the given scale degrees 1 3 6 4 7 5 8 :

l,- m,- C - G   d - si,- E♭-B   f - d - A♭-E♭

The intervals of the harmonic minor pentachords

1. (M) Practise to solfa the intervals of the ascending pentachords in increasing and decreasing order from the same starting pitch. Give only the respective "l" for each set of notes to be sung.

For example if we begin singing from the note "D", the notes "l" belonging to the single pentachords are as follows:

Without sounding the note "l" the clear intonation of the pentachords containing the augmented second is not secure.

The singing procedure otherwise is the same as in the case of the diatonic pentachords (see Chapter III, page 207 and Chapter IV, page 297).

For example, the intervals of the pentachords with "r" and "si" as lowest note in decreasing succession from the starting note C:

2. Similarly sing the intervals of the descending pentachords.

New forms of practising the sixths

1. (M) Sing the sequence of sixths in E and E♭ major.
a/ Upwards to solfa; b/ downwards to solfa; c/ upwards to solfa + note names;
d/ downwards to solfa + note names.
   For example, exercise d/ in E major:

(Cf. Chapter IV, page 296, 7.)
2. (M) Practise with solfa + note name singing the different types of sixths in E
and E♭ major both in upward and downward direction:
   a/ Minor sixths upwards;   b/ minor sixths downwards;
   c/ major sixths upwards;   d/ major sixths downwards.
   For example, exercise b/ in E♭ major:

59

The intervals of the first and second inversion
(6, $\frac{6}{4}$) triads in major

1. (M) Sing the intervals of the different kinds of first and second inversion chords within the major key at the pitch of E and E^b major in increasing or decreasing progression compared to their lowest note, to solfa. The possible variants for practice:

a/ Intervals of the 6 chords using the progression of 3↑ 6↑

b/ singing the same intervals in decreasing order: 6↑ 3↑

c/ Intervals of the $\frac{6}{4}$ chords using the progression of 4↑ 6↑

d/ singing the same intervals in decreasing order: 6↑ 4↑

The quality of the intervals (major or minor, perfect or augmented, etc.) depends on the type of the given triad. Thus for the minor triad sung as in variant a/ the major third and major sixth will be heard; for the diminished triad sung as in variant d/ the major sixth and augmented fourth, etc.

(Cf.: Inversions of the triad, Chapter IV, page 301)

For example, the minor triad sung as in variant c/ within E major:

2. (M) Singing now the downward intervals, practise the exercises given in 1. (a—d):

a/ Intervals of the 6 chord, in the order 4↓ 6↓

b/ in decreasing order: 6↓ 4↓

c/ Intervals of the $\frac{6}{4}$ chord, in the order 3↓ 6↓

d/ in decreasing order: 6↓ 3↓

For example, the major triads according to variant b/ in E^b major:

60

Chords
Triadic functions

The music of the Baroque and Viennese classical styles is usually described as being based on a system of functional harmony. The term refers to an inner order, prevalent in the harmonic vocabulary of the two styles, which governs the movement of chords, following a system of functional logic.

The most important element of this functional logic is the dominant-tonic relationship: tje dp,omamt, which contains the leading tone, strives to reach the tonic, which brings resolution and tranquility. The third function, the subdominant, is built on the fourth scale degree not to be found in either the tonic or dominant triads, and thereby forms, together with the dominant-tonic chord progression, a complete and unambiguous tonality.

Since the tonic, the chord which indicates close and rest, is heard as the resolution of the dominant, which contains the leading tone, the subdominant must precede the dominant. This type of functional chord order is known as an authentic progression.

Each of the three functions within the major and minor tonalities is represented by more than one chord. For each function there is at least one secondary degree which serves as a substitute to the main degree and contains the most essential functional element of the main triad. The relationship existing between main and secondary triads is the following:

1. In major:

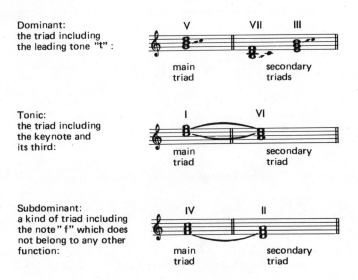

61

2. In harmonic minor:

Dominant:
triad including the
leading tone "si":

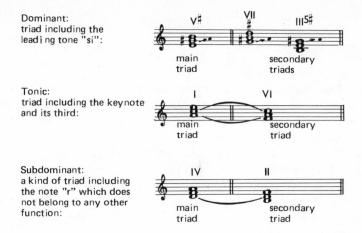

main
triad

secondary
triads

Tonic:
triad including the keynote
and its third:

main
triad

secondary
triad

Subdominant:
a kind of triad including
the note "r" which does
not belong to any other
function:

main
triad

secondary
triad

(The third degree of the key is known as mediant, the sixth degree in known as submediant as well.)

Singing exercises for practising chord functions

1. (M) Sing with solfa + note names the sequence of triads belonging to each function in E major and C# harmonic minor.

For example, the triads belonging to the subdominant function in E major:

given
tone   IV   II

d   f - l - d'   r - f - l
tonic   A - C#- E   F#- A - C#

2. (M) Practise the above exercise (1.) with first and second inversion (6, $\frac{6}{4}$) triads as well.

For example, the $\frac{6}{4}$ chords belonging to the dominant function in C# minor:

given
tone   V$\frac{6}{4}$ VII$\frac{6}{4}$ III$\frac{6}{4}$

l   t,- m - si   r- si - t   si,- d - m
          D#- G#- B#   F#- B#- D#   B#- E - G#

3. (M) Sing the exercises in 1. and 2. in E♭ major and C harmonic minor.

Other forms of practising the triads

1. Sing the 6 chords in a predetermined order to solfa + note names in the keys with 4 sharps and 3 flats.

For example, I^6–V^6–II^6–VII^6–IV^6–III^6–VI^6 in C minor:

etc.

$$I^6 \qquad V^6 \qquad II^6$$

d – m – l   si,- t, - m   r – f - t
Eᵇ- G - C   B - D - G   F - Aᵇ- D

2. Practise the $\frac{6}{4}$ chords in a similar way.

For example, V^6_4–IV^6_4–I^6_4–III^6_4–VII^6_4–II^6_4–VI^6_4 in E major:

etc.

$$V^6_4 \qquad IV^6_4 \qquad I^6_4$$

r – s - t   d - f - l   s,- d - m
F# B - D#   E - A - C#   B - E - G#

3. Sing to solfa syllables the 6 and $\frac{6}{4}$ chords of the different degrees of the major and minor tonality, from the same starting note.

For example, the $I^6_4 - II^6_4 - IV^6_4 - III^6_4 - VII^6_4 - VI^6_4 - V^6_4$

(major, minor, major, minor, dim., minor, major)

progression in the major key:

starting pitch   singing   etc.

s,- d - m   l,- r - f   d - f - l   t,- m - s

4. (M) Practise with solfa singing the root position and the first and second inversions (6, $\frac{6}{4}$) of a given triad of the major or minor tonality from the same starting pitch.

For example, the triad built on the second degree of the minor key, in the succession of first inversion, root position and second inversion:

starting pitch   6   root $\frac{6}{4}$

r - f - t   t,- r - f   f - t - r'

Seventh chords

It is very frequent that another third is added to the triad built up of thirds:

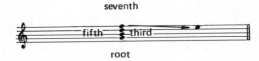 The resulting chord contains a seventh interval as well which needs

a melodic resolution:

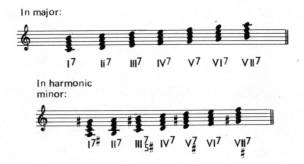

Because of its characteristic interval of the seventh, the chord is called seventh chord.

Seventh chords in the major and harmonic minor keys

In major:

I⁷ II⁷ III⁷ IV⁷ V⁷ VI⁷ VII⁷

In harmonic minor:

I⁷# II⁷ III⁷₅# IV⁷ V⁷ VI⁷ VII⁷#

(The basic principles for indicating the altered note can be found in Chapter III, page 209)

The types of seventh chords

Type	Where it occurs	
	in major	in harmonic minor
Major triad with minor seventh	V	V
Major triad with major seventh	I, IV	VI
Minor triad with minor seventh	II, III, VI	IV

64

Minor triad with major seventh	–	I
Diminished triad with minor seventh	VII	II
Diminished triad with diminished seventh	–	VII
Augmented triad with major seventh	–	III

Inversions of the seventh chords

As in the case of the triads, any chord note may become the lowest sounding tone. The inversions brought about in this way produce new types of chord structure:

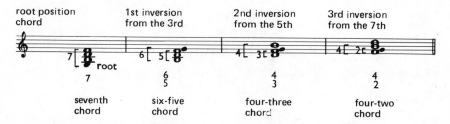

The original root of the chord is always to be found as the upper note of the second interval found in the given inversion.

Singing exercises with the seventh chords

1. (M) Sing the seventh chord sequence in the keys with 4 sharps and 3 flats to solfa + note names.

For example, in C minor:

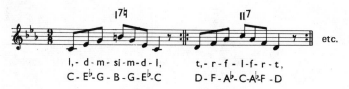

l, - d - m - si - m - d - l,
C - E♭ - G - B - G - E♭ - C

t, - r - f - l - f - r - t,
D - F - A♭ - C - A♭ - F - D

etc.

2. (M) Practise all inversions of the seventh chords in the same manner.
For example, the sequence of $\frac{6}{5}$ chords in E major:

$I\frac{6}{5}$ $II\frac{6}{5}$ etc.

m,- s,- t,- d,- t,- s,- m,   f, - l,- d - r- d - l,- f,
G♯- B - D♯E -D♯-B-G♯   A - C♯-E - F♯-E - C♯-A

3. Sing the seventh chords in a given order in the keys with 4 sharps and 3 flats, a/ to solfa names, b/ to solfa + note names.
For example, the sequence $II^7–V^7–I^7–VI^7–IV^7–VII^7–III^7$ in E major according to exercise b/:

II^7 V^7 I^7 etc.

r - f - l - d'   s,- t,- r - f   d - m - s - t
F♯A - C♯E   B - D♯F♯ A   E - G♯B - D♯

4. Practise the $\frac{6}{5}$ chords as well in a similar way.
For example, $V\frac{6}{5}–VI\frac{6}{5}–II\frac{6}{5}–IV\frac{6}{5}–III\frac{6}{5}–VII\frac{6}{5}–I\frac{6}{5}$ in C minor:

$V\frac{6}{5}$ $VI\frac{6}{5}$ $II\frac{6}{5}$ etc.

si,- t,- r - m   l,- d - m - f   r - f - l - t
B - D - F - G   C - E♭G - A♭   F - A♭C - D

5. (M) Sing from each note of E and E♭ major a root position seventh chord, a $\frac{6}{5}$, $\frac{4}{3}$ and $\frac{4}{2}$ chord to solfa + note names, then name the degree number of the individual chords within the given key.
For example, the exercise in E♭ major from the note "l":

The structure of the chord:	7	$\frac{6}{5}$	$\frac{4}{3}$	$\frac{4}{2}$
	[3 ↑ [3 [3	[2 ↑ [3 [3	[3 ↑ [2 [3	[3 ↑ [3 [2

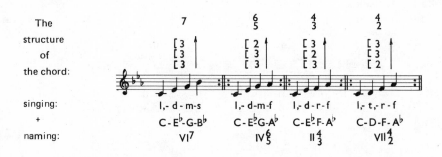

singing:	l,- d - m - s	l,- d - m - f	l,- d - r - f	l,- t,- r - f
+	C - E♭-G-B♭	C - E♭G - A♭	C - E♭F - A♭	C - D - F - A♭
naming:	VI^7	$IV\frac{6}{5}$	$II\frac{4}{3}$	$VII\frac{4}{2}$

66

Harmonic analysis

The chord progressions in the following extracts are much more varied than were those of the preceding chapters (Chapters III and IV). Not only triads but also seventh chords are now used. The method of analysis and the forms of practice, however, are the same as before (see Chapter III, pages 214–216).

Musical quotations for harmonic analysis

591. HANDEL: RODELINDA. I.

592. J.HAYDN: PIANO SONATA IN D MAJOR. II.

593. A.SCARLATTI: PENSIERI.

594. MOZART: THE MAGIC FLUTE. II.

595. MOZART: IL SERAGLIO. II.

596. MOZART: THE MARRIAGE OF FIGARO. I.

597.   MOZART: THE MARRIAGE OF FIGARO. II.

598.   MOZART: THE MAGIC FLUTE. II.

599.   MOZART: THE MARRIAGE OF FIGARO. II.

600. BEETHOVEN: ICH LIEBE DICH.

601. BEETHOVEN: SEPTET. OP. 20. III.

602. MOZART: IL SERAGLIO. I.

603. MOZART: PIANO SONATA IN F MAJOR. I. (K.332)

604. MOZART: IL SERAGLIO. II.

605. BEETHOVEN: GERMAN DANCE.

606. J.S.BACH: SCHMÜCKE DICH, O LIEBE SEELE. CHORALE.

607. MOZART: SONATA FOR TWO PIANOS IN D MAJOR. III. (K.448)

608. J.S.BACH: CHRISTE, DU BEISTAND DEINER KREUZGEMEINDE. CHORALE.

609. CORELLI: CONCERTO GROSSO IN D MAJOR. OP.6, NO 1.

610. J.S.BACH: JESU, MEIN HORT UND ERRETTER. CHORALE.

611. MOZART: IL SERAGLIO. OVERTURE.

612. J.S.BACH: LEIT' UNS MIT DEINER RECHTEN HAND. CHORALE.

613. MOZART: THE MAGIC FLUTE. I.

614. J.S.BACH: LOBT GOTT, IHR CHRISTEN ALLZUGLEICH. CHORALE.

615. HANDEL: SAMSON. III.

616. J.S.BACH: WARUM SOLLT' ICH MICH DENN GRÄMEN. CHORALE.

617. J.S.BACH: ENGLISH SUITE IN G MINOR. PRELUDE.

618. J.S.BACH: JESU, DER DU MEINE SEELE. CHORALE.

619. MOZART: PIANO SONATA IN F MAJOR. I. (K.332)

620.   J.S.BACH: ES IST GEWISSLICH AN DER ZEIT. CHORALE.

621.   J.HAYDN: PIANO SONATA IN B FLAT MAJOR. II.

622.   J.S.BACH: ACH GOTT, VOM HIMMEL SIEH DAREIN. CHORALE.

623.   LULLY: ALCESTE. IV.

75

624. J.S.BACH: ICH DANK' DIR SCHON DURCH DEINEN SOHN. CHORALE.

625. J.S.BACH: HILF, HERR JESU, LASS GELINGEN. CHORALE.

626. VIVALDI: BASSOON CONCERTO IN B FLAT MAJOR. OP.45, NO 8.

SIGHT-SINGING
Unison Extracts from the Musical Literature
MATERIAL IN STAFF NOTATION

Melodies in pentatonic and church modes

627. LISZT: INNO A MARIA VERGINE. (OR.: 1♯)

628. KODÁLY: PSALMUS HUNGARICUS. (OR.: 3♯)

629. BORODIN: THIRD SYMPHONY (A MINOR). II. (OR.: 2♭)

630. SAINT SAËNS: HENRY VIII. BALLET. (OR.: 1♭)

631. BORODIN: PRINCE IGOR. PROLOGUE.

632. KODÁLY: JESUS AND THE TRADERS. (OR.: 1♭)

633. PUCCINI: TURANDOT. II. (OR.: 1♯)

634. MUSSORGSKY: BORIS GODUNOV. II. (OR.: 1♭)

635. KODÁLY: TREACHEROUS GLEAM. (OR.: 1♭)

636. MUSSORGSKY: PICTURES AT AN EXHIBITION. (OR.: 2♭)

637. DEBUSSY: LE PETIT NÈGRE. (OR.: 0)

638. BRITTEN: PETER GRIMES. III. (OR.: 4♭)

639. BARTÓK: CANTATA PROFANA.

640. PUCCINI: TURANDOT. II.

641. KODÁLY: PEACOCK VARIATIONS. (OR.: 1♭)

642. BARTÓK: CANTATA PROFANA. (OR.: 5♭)

643. KODÁLY: JESUS AND THE TRADERS.

644. BARTÓK: MICROCOSM II. NO 66. (OR.: 2♯)

645. BORODIN: PRINCE IGOR. I. (OR.: 6♭)

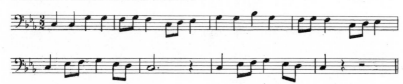

646. BARTÓK: BLUEBEARD'S CASTLE. (OR.: 0)

647. LISZT: VIA CRUCIS. (OR.: 1♭)

648. BARTÓK: SECOND SUITE. IV.

649. KODÁLY: MAROSSZÉK DANCES. (OR.: 2♭)

650. VAUGHAN WILLIAMS: STRING QUARTET IN G MINOR. II. (OR.: 1♯)

Major and minor melodies

Remaining in the same key signature

651. HANDEL: TAMERLANO. III. (OR.: 2♭)

652. PERGOLESI: SE TU M'AMI.

653. HANDEL: SAMSON. III.

654. LULLY: PHAÉTON. III. (OR.: 2♭)

655. J.HAYDN: THE SEASONS. IV.

656. J.S.BACH: DOUBLE CONCERTO IN D MINOR. I. (OR.: 1♭)

657. D.SCARLATTI: QUAL FARFALLETTA. (OR.: 2♭)

658. MOZART: THE MAGIC FLUTE. II. (OR.: 4♭)

659. CORELLI: VIOLIN SONATA IN G MINOR. OP.5. (OR.: 2♭)

660. MOZART: IL SERAGLIO. II. (OR.: 1♯)

661. MOZART: THE MAGIC FLUTE. II. (OR.: 2♭)

662. HANDEL: SAMSON. III.

663. MOZART: IL SERAGLIO. II. (OR.: 0)

664. LULLY: PSŸCHE. II. (OR.: 0)

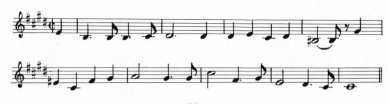

665. CORELLI: VIOLIN SONATA IN C MAJOR. OP.5. (OR.: 0)

666. HANDEL: GIULIO CESARE. II. (OR.: 2♭)

667. H.PURCELL: THE HISTORY OF DIOCLESIAN. (OR.: 2♭)

668. VIVALDI: THE FOUR SEASONS. OP.8, NO 1.

669. MOZART; THE MAGIC FLUTE. II. (OR.: 2♭)

With "d" change

670. VIVALDI: THE FOUR SEASONS. OP.8, NO 2.

671. HANDEL: TAMERLANO. III. (OR.: 1♭)

672. VIVALDI CELLO SONATA IN F MAJOR. (OR.: 2♭)

673. LULLY ISIS. III.

674. H.PURCELL: THE HISTORY OF DIOCLESIAN. (OR.: 2♭)

675. HANDEL: SAMSON. III.

Suggested further material: Legányné Hegyi Erzsébet: Collection of Bach Examples I/1,15,24,26,28; 38,40,56,65,70,73,81,101,182,183,202,210,219,223,227, 231,232,239.

EXTRACTS IN SOLFA NOTATION

The following extracts should be sung only to note names, using key signatures of 3 flats or 4 sharps, and are to be accompanied by beating time.

676. MOZART: COSÌ FAN TUTTE. I. (OR.: 3♯)

s, dm d f l f r s f md

677. VIVALDI: THE FOUR SEASONS. OP.8, NO 1. (OR.: 4♯)

l, m r d r m f m l, m r d r m f m l, f m r d t, l, t, l,

678. J.HAYDN: STRING QUARTET IN D MAJOR. OP.20, NO 4. III (OR.: 2♯)

s, s f   m l f   f r   t,d r t,s   s m   d   l, t,

d l, f   r   t,s d   d   t,s,d t, s, d r f r t, d

85

679. CORELLI: VIOLIN SONATA IN B FLAT MAJOR. OP.5. (OR.: 2♭)

l, t, d r d l,   d   r m f m d   m   l m   f m d r m   m

d l,   f r t,   s   m d   s l d f   f   m r m   r   d

680. HANDEL: SAMSON. II. (OR.: 1♭)

m f m f r l   d r m   m f   f m r l   l,   m,   m, l,

681. HANDEL: SAMSON. III. (OR.: 3♭)

l, m r d t, l,   m r d t, l,   m fi si   l

682. H.PURCELL: KING ARTHUR. III. (OR.: 0)

s   m d s   s,   d   l, f   r   s d f   m   d   r t,   d   s, d   s, l,   r t, m d

f   f r s r m   r m fi s   s   m d s,   d   l, f r   s d f   m   d r t,   d

683. CORELLI: VIOLIN SONATA IN A MAJOR. OP.5. (OR.: 3♯)

d m   l,   r f si,   m l   f   f m r d t, d r t,   l,

684. H.PURCELL: THE HISTORY OF DIOCLESIAN. (OR.: 2♭)

d | d t, l, | l, si, f m | d t, l, | l,

685. HANDEL: SAMSON. II. (OR.: 2♭)

m l | s f m r d | t, r s f | m r d t, | l, d f m r d t, l,

si, m d | l, d m l | s f m r | d t, l, l,

686. J.HAYDN: THE CREATION. I. (OR.: 1♭)

l | m d l, | t, d | r t, | t, r | f si, | t, m r | d

687. J.HAYDN: MASS IN B FLAT MAJOR. AGNUS. (OR.: 2♭)

l m | f si, l, | t, d t, | d r | di r f | m ri m | m,

Material in Several Parts

690. SCHÜTZ: ST.MATTHEW PASSION. (OR.: 1♭)

691. TELEMANN: CANON.

692. PALESTRINA: FECIT POTENTIAM. MOTET. (OR.: 1♭)

693. LASSUS: ADORAMUS. MOTET. (OR.: 1♭)

694. PALESTRINA: SICUT LOCUTUS EST. MOTET. (OR.: 1♭)

95

695. VICTORIA: ET MISERICORDIA. (OR.: 1♭)

696. PALESTRINA: CULTOR DEI, MEMENTO. MOTET. (OR.: 1♭)

98

697. J.S.BACH: THREE–PART INVENTION IN F MINOR. (OR.: 4♭)

698.   CROCE: O VOS OMNES. MOTET. (OR.: 1♭)

699.   SCHÜTZ: ST.MATTHEW PASSION. (OR.: 1♭)

101

700. J.S.BACH: ERKENNE MICH, MEIN HÜTER. CHORALE.

701. LULLY: PROSERPINE. V. (OR.: 1♭)

702. J.S.BACH: JESU; JESU, DU BIST MEIN. CHORALE.

703. J.S.BACH: SO WAHR ICH LEBE. CHORALE.

704. J.S.BACH: WIE SCHÖN LEUCHTET DER MORGENSTERN. CHORALE.

DEVELOPMENT OF MUSICAL MEMORY
Memorizing and Transposing
a Unison Melody

For this purpose, use those melodies of the sight-singing material in this chapter which contain modulations (examples 670—675). As these melodies are rather long, they may be memorized in two or three sections.

For example, the Purcell melody (674), may be learned as a succession of three melodic units:

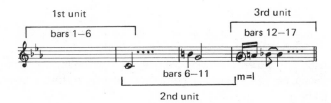

While learning the melody, several essential steps may not be omitted from the checking process. The students may begin learning the next melodic section only after they have faultlessly sung the preceding unit.

In the case of the above melody, therefore, the steps for memorizing, checking, and finally writing down the melody are as follows:

1. Learn the melody.

a/ Memorize, with the help of inner hearing, the first section with solfa;

b/ sing the memorized section by heart, accompanied by beating time;

c/ memorize, then sing, the second unit;

d/ connect the first two units in performance;

e/ memorize, then sing, the third unit in which the "d" change occurs;

f/ repeat the entire melody, singing from memory, with solfa names, accompanied by beating time.

2. After singing the melody faultlessly in solfa, sing it next with note names, again beating time as well.

3. Write down the melody in staff notation using the given key signature.

4. Describe and discuss those bars in which the more difficult rhythmic patterns occur.

5. The students sing what they have written down from their own exercise books while tapping the metric beats.

Depending on the range of the melody, *transposed singing* can be practised using the "d" systems with $7^\sharp$, $7^\flat$, $1^\flat$, $6^\sharp$, $2^\flat$, $5^\sharp$, as key signature:

1. The teacher gives the name of the new starting key. The students then determine to what key the modulating melody will arrive.

2. They sing the musical extract faultlessly to solfa, from memory, at the pitch of the new key.

3. The students name the new starting note and the note where they change "d".

4. Following this they sing the whole melody with note names appropriate to the new key signature, by memory.

Memorizing and Transposing
Two-Part Material

The learning process is the same as in the preceding chapters (see Chapter III, page 244 and Chapter IV, page 338).

If memorizing the chosen quotation does not take up too much time transposition can also be practised after checking the extract already learned and written down in the original key:

1. Repeat the musical material with solfa singing at the pitch of the new key signature a/ part by part, b/ in two parts.

2. Practise repetition as in 1., singing note names in the new key.

3. The two-part performance should be carried out by one person:

a/ A student plays one part on the piano and sings the other part in solfa. He then repeats the exercise changing parts.

b/ The student plays both parts at the piano.

c/ The student plays one part on the piano and at the same time sings the other to note names, exchanging parts afterwards.

4. A volunteer writes the two-part extract on the blackboard. The students then sing it again in groups.

The two-part extracts

705. BUXTEHUDE: MAGNIFICAT PRIMI TONI. (OR.: 1♭)

706. BUXTEHUDE: LOBT GOTT, IHR CHRISTEN ALLZUGLEICH. (OR.: 1♯)

707. HANDEL: DETTINGEN TE DEUM. NO 11. (OR.: 2♯)

708.   J.S.BACH: THE MUSICAL OFFERING. NO 8.

709.   BEETHOVEN: 15 VARIATIONS IN E FLAT MAJOR. OP.35.

710.   HANDEL: CONCERTO GROSSO IN G MINOR. OP.6, NO 6. II. (OR.: 2♭)

Memorizing Three-Part Material

Of the three parts, select one to be sung and play the other two on the piano.

Suggested way of memorization

1. Memorize the part chosen to be sung first in solfa, then to note names.
2. Similarly learn one of the other parts, too.
3. In the now familiar manner (solfa singing + piano playing) perform the two parts from memory.
4. After memorizing the third part, practise it with the sung part as described above (3.).
5. Leaving out the singing part, play the other two parts on the piano.
6. After repeating steps 3—5 many times, three-part performance can be practised:
a/ The singing part to solfa names, the others on the piano;
b/ the singing part to note names, the others on the piano.
7. Write down the complete musical quotation from memory according to the original staff notation.
8. Check the written extract with note name singing.

The three-part extracts

711.   VIVALDI: SYMPHONY FOR STRINGS IN C MAJOR.

712. MONTEVERDI: SE PER HAVERNE OIMÈ DONATO. MADRIGAL.

(Dorian start, coloured by "ta". Cf. Chapter III, page 235.)

713. MOZART: THE MAGIC FLUTE. OVERTURE.

714. MONTEVERDI: COR MIO! MENTRE VI MIRO. MADRIGAL. (OR.: 0)

(Dorian start, coloured by "fi", "ta" and "di".)

715. MONTEVERDI: CH' AMI LA VITA MIA. MADRIGAL. (OR.: 1♭)

(Aeolin start, coloured by "di" and "ta".)

716. MONTEVERDI: O ROSSIGNUOL, CH' IN QUESTE VERDI. MADRIGAL. (OR.: 1♭)

717. PALESTRINA: DOMINE FILI. MOTET. (OR.: 1♭)

718. PALESTRINA: POENAS CUCURRIT. MOTET. (OR.: 1♭)

Memorizing Chord Progressions

The following figured bass examples are given complete with a suggested soprano line. The chord progressions are those of previously analysed selections. Directly related to the study of harmony is the ability to commit these progressions to memory as this presupposes and reinforces knowledge of the basic principles of four-part chord construction. The presence of a second voice, here a given soprano, is of great help in forming framework within which the students may consciously complete and memorize a four-part chord progression.

Suggested method of memorization

1. Analyse the exercise, identifying the key and the scale degree number of each chord.

2. Memorize the lowest part (bass): a/ with solfa, b/ with degree numbers, c/ with note names.

3. Memorize the soprano: a/ to solfa, b/ to note names.

4. The students individually perform the two parts at the piano while singing a/ the bass part to solfa then with degree numbers, b/ the soprano part to solfa.

5. With the help of the given soprano, let us imagine the missing alto and tenor parts, and then consciously complete the four-part structure of each chord.

6. Check to see that the above progressive steps are consciously understood and firmly memorized by the entire group: the two parts given in staff notation are played on the piano from memory by one of the students while the others then sing a/ to solfa, b/ to note names the three upper parts of each chord in descending order from the soprano.

7. A volunteer can play the four-part progression from memory at the piano while a/ singing the bass part to degree numbers, to solfa and then to note names; b/ singing the three upper parts of the chord sounding at the moment in downward direction, starting with the soprano, to solfa then to note names.

8. After several individual performances, have the entire group sing the exercise in the same way (7.).

Figured bass progressions

EAR TRAINING
Recognition of Intervals

Interval progressions within the major and minor tonality

After giving the tonic note the teacher plays a tonal sequence on the piano. It is made up of second, third, fourth and fifth intervals belonging to the major or minor key and the students write down the successive intervals with solfa names.

To carry out this task successfully the students have to recall and sing the keynote "d" or "l" of the given key before sounding the new intervals.

For example, a sequence in harmonic minor:

1. Recognition.

2. Checking:

a/ Sing each interval upwards to solfa, identifying the interval each time (l,—m: perfect 5th; d—f: perfect 4th; etc.).

b/ Sing all the intervals upwards (l,—m; d—f; r—m; etc.) then downwards (m—l,; f—d; etc.).

Intervals in the diatonic hexachords

Practise in ways similar to those used for the pentachords (see Chapter IV, page 342).

Intervals within the pentatonic modes

Practise interval recognition with the five pentatonic modes in ways similar to those used for the intervals of pentatonic trichords, tetrachords, and for the set of notes within the sixth range (see Chapter I, pages 76—79, Chapter II, page 158).

Interval recognition from "Let Us Sing Correctly"

In this chapter exercises 47, 48, 56, 60, 61, 66, 69 and 70 are used for ear training purposes. Use them in the already familiar methods of practice (see Chapter III, page 248).

Chord Recognition

Root position triad, 6 chord
and $\frac{6}{4}$ chord from a given scale degree

The teacher plays on the piano a root position triad, a 6 chord and a $\frac{6}{4}$ chord in an optional sequence from a certain scale degree—taken as the lowest note—of any major or harmonic minor key belonging to the "d" systems practised so far. The students put down a/ the structure of the single chords (root, or one or the other of the inversions), b/ the solfa name of the lowest note which remains unchanged and c/ the degree number of the chord within the tonality.

For example, the progression of 6 chord, root, $\frac{6}{4}$ chord in harmonic minor, from "r" as lowest note, at the pitch of C (G minor):

1. Recognition.

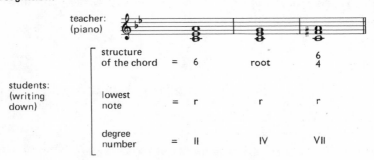

teacher: (piano)				
students: (writing down)	structure of the chord	= 6	root	$\frac{6}{4}$
	lowest note	= r	r	r
	degree number	= II	IV	VII

2. Individual checking: during the second playing the students check their own work and make correction where necessary.

3. Check the entire group. Ask them to:

a/ identify the chord structure,

b/ give the solfa name of the lowest (bass) note,

c/ give the appropriate Roman numeral for each chord.

4. Sing the chords in broken form starting from the same lowest note: a/ to solfa, b/ to note names (in the given key).

Seventh chords

Type recognition

The teacher plays the different types of the seventh chord (see Chapter VI, page 64). on the piano, while the students, using the aid of solfa names, write down the progressions.

For example, the sequence minor+minor 7th — augmented+major 7th — major+ major 7th — diminished+dim. 7th — major+minor 7th — diminished+minor 7th — minor+major 7th from C as starting note:

1. Recognition.

teacher: (piano)		
students: (writing down)	l,- d - m - s or: r - f - l - d' or: m - s - t - r'	d - m - si - t

2. Checking: The students

a/ sing the individual chords with all solfa possibilities,

b/ identify the type (minor+major 7th, etc.),

c/ enumerate the degree numbers of the chords within the major and harmonic minor tonality.

3. Making the chords conscious: after group discussion and correction, the teacher plays the progression once more to help the students retain the types of chords in their inner hearing as firmly as possible.

Seventh chords placed within tonality

After giving the tonic in major or minor the teacher plays the seventh chords of different degrees of the chosen tonality. Before he sounds a new chord the students sing the "d" or "l" keynote and compared to that they establish the degree number of the new seventh chord. They then write the number in their exercise-books. As a check they name the degree numbers and then sing the whole progression to solfa.

For example, the sequence I⁷–VI⁷–II⁷–V⁷–IV⁷–VII⁷–III⁷ in C harmonic minor:

1. Recognition.

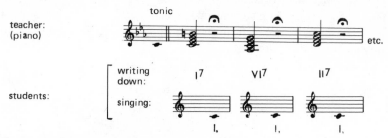

2. Group checking by naming the degree numbers.
3. Singing for making the chords conscious.

First inversion seventh (⁶₅) chords

Type recognition

Let us practise in the same way we have already practised root position seventh chords (see Chapter VI, page 119).

⁶₅ chords placed within tonality

Practise in the manner already used for root position seventh chords (see Chapter VI, page 119).

Chord progressions

The figured bass examples on page 115 in Chapter VI can be used not only for memorizing but also for ear training purposes.

Suggested stages in practice

1. The teacher presents the selected progression in four parts on the piano then plays it again while the students accompany it by singing the bass melody to solfa.

2. The teacher then repeats the progression while the students, individually if possible, sing each chord in broken form. Since the bass line is already familiar, this should not prove too difficult to do. The chords are to be sung from the lowest note upward.

3. After the above singing they name the degree numbers of the chords within the tonality then write the progression of these degree numbers on the blackboard.

4. Finally, the teacher plays the sequence once more while the students repeat the singing of chords to solfa from the degree numbers put down on the blackboard. In this way the conscious singing and the total sounding of the chords form an organic unity in the students' inner hearing.

Rhythm Dictation

(Musical material on page 467 of the Supplement)

Suggested method of practice

1. The teacher selects three or four excerpts in the same metre for dictation, identifies the given time signature, and then plays the extracts one at a time. The students are to write down the rhythm from memory only after the excerpt has been played. Repeat only if necessary, each extract several times so that the students are able to write down the rhythm of the topmost voice.

2. After dictating all the excerpts, the teacher plays each one again while the students check what they have written.

3. A volunteer then write the rhythm of each excerpt on the board. After the group makes any necessary corrections, the teacher once more plays the examples so that the students may consciously relate the sound to its written representation.

Kodály: 24 Little Canons

In this chapter, practise exercises 4, 8, 10, 12 and 15 in the already familiar manner (see Chapter III, page 252, and Chapter IV, page 348). Now, however, place the "d" on E or E♭. If, after the canon has been successfully sung, there is a student who has memorized the entire melody, we may include two further practice procedures:

1. The above student begins the melody from memory, singing it on solfa syllables, while the rest of the group, or one other student, answer in canon.

2. The student who can sing the melody also to note names by memory performs the two-part canon individually: a/ sings the first part to solfa and plays the other on the piano, b/ plays the first part and sings the second one.

Melody Dictation

One-part dictation

This area of ear training will be practised as previously (preparation — memorizing+ singing+writing, see Chapter II, pages 162—164) but, keeping pace with the students' more advanced level, we shall now include new and more difficult tasks to be carried out. These are as follows:

1. The students a/ memorize the melody with the help of their inner hearing, then b/ perform it on the piano (or on another instrument), finally c/ write it down by heart.

2. In the case of shorter extracts, any of the above mentioned procedures (memorizing+singing+writing down or memorizing+instrumental performance+writing down) can be brought into play by memorizing two or three melodies, one after another, but not writing them down, however, until the students have shown that they have learned them and are able to perform them, vocally or instrumentally. Only then shall we ask the students to write them down.

This is a very difficult task but the students' ability to concentrate will be greatly intensified and strengthened through its practice.

3. The students a/ memorize the melody with the help of their inner hearing, then b/ write it down immediately.

4. The students use "continuous writing"—that is they write the melody simultaneously as it is being performed without memorizing it—and correct the written material during the pauses between playings.

Melodies in pentatonic and church modes
(Musical material on page 471 of the Supplement)

From the above-mentioned methods of dictation, choose those which seem to be most useful from the standpoint of the musical material and the needs of the students. In regard to 4. above, continuous writing type dictation should be used only with pentatonic melodies, and only after the students are well able to sing melodies of the Pentatonic Music to note names.

Major and minor melodies
(Musical material on page 474 of the Supplement)

The musical material found under this heading contains many melodic turns with altered notes. Therefore, whichever type of dictation we choose for ear training purposes, we must take great care to prepare these sections of the given melody (see Chapter II, page 162).

Do not attempt continuous writing dictation for the melodies in this group.

Two-part dictation

CONCENTRATION ON THE VERTICAL SOUNDING
(Musical material on page 477 of the Supplement)

When two-part dictation was discussed in Chapter IV, the teacher was asked to play the chosen quotation several times so the students had the opportunity to hear each part as an independent melody (see Chapter IV, page 349, point 1). The vertical sounding of two-part material was only concentrated upon when checking the memorized extract (see Chapter IV, page 349, point 2).

In this chapter we must now attempt to memorize material after only one hearing. This can only be done if the students concentrate on the lower part when listening to the extract. Thus, while focusing on the lower part, which gives a sense of harmonic orientation, the students involuntarily hear the complementary melodic part at the same time.

The procedure for this area of ear training is otherwise the same as described in Chapter IV (see page 349).

When dictating excerpts which contain altered notes, leave out those steps involving hand-signs.

CONCENTRATION ON THE HORIZONTAL MELODIC MOVEMENT
(Musical material on page 479 of the Supplement)

When dictating these longer quotations the students should memorize both parts as independent melodies. Otherwise they will not remember either part securely. It is still very important and is an assurance for the students' further development that they memorize the lower part first.

Suggested procedure for ear training

1. During the first performance the students establish the key and metre of the quotation, the metrical position of the opening, and the beginning note of the bass part (to solfa).
2. They then memorize the lower part and sing it a/ to solfa, b/ to note names.
3. Similarly they memorize and sing the upper part.
4. The above part-singing is followed by two-part performances: a/ Two groups then two persons sing the extract with solfa (exchanging parts as well), b/ a volunteer plays one part on the piano while the other students sing the second part to note names (also exchanging parts), c/ the entire two-part selection is performed by one student who plays either of the parts on the piano and sings the other to solfa (exchanging parts, too).
5. The students write down the excerpt in their exercise-book.
6. As a check a/ one of the students who was able to write the two-part extract without any mistakes plays it from the exercise-book then b/ another volunteer sings the written melodic lines to note names, finally c/ they do the same as a group.

Bach Chorale Extracts

Two-part continuous writing
(Musical material on page 481 of the Supplement)

As the essentially new step in this form of ear training, the students take down the outer voices of the quoted chorale excerpt as they are played. The primary conditions for carrying out this task successfully are the following: a/ a secure tonal feeling developed also in the students' inner hearing, b/ conscious, concentrated and steady observational ability, c/ immediate and accurate recognition of successive tones, d/ rapid association of the aurally recognized intervallic movement with staff notation in the given "d" system.

If, in previous chapters, the many varied procedures aimed at developing aural comprehension have been intensively practised, this new task should not cause any special difficulty for the students.

Two-part continuous writing realized in practice

1. The teacher plays the chorale extract and the students establish a/ the tonality of the quotation (major or minor), b/ the opening note of the bass part and that of the melody (to solfa then to note names), c/ the metre of the excerpt and d/ the metrical position of the opening.

2. As the teacher plays the example a second time, the students write down the bass part, trying to remember the soprano melody which is then to be written out from memory.

3. When the chorale is played for a third time, the students complete the soprano line and check the bass.

4. While the teacher plays the quotation once more the students fill in possible omissions and check the two-part vertical sounding.

5. As group checking a/ a volunteer sings the written parts one by one with note names (first the bass then the soprano), b/ two persons sing the two-part material to solfa then to note names, c/ divided into two groups they sing the bass + soprano parts with solfa while the teacher plays the complete four-part material on the piano.

Memorizing and writing down the bass
(Musical material on page 484 of the Supplement)

We shall follow the procedures given in previous chapters, but in a more concentrated fashion:

1. At the first performance the students establish a/ the key of the extract, b/ the opening and closing note of the bass, c/ the metre, d/ the metrical position of the opening.

2. During the second dictation they follow the bass melody by themselves to solfa.

3. After the third performance they sing the melody of the lower part by memory a/ to solfa, b/ to note names.

4. After several perfect performances, they write down the bass.

5. As a control, the students sing the excerpt with note names from their exercise-books.

6. Finally, they perform the excerpt in groups: the four-part material is played by the teacher on the piano while the students sing the written bass in solfa.

PLANNING SUGGESTION

(See the diagram at the end of the book.)

CHAPTER VII
(Material in staff notation uses A and A flat as "d")

KODÁLY MATERIAL
Unison Pentatonic Melodies
MATERIAL IN SOLFA NOTATION
(Pentatonic Music I—IV; 333 Reading Exercises)

New elements

Alternation of $\frac{5}{4}$ and $\frac{4}{4}$: IV/131

The beating time for the $\frac{5}{4}$ bars will conform to the 2+3 division contained therein (see Chapter IV, page 265). Have the students sing the melody individually and as a group. Beating time should always accompany the singing so that the alternation of $\frac{5}{4}$ and $\frac{4}{4}$ time-beating become very well ingrained.

Major tenth upwards: IV/134

The final note of line 1 and the initial note of line 2 is an upward major tenth. Intonation will not be difficult as the first three notes of line 2 repeat the final three notes of line 1 transposed one octave higher. (The melody is in $\frac{6}{8}$ with the ♪ as metrical unit.)

Before singing the melody, practise the following sequence several times:

The students may sing the melody only after the d—m' interval of tenth is secure, and then always with beating time.

Alternation of $\frac{3}{8}$ and $\frac{4}{8}$: IV/127

Practise the exercise with a two-part rhythmic accompaniment in which the stressed metrical units are sounded by the left hand and the unstressed metrical units by the right hand.

Pattern for bars in $\frac{4}{8}$:

(compound metre: $\frac{2}{8}$ + $\frac{2}{8}$)

Pattern for bars in $\frac{3}{8}$:

(simple metre)

Alternation of metres with different metrical units: IV/139, 107

a/ No 139: the melody is based on the same principles as the above piece (No 127). Practise it with a two-part rhythm accompaniment.

The rhythmic accompaniment corresponds to the metric structure of each bar:

(compound metres)

b/ No 107: sing the melody with the following one-part rhythm accompaniment:

130

Easy melodies for practising note name singing

(333/327–330; III/62,64,65,66,85,86,87,88,90,91, IV/133)

The melodies in this group all contain familiar pentatonic melodic turns and simple rhythmic patterns. They may therefore be sung with note names after appropriate preparation with hand-signs (see Chapter VII, page 153).

Since the melodies remain within the frame of the d—m' tenth, A or A♭ "d" will provide a comfortable singing range:

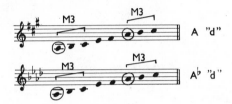

A "d"

A♭ "d"

Note name singing may be accompanied by a/ tapping the metrical unit, b/ beating time, c/ an ostinato.

For example, III/66 from Pentatonic Music in the system with A as "d" with the two-bar ostinato $\frac{2}{4}$ ♩ ♫ | ♪♩ ♪ :

singing:

A F♯ E A   B A F♯   A F♯E   B   A   etc.

ostinato:

131

Two-Part Material

PREPARATORY EXERCISES:
"LET US SING CORRECTLY"
(Nos. 82,83,84,85,86,87)

Sing the exercises in the usual way.

TWO-PART WORKS

Pentatonic range of notes

Those two-part pentatonic exercises of the Kodály Choral Method using A as "d"
all contain two-system pentatonic themes. Since these themes combine two pentatonic
systems with A and D as "d" they will be left for Chapter VIII.

The unison material of this chapter does not include melodies in staff notation
nor does the two-part material include one-system pentatonic exercises. Therefore
it is important that we intensify our practice of note-finding from staff notation.

The new pentatonic set of notes using A or A $^\flat$ as "d":

a/ with A as "d":

b/ with A $^\flat$ as "d":

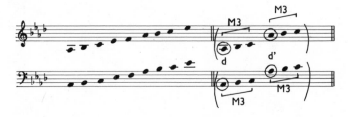

44 Two-Part Exercises/22, Var. 11

1. The original minor theme appears as a variant, transformed to major, in the alto part. The rhythm is varied only in bar 6: ♩ instead of ♩.

2. The melodic patterns are not difficult. However, a composition beginning on the subdominant function is unusual. Clear intonation of the simultaneous f–d' will be insured by playing the harmonic outline of the first bar as a prelude:

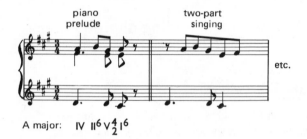

A major: IV   II⁶ V⁴₂ I⁶

It is advisable to immediately repeat the exercise in this way. The second subdominant beginning following the cadential tonic is more easily established in the students' inner hearing.

Bicinia Hungarica III/110

1. The theme is mixolydian, the form A B B, A . As both the fourth ("d") and the sixth ("m") above the final note play prominent roles in the course of the melody, singing with comparative names, that is with "d" final note, is not justified.
    Folk melodies of this type are identified as being "$\frac{6}{4}$ mixolydian".

2. The melody note "d" is also prominent in the imitative material of the accompanying line:

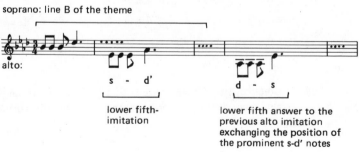

soprano: line B of the theme

alto:

s - d'   d - s

lower fifth-
imitation

lower fifth answer to the
previous alto imitation
exchanging the position of
the prominent s-d' notes

133

We find many unusual mixolydian turns in the course of this "s"-ending melody. Especially awkward are those sections of the melody in which "f" appears as a lower changing note:

Let us make sure in these instances that the "f" is low enough.

Range including altered notes

55 Two-Part Exercises/5

Special attention must be paid to two patterns of the alto part:
  a/ the altered note "ta" in the ascending melody line (bar 4);
  b/ the unresolved augmented fourth:

To insure correct intonation of these difficult melodic sections practise the following material from bars 1—8
  a/ with "d" change (alternating "f" and "fi")
  b/ without "d" change (alternating "ta" and "t"):

Of these two types of practice, the first (a) insures that the note G in bar 4 will be sufficiently low, and the second (b) insures that the G♯ melodic turning-point in bar 6 will be sufficiently high.

1. The absence of bar lines is a significant characteristic of this exercise. In this case more concentration is generally demanded of the performer than in the case of musical material delineating bar lines. Even greater concentration is required in this particular instance as the outward appearance of the musical material, due to the notation itself, does not conform to the inner, metrical pulse of the motivic material.

For example, the soprano:

a/ The written staff notation:

b/ Inner musical pulse:

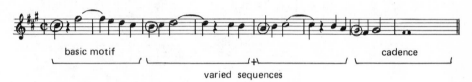

basic motif   varied sequences   cadence

c/ An exact sequence would sound thus:

To overcome these metrical difficulties it is very useful to practise the individual parts separately in the following ways:

a/ The students sing one part while tapping (or clapping) the other.

b/ Practise each voice to the $\math112{C}$ two-part rhythmic accompaniment.

c/ Maintaining the ♩ as the metrical unit, the students accompany part-singing with beating duple time.

2. The other significant feature found in the first third of this exercise is the appearance of melodic elements of a typically Baroque chord progression (see Chapter III, page 219):

F# minor: I   IV VII III VI II V# I

natural
minor

(A major: V - I)

The last five chords of this sequential progression appear in the exercise, some in first inversion:

Before singing this exercise in two parts, it is most important that the students are clearly aware of the root of each chord in the sequential progression. The entire group should therefore practice the following melodic lines:

66 Two-Part Exercises/40

The presence of the leap of the seventh in the theme demands that this exercise receive thorough preparation.

1. Identify the melodic outline of the theme as it appears through the exercise. Practise singing these melodic outlines only as a continuous melodic sequence. The students sing first as a group, then individually:

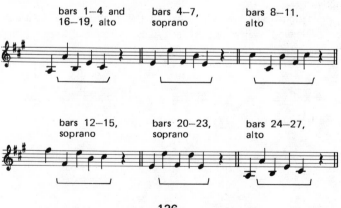

2. When the intonation of these melodic figures is correct and secure, sing the original material of the above-mentioned bars:

a/ each voice separately, for example, the alto:

bars 1—4   bars 8—11

b/ both voices together, continuously, one voice answering the other:

3. Two-part singing of the entire exercise should be attempted only after this preparation.

Suggested further exercises: 55 Two-Part Exercises/22; 44 Two-Part Exercises/22, Var. 10.

Modulating musical material

66 Two-Part Exercises/27

1. The melodic outline of the theme (in the soprano):

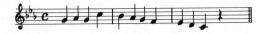

The melody is tripodic in C aeolian (natural minor). We find two points worthy of our attention in the further appearances of the time:

a/ The F aeolian theme (bars 7—8) is heard in a shortened variant:

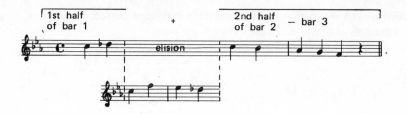

Here the theme becomes bipodic and remains within the range of a hexachord.

b/ A transformed variant is heard in bars 9 and 12: the soprano presents the theme in E♭ ionian (major), the alto follows with the theme in G phrygian.

2. The sequence containing leaps of diminished fifths (soprano, bars 14—17) demands special practice. Sing, in succession these melodic segments:

3. The theme appears successively in the following keys:

Theme (dux) bars 1—3		Theme 7-8	Theme 9-11				Theme 17—19	
C aeolian		F aeolian (shortened variant)	E ionian (transformed)		leading back (sequence)	C aeolian		
	Theme (comes) 4—6			Theme 12—14			Theme 20—22	
	G aeolian (real answer)			G phrygian (transformed)			C aeolian	
3♭ → 2♭ ——— → 4♭ → 3♭								
T → D ⟍ S ↗ T								

4. The outline of keys and the formal structure combine to present an interesting blend of Baroque and Renaissance stylistic elements:

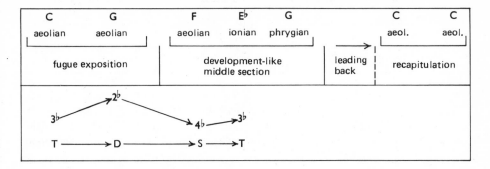

The order of key signatures establishes an outer Baroque (plagal) frame, while the modal thematic content is characteristically Renaissance in style. The first three successive keys (with signatures of 3^b, 2^b, and 4^b respectively) each present the theme once in aeolian mode. The final section (signature of 3^b) presents the so-called modality, most characteristic to the Renaissance style: the relative modes within the same key signature follow one another. Thus the proportions of the Baroque order of keys (see Chapter III, page 277, point 4) have been shifted: the ascending subdominant-tonic fifth movement does not occur in its customary position at the close of the composition, but rather at an earlier point. (Cf.: 66 Two-Part Exercises/49; Chapter IX, page 359).

5. Suggested places for "d" change:

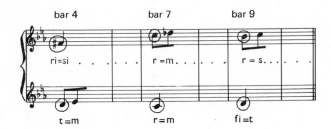

33 Two-Part Exercises/2

1. The exercise has clearly two main sections. The same thematic material is presented in the first period in the soprano, in the second period in the alto. Thus we can designate the form as A A, :

A			A,		
a		b	a		b,
A major : opens, A minor → C major : closes			C major : opens, C major → A minor → A major : closes		
1st period (section 1)			2nd period (section 2)		

2. There is an interesting order of keys within each section: "A" period: tonic major→minore (parallel minor)→relative major of the minore. "A," period: the new major as tonic → relative minor → maggiore (parallel major) of the relative minor. (Minore — parallel minor — is the minor key starting from the same keynote as the given major; maggiore — parallel major — is the major key starting from the same keynote as the given minor.)

3. Suggested places for "d" change:

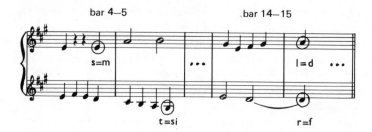

44 Two-Part Exercises/18

1. The tripodic theme and its real answer are related in the following manner: the final note of the dux and the initial note of the comes coincide at a same point of main accent. Thus in the dux and comes together we find only 5 points of main accent:

main accents of comes:			1. starting main accent	2.	3.
main accents of dux:	1.	2.	3. closing main accent		

2. As the tonic closing note of the dux is particularly prominent, the simultaneous dominant starting note of the comes may present difficulty in intonation. As preparation, practise, in succession, the following melodic segments:

a)

3. The theme appears successively in the following keys:

	Comes 3–5						Theme 16–19	
	C minor (real answer)	leading back		trans-ition		trans-ition	A♭ major (trans-formed)	leading back
Dux bars 1–3			Theme 8–10		Theme 12–14			Theme 23–25
F minor			F minor		E♭ major (transformed)			F minor

4♭ ——→ 3♭ ————→ 4♭ ————→ 3♭ ————————→ 4♭

The final return is achieved by a modulating variant of the theme in which we move from A♭ major to the dominant of F minor (bars 18–21 in the soprano).

4. Suggested places for "d" change:

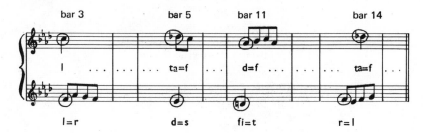

33 Two-Part Exercises/3

This eight-bar exercise in A major has a central cadence in C# major, i.e. in the major dominant of the F# relative minor. Following the A major opening, the E# in the soprano can easily be sung too low as it is the upper note of an unresolved augmented fifth approached by consecutive ascending major seconds. To insure proper intonation:

1. Practise bars 3—4 only a/ as being in C# major and then b/ as being in F# minor:

2. Practise the entire alto part alone, in unison, with A as "d". Proper intonation

of the descending trichord 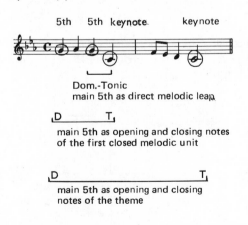 will ensure a firm tonal framework for

the difficult melodic pattern in the soprano.

Perform the entire exercise in two parts, without "d" change, but only after having sung the above preparatory steps.

66 Two-Part Exercises/44

1. The most important melodic element of this minor hexachord theme, based on keynote C, is the repeatedly prominent main fifth:

Dom.-Tonic
main 5th as direct melodic leap

main 5th as opening and closing notes of the first closed melodic unit

main 5th as opening and closing notes of the theme

2. The comes (soprano, bars 3—4) is a tonal answer and modulates, in a characteristically Baroque manner, to the dominant. In place of the opening—closing (D–T) descending main fifth of the dux we now find the descending main fourth (T–D):

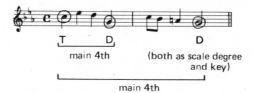

(Cf.: Bach, The Well-Tempered Clavier I, Fugue in C minor.)
The direct melodic leap of the main fifth determines the key of arrival in the comes as well:

The differentiation of dux and comes is clear from the very first melodic turn: the ascending third characterizes the comes form of the theme.

3. The remainder of the composition presents the dux and comes in the following order of appearance:

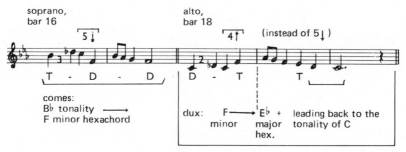

varied theme with the role of leading back

143

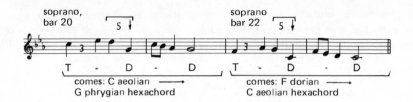

comes: C aeolian ⟶
G phrygian hexachord

comes: F dorian ⟶
C aeolian hexachord

The order of the final two appearances of the theme is in many respects worthy of close attention: a/ They relate in a manner which realizes the familiar Renaissance "modal" answer (an answer with the same intervallic structure but sounding in a relative mode); b/ The order of the modes contains the logical essence of the Baroque order of keys: the theme beginning with a "l" keynote ends with a "m" keynote, the theme beginning with a "r" keynote ends with a "l" keynote, only here the use of Renaissance modes replaces the major–minor tonalities of the Baroque:

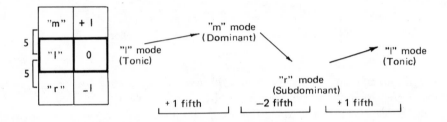

(Cf.: Bach, The Well-Tempered Clavier I, Fugue in G# minor.)

4. If we consider the vertical sound of the two-part material, as well as the appearance of the theme, we notice an interesting stylistic feature: the first dux–comes succession brings about a real modulation from C minor to G minor. From bar 5, however, the thematic material appears within the framework of the eleven-note Renaissance tone-set (see Chapter III, page 235) which includes typical "waving-notes" (t+ta; f+fi; d+di; s+si). Thus the major- and minor-sounding hexachords are not transpositions with changes of key signatures, but rather hexachords of the relative modes within the 3$^\flat$ system:

144

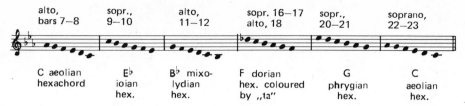

alto, bars 7–8	sopr., 9–10	alto, 11–12	sopr. 16–17 alto, 18	sopr., 20–21	soprano, 22–23
C aeolian hexachord	Eb ioian hex.	Bb mixo-lydian hex.	F dorian hex. coloured by „ta"	G phrygian hex.	C aeolian hex.

(Modes similar to the fourth set of notes, with "ta" as colouring note, are often found in the two-part motets of Lassus.)

This modal interpretation is further supported by the F dorian theme following the Bb mixolydian cadence (bars 15–17) placing the D and Db ("t" and "ta") in close proximity:

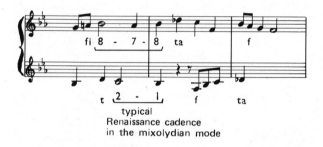

typical
Renaissance cadence
in the mixolydian mode

The "t" becomes partner to the leading tone "fi" (A) of the mixolydian cadence. The "ta", however, which appears in close proximity to the "t", is necessitated, in the spirit of the style, by the "f" (Ab) notes. As a consequence, an octave imitation, coloured by the alternating t–ta comes about in the musical material:

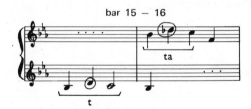

bar 15 – 16

5. Therefore, when performing the exercise with solfa names, we are faithful to the style if we change the "d" only at the appearance of the first comes and interpret the rest of the music material on the basis of the Renaissance eleven-note system according to 3b key signature. The suggested places for "d"-change are thus:

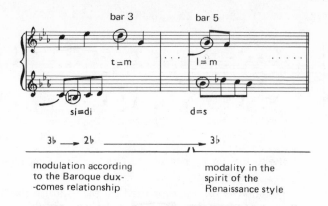

modulation according
to the Baroque dux-
-comes relationship

modality in the
spirit of the
Renaissance style

6. The relation to the Renaissance style is strengthened by a further element as well: the inner cadences, which delineate the compositional sections, contain melodic elements typical of two-part Renaissance cadences.

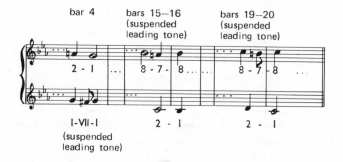

Suggested further exercises: 55 Two-Part Exercises/48; Fifteen Two-Part Exercises/11.

Three-Part Material

Tricinia/3

1. The composition is divided into three sections:

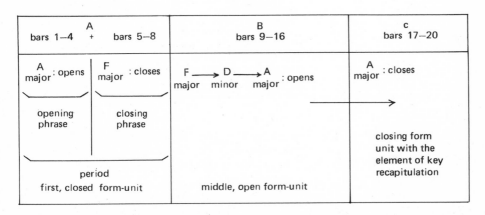

A bars 1—4 + bars 5—8	B bars 9—16	c bars 17—20
A major: opens F major: closes	F —→ D —→ A : opens major minor major	A major: closes
opening closing phrase phrase		
period first, closed form-unit	middle, open form-unit	closing form unit with the element of key recapitulation

Examining the musical material of the final "c" section, we can see that its seemingly new melodic line is actually built from turns and phrases of the two preceding sections. The organic development of the previous melodic elements becomes intensified by the alteration, itself consequential to the organic melodic development, of metrical function in certain bars: the unstressed bar within the motif becomes a stressed bar of the new motif.

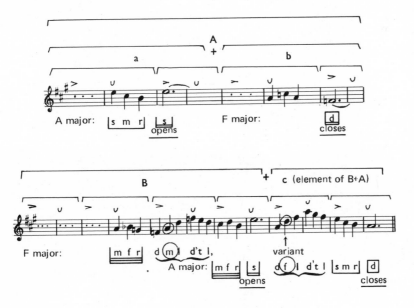

2. The modulation places two so-called third-related keys next to each other (A major − F major − A major; two major keys a third apart), a common occurence in the Romantic style. The chord progressions of the modulation are likewise of a new type, but can be explained within the framework of functional analysis:

a/ A major → F major:

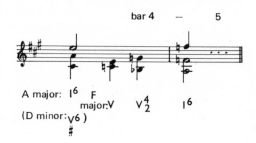

b/ F major → A major:

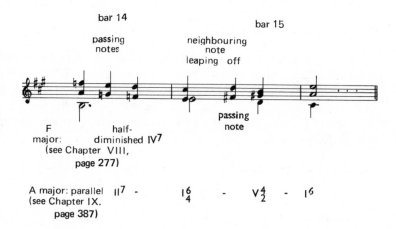

3. Suggested places for "d" change:

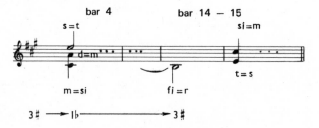

148

4. Intonation difficulties in the composition:

a/ Alto, bars 3—5: Practise only with the already secure mezzo part. Because of the unusual modulation the  melodic segment will itself be always uncertain.

b/ Soprano, bar 11: The "t" (E) as the fifth of the $V\frac{6}{5}$ in D minor, is preceded by its altered lower neighbouring note "li" (D♯) approached by leap, which is usually sung higher than necessary. Practise the soprano and alto parts only (bars 11—13), first without the above-mentioned lower neighbour (), then with the lower neighbour as written. After a successful performance with the two parts, sing the same bars in three parts, at first without the "li", and then again with the "li".

c/ In the modulating material of the mezzo, bars 14—15, the F♯—G♯ within the ascending melodic line can easily be sung lower than necessary. Therefore it is most useful to sing this three-bar melodic section taken out of context, as if it were in A minor:

When singing either the entire line, or the several parts together, we must interpret this section in the context of the ongoing modulation of the musical material:

149

Melody with Piano Accompaniment

Epigrams/4

1. This wide-ranging melody is essentially built on two basic motifs of contrasting character, and their respective variants. Together they give rise to an A B two-section form. The main motif of section A contains large and decisive leaps (motif "α"), while section B begins with descending major seconds forming a tetrachord (motif "β").

Section A:

key	A major			→ F# minor		→ C# minor		
number of bar	I	2	3	4	5	6	7	8
music material	α 5			α³ᵥ	αᵥ	β⁶		α³ᵥᵥ

C# minor			→ A major									
I	2	3	4	5	6	7	8	9	10	II	12	13
β		β⁵	α⁵ᵥ		α⁴ mirror and crab invers.		γ		α³ᵥᵥᵥ with 2nd↑ closing element instead of 7th↓	α⁵ᵥᵥᵥ	γᵥ	

150

2. Suggested places for "d" change:

bar 6   bar 12

s=d   d = s

3. The exceptionally difficult melodic turns of bars 6, 11—12 (twelfth and diminished octave, both upwards) must be prepared tonally.

a/ Sing the entire A section four times in succession with the following variants for the final three bars:

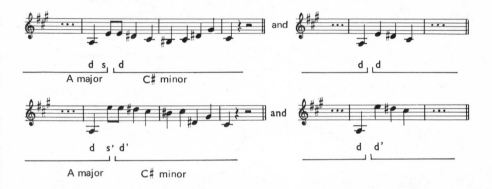

and

d s d
A major   C# minor

d d

d s' d'
A major   C# minor

d d'

b/ Proper intonation of the melodic segment containing the diminished octave can be helped by practising the following motivic sequence:

C#
minor: m ....

Epigrams/1

The composition is a succession of four-bar melodically open musical units. Decidedly cadential elements, from a harmonic, rhythmic, and melodic viewpoint, occur only in the last five bars, which open out as a coda.

The main key of the musical material is A♭ major, then moves through the minore A minor into C♭ major, remaining in that key for a short while. Extremely interesting are the harmonic progressions, albeit familiar in context of functional harmony, which determine the manner and points of the "d" changes:

151

bar 9

ta = s

(F minor: V⁷) ⟶ I

passing
note

A♭ major: VI   -   IV⁶ - II$\frac{4}{3}$ - I$\frac{6}{4}$ - I$\frac{4}{3}$ -   - Neap.⁶

parallel
sec.
dom.

A♭
minor: Neap.⁶ - V$\frac{4}{2}$ -

— III⁷ ⎤ enharmonic
dim. ⎦ C♭ major: III$\frac{4}{2}$ - I⁷ - I$\frac{9}{7}$ - IV⁷ ⎤ A♭ minor: aug.5 —

enharmonic
6

dim.

secondary
dominant

sec.
dom.

si=t

— aug. $\frac{6}{5}$ + $\frac{4}{3}$ A♭ major: I$\frac{6}{4}$ - V$\frac{9}{7}$ - VI⁶ — VII⁷♭— I

alter-
nation

parallel + tonic

deceptive
cadence

pedal

(Cf.: Altered chords, Chapter VIII, pages 276–283 and Chapter IX, pages 387–392; Enharmonic re-interpretations, Chapter IX, page 392)

THEORETICAL INFORMATION
AND TECHNICAL EXERCISES
Range of Notes, Hand-Signs

Pentatony

Note name singing to hand-signs

Practise in the usual way but now with A and A^b as "d".
(Cf.: Chapter VI, page 41).

Diatony

Note name singing to hand-signs

Practise as before, using key signatures of 3$^\sharp$ or 4^b.
(Cf.: Chapter VI, page 41).

Diatony + alteration

Solfa singing from staff notation

Use the following set of notes for practice:
    a/ in the G clef:

b/ in the F clef:

Solfa – note name singing in answering form

Practise more difficult melodic patterns with 3 sharps or 4 flats as key signature.
(Cf.: Chapter VI, page 42)

Note name singing to hand-signs with change of key

We have already practised changes of key brought about by the notes "fi" and "ta"
in Chapter VI (see page 43). Since the principle of modulation (fi=t and ta=f)
is well-known to the students, we must now emphasize note name singing.

For example, if the starting key is B major:

| the teacher's hand-sign melody: | right hand: | d - l,- t,- d - f,-m,- s, - ta, | | t,- d | etc. |
| | left hand: | | f - m- r- t,-d - l - fi | | |

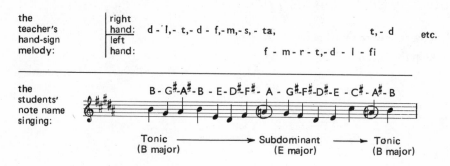

Tonic ⟶ Subdominant ⟶ Tonic
(B major)　　　　(E major)　　　　(B major)

154

Keys and Modes

The pentatonic modes

With A and A♭ as "d"

Practise as in Chapter VI (see page 44).
    For example, the succession of r↑–l↓–m↑–d↓–s↑ pentatonic modes with A♭ as "d":

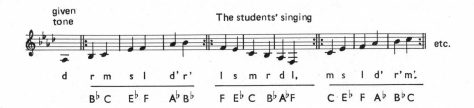

given tone   The students' singing

d   r m s l   d'r'   l s m r d l,   m s   l d' r'm'.
    B♭ C   E♭ F   A♭ B♭   F E♭ C   B♭A♭F   C E♭ F A♭ B♭C

From the same keynote

Sing the modes descending in a previously determined, written order with note names from the same starting pitch, moving in equal quarters.
    For example, the succession of d–, s–, r–, l–, m– modes from C as starting note:

"d" pentatonic   "s" pentatonic   "r" pentatonic   etc.

Major and minor keys with three sharps or four flats

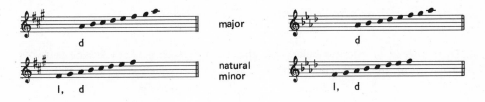

major   d

natural minor   l, d

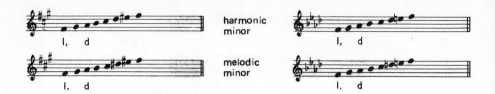

| | harmonic minor | | |
| I, d | | | I, d |

| | melodic minor | | |
| I, d | | | I, d |

Forms of practising the minor

(M) As in Chapter VI, sing the three types of F♯ and F minors in an alternating metre. Use $\frac{3}{4}$ and $\frac{6}{8}$ metres for this alternation. Considering the two kinds of metrical unit, we must choose a different rhythm pattern for each metre.

For example, the different types of F minor with the alternation of $\frac{3}{4}$ ♫ ♩. ♪

and $\frac{6}{8}$ ♩ ♪♩ ♪ :

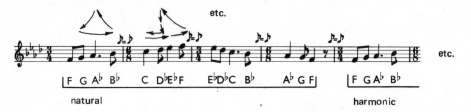

| F G A♭ B♭ | C D♭E♭F | E♭D♭C B♭ | A♭ G F | F G A♭ B♭ |
| natural | | | | harmonic |

Note finding exercices in major and harmonic minor

For all forms of practice (see Chapter VI, page 46) use the following range:

Church modes

The characteristic intervals of the modes

To this series of intervals belong the third, which determines the major or minor character of the mode, and further those intervals which will finally determine the specific church mode with major or minor character. The ability to recognize the modes by ear is greatly helped by singing these intervals and making them conscious.

Before beginning the exercises, study the summary outlined in the following diagram:

Key	1st degree triad		Variable intervals within the modes of major or minor character		
	with diatonic names	with comparative names	with diatonic names		with comparative names
Ionian:	d - m - s major	the same	d - f p 4	d - t M7	the same
Lydian:	f - l - d' major	d - m - s	f - t a4	f - m' M7	d - fi d - t
Mixo- lydian:	s - t - r' major	d - m - s	s - d' p4	s - f' m7	d - f d - ta
Dorian:	r - f - l minor	l, - d - m	r - m M2	r - t M6	l, - t, l, - fi
Phrygian:	m - s - t minor	l, - d - m	m - f m2	m - d' m6	l, - ta, l, - f
Aeolian:	l, - d - m minor	the same	l, - t, M2	l, - f m6	the same

(Cf.: Chapter IV, pages 291—293)

157

Forms of practising the intervals

1. (M) Sing the first degree triad then the variable intervals (fourth and seventh) of the modes of major character with diatonic + comparative + note names.
For example, starting from D:

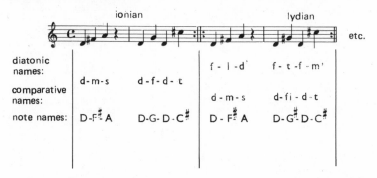

diatonic names:			f - l -d'	f - t -f - m'
	d-m-s	d-f-d- t		
comparative names:			d-m-s	d-fi - d -t
note names:	D-F♯-A	D-G- D -C♯	D - F♯ A	D-G♯-D-C♯

2. (M) Practise similarly the modes of minor character (1st degree triad and characteristic intervals).
For example, from C as keynote:

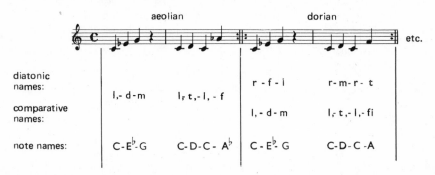

diatonic names:			r - f - l	r- m- r - t
	l,- d - m	l, t,- l,- f		
comparative names:			l, - d - m	l, t,- l,- fi
note names:	C - E♭-G	C-D-C- A♭	C - E♭ G	C-D- C -A

3. (M) After having practised assignments 1. and 2. above from many different starting pitches, we may now omit solfa singing and practise with note names only.
For example, modes of major character from D, or modes of minor character from C; etc.

Note name singing of the modes

(M) Practise now the lydian mode, as previously the dorian and phrygian, with note names proceeding in order according to the fifth pillar.
For example, with key signatures 7♯→0:

key signature:	7#	6#	5#	4#	3#	2#	1#	0
keynote:	F#	B	E	A	D	G	C	F

Note name singing accompanied by beating time:

etc.

(Cf.: Chapter VI, page 47)

Transformed singing

The quotations which follow now have the range of a sixth with the keynote generally the lowest note of the hexachord. The greater range allows more possibilities for transformation than the trichord, tetrachord or pentachord melodies of the preceding chapter.

Carry out transformed singing as described in Chapter VI (see page 50) but include now comparative solmisation and note name singing as well.

Use, for example, the following melody for practice:

1. The students establish the mode of the extract (lydian hexachord), they then memorize it with diatonic solfa names ("f" as final note).

2. When they all know the melody securely they then list the other diatonic hexachords (see Chapter VI, page 49). As in the present case there is no mode sounding the same as the original, we can immediately turn to transformed singing. Practise the melody by memory, from the same starting pitch, using diatonic names:

major hexachord:

d r m d   m f s l   etc.

mixolydian hex. of the same sounding:

s, l, t, s,   t, d r m   etc.

dorian hex.:

r m f r   f s l t   etc.

etc.

3. Following this, sing the melody only in those hexachords containing a perfect fifth. Now using comparative names with "d" or "l" as keynote (by memory and from the same starting note):

the original
lydian hex.:

d r m d | m fi s l | etc.

major and mixo-
lydian hex.:

d r m d | m f s l | etc.

minor hex.:

l, t, d l, | d r m f | etc.

dorian hex.:

l, t, d l, | d r m fi | etc.

phrygian hex.:

l, ta d. l, | d r m f | etc.

4. Finally, practise with note names in all the diatonic hexachords. For example, from E:

the original major
lydian (mixol.) dorian phrygian minor locrian

Musical quotations for transformed singing

719.   KODÁLY: 66 TWO–PART EXERCISES. NO 27.

720.   KODÁLY: 66 TWO–PART EXERCISES. NO 44.

721.   J.S.BACH: AUS TIEFER NOT SCHREI ICH ZU DIR. CHORALE.

722.   KODÁLY: 55 TWO–PART EXERCISES. NO 35.

723.   KODÁLY: 55 TWO–PART EXERCISES. NO 47.

724.   J.S.BACH: ERBARM' DICH MEIN, O HERRE GOTT. CHORALE.

725.   BARTÓK: 10 EASY PIECES. NO III.

726.   KODÁLY: 22 TWO–PART EXERCISES. NO 3.

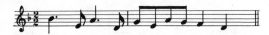

727.   BARTÓK: THREE RONDOS. NO III.

728.   J.S.BACH: CHRISTUS, DER UNS SELIG MACHT. CHORALE.

729. BARTÓK: MICROCOSM III. NO 94.

730. KODÁLY: FIFTEEN TWO–PART EXERCISES. NO 13.

731. BARTÓK: THREE RONDOS. NO 1.

732. J.S.BACH: ES WOLL' UNS GOTT GENÄDIG SEIN. CHORALE.

733. DEBUSSY: TROIS CHANSONS DE CHARLES D'ORLÉANS.

734. KODÁLY: 66 TWO–PART EXERCISES. NO 25.

735. KODÁLY: FIFTEEN TWO–PART EXERCISES. NO 14.

736. BARTÓK: 2ND PIANO CONCERTO. II.

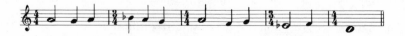

Intervals

New forms of practising fifths and sixths

1. Sing upward or downward fifths with solfa + note names from the given degrees of the major and harmonic minor keys using 3 sharps or 4 flats as key signature.
For example, in F# minor downwards from degree numbers 1 5 3 4 2 VII 5:

the numbers written
on the blackboard:

(Cf.: Chapter VI, page 58, point 8)

2. (M) Practise the sequences of fourth–fifth and fifth–fourth progressions using solfa names within F# and F minor.
a/ Fourth–fifth progression in ascending sequence; b/ fourth–fifth progression in descending sequence; c/ fifth–fourth progression in ascending sequence; d/ fifth-fourth progression in descending sequence.
For example, sequence b/ in F minor:

3. (M) Sing the sequence of sixths in F and F# harmonic minor:
a/ Upwards with solfa; b/ downwards with solfa; c/ upwards with solfa + note names; d/ downwards with solfa + note names.
For example, exercise b/ in F# minor:

(Cf.: Chapter VI, page 59, point 1)

4. (M) Practise the different types of sixths in F and F# minor with solfa + note names, both upwards and downwards.

a/ Minor sixths upwards; b/ minor sixths downwards; c/ major sixths upwards; d/ major sixths downwards.

For example, exercise c/ in F[#] minor:

The intervals of the first and second inversion (6, $\frac{6}{4}$) triads in harmonic minor

1. (M) Sing the variations already practised in major (see Chapter VI, page 60. points 1–2) in F and F[#] minor.

a/ Intervals of the 6 chords in $\underline{3\uparrow6\uparrow}$ increasing order and b/ in $\underline{6\uparrow3\uparrow}$ decreasing order.

c/ Intervals of the $\frac{6}{4}$ chords in $\underline{4\uparrow6\uparrow}$ increasing order and d/ in $\underline{6\uparrow4\uparrow}$ decreasing order.

e/ Intervals of the 6 chords in $\overline{4\downarrow6\downarrow}$ increasing order and f/ in $\overline{6\downarrow4\downarrow}$ decreasing order.

g/ Intervals of the $\frac{6}{4}$ chords in $\overline{3\downarrow6\downarrow}$ increasing order and h/ in $\overline{6\downarrow3\downarrow}$ decreasing order.

164

The intervals of the harmonic minor hexachords

Sing the intervals of the ascending and descending hexachords with solfa in a previously set order from the same starting pitch after sounding the tonic note "l" belonging to the given set of notes.

For example, the intervals of the descending hexachords starting from "t" and "d", in the order 3, 5, 2, 6, 4, at the pitch of G:

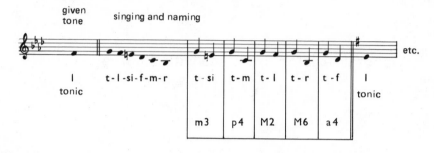

	given tone	singing and naming								
	l	t-l-si-f-m-r	t-si	t-m	t-l	t-r	t-f	l		etc.
	tonic							tonic		
			m3	p4	M2	M6	a4			

Practice of sevenths

1. (M) Sing the inversion combinations of second–seventh intervals in both directions from any given pitch, using all the major and harmonic minor solfa possibilities.

a/ Major 2nd↓ − minor 7th↑; b/ minor 2nd↓ − major 7th↑; c/ major 2nd↑ − minor 7th↓; d/ minor 2nd↑ − major 7th↓.

For example, variation b/ from the note A:

d - t,   d - t´
f - m   f - m´
l - si   l - si´

2. (M) Sing the sequence of sevenths in A and A♭ major.

a/ Upwards with solfa; b/ downwards with solfa; c/ upwards with solfa + note names; d/ downwards with solfa + note names.

For example, exercise d/ in A major:

d´- r - A - B   t - d - G♯ - A   etc.

3. (M) Practise with solfa + note name singing the different types of sevenths in A and A♭ major in both upward and downward directions.

a/ Minor seventh upwards; b/ minor seventh downwards; c/ major sevenths upwards; d/ major sevenths downwards.

For example, exercise c/ in A♭ major:

General revision exercises with the interval types of pentatony

1. (M) Sing the interval types of the pentatonic system remaining within the range of an octave, from the same starting pitch, upwards and downwards, with all pentatonic solfa possibilities.

a/ Starting with the smallest interval, b/ starting with the largest interval, c/ in a previously established order.

For example, starting with the smallest interval, from C:

M2	m3	M3	p4	p5	m6	M6	m7
d - r	l, - d	d - m	l, - r	r - l	m - d'	d - l	r - d'
r - m	m - s		r - s	s, - r		s - m'	m - r'
s - l			s, - d	l, - m			l - s'

2. Sing the exercises in 1. with note names as well.

For example, the downward intervals in the order m3, M6, M2, p4, m7, p5, M3, m6 from starting pitch A:

m3	M6	M2	p4	
A - F♯	A - C♯	A - G	A - E	etc.

166

Chords

Triads

(M) Use the exercises for practising chord function singing as described in Chapter VI (see page 62, points 1–3) in the major and harmonic minor keys with three sharps or four flats as key signature.

Seventh chords

1. (M) Sing the series of root position, first inversion ($\frac{6}{5}$), second inversion ($\frac{4}{3}$) and third inversion ($\frac{4}{2}$) seventh chords with solfa + note names in the keys using 3 sharps and 4 flats as key signature, starting from any scale degree.
For example, the sequence of $\frac{4}{3}$ chords in F# minor beginning on VI:

given tone   VI$\frac{4}{3}$ VII$\frac{4}{3}$ etc.

I   d - m - f - l - f - m - d   r - f - si - t - si - f - r
tonic   A - C#D - F#D - C#-A   B - D - E# - G#-E#- D - B

2. (M) Sing the seven types of seventh chords in a set order from the same starting pitch upwards, with all solfa possibilities of the given type (see Chapter VI, page 64).
For example, the succession

   a/   b/   c/   d/   e/
major+M7 – minor+m7 – diminished+dim.7 – augmented+M7 – major+m7 –
   f/   g/
minor+M7 – dim.+m7 from D as starting note:

      a)   b)   c)   d)   etc.

d - m - s - t   l, - d - m - s   si - t, - r - f   d - m - si - t
f - l - d'- m'   r - f - l - d'
                  m - s - t - r'

3. (M) Practise the $\frac{6}{5}$, $\frac{4}{3}$ and $\frac{4}{2}$ chords in the same way.

For example, the succession

a/	b/	c/	d/	e/	f/

minor+M7 — aug.+M7 — major+m7 — dim.+m7 — minor+m7 — dim.+dim7 —

g/

major+M7 with third inversion chords from the note C:

    si,- l, - d -m   t,- d -m -si   f- sl- t - r'   l,- t, - r - f
                                      r - m -si- t

4. (M) Sing the root position seventh chords downwards as well.

For example:

    s - m -d - l,   t - si -m - d   l - f - r - t,
    d' - l - f - r
    r' - t - s - m

5. Sing the $\frac{4}{3}$ chords in a given order in the keys using 3 sharps or 4 flats as key signature a/ with solfa, b/ with solfa + note names.

For example, the progression $V_3^4 - IV_3^4 - I_3^4 - VII_3^4 - III_3^4 - II_3^4 - VI_3^4$ in F minor as described in a/:

    t, - r - m - si   l,- d -r - f   m,- si,- l,- d

6. Practise the progressions of the $\frac{4}{2}$ chords in the same manner.

7. (M) Sing a root position seventh chord, a $\frac{6}{5}$, $\frac{4}{3}$ and a $\frac{4}{2}$ chord from each note of F♯ and F minor with solfa and with note names. Then give the degree number of the individual chords within the given key.

In F♯ minor from the note "r", for example:

(Cf.: Chapter VI, page 66 , point 5)

8. (M) Choose any seventh chord in the major or harmonic minor tonality and sing it in root position, in first ($\frac{6}{5}$), second ($\frac{4}{3}$) and third ($\frac{4}{2}$) inversion from the same lowest note, with solfa.

For example, the I[7] chord in major:

or the I[7] chord in harmonic minor:

Practise all the other seventh chords in the same manner.

Harmonic analysis

The quotations below include all inversions ($\frac{6}{5}, \frac{4}{3}, \frac{4}{2}$) of the seventh chords.

In some excerpts we also find a so-called diatonic modulation. In the course of this modulation, one of the chords plays a double role in the musical material: it appears as a chord belonging to the original key (starting key) but at the same time it becomes an organic part of the musical material which is already in the new key (key of arrival). Almost imperceptibly, the musical material moves from one key to the next.

The chord progression of the modulating sections must be analysed carefully and put down clearly so that when we sing, the double role of the common chord will not cause difficulties. If the modulation connects keys of different key signatures, the re-interpretation of the common chord naturally brings about a "d" change.

For example, in quotation 781:

169

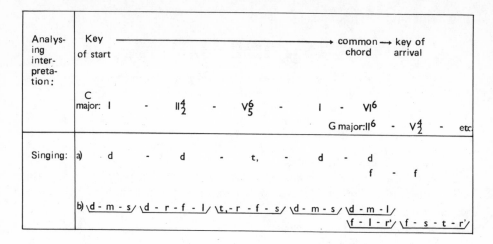

Analysing interpretation:	Key of start								common → chord	key of arrival
	C major: I	-	II$\frac{4}{2}$	-	V$\frac{6}{5}$	-	I	-	VI^6	
									G major:II^6 - V$\frac{4}{2}$ - etc.	

Singing:	a)	d	-	d	-	t,	-	d	-	d
										f - f

b) \d - m - s/ \d - r - f - l/ \t, - r - f - s/ \d - m - s/ \d - m - l/
\f - l - r'/ \f - s - t - r'/

(Cf.: Chapter III, page 216)

Musical quotations for harmonic analysis

737.   VIVALDI: VIOLIN CONCERTO IN G MAJOR.

738.   CORELLI: CONCERTO GROSSO IN D MAJOR. OP.6, NO 4.

739.   MOZART: IL SERAGLIO. I.

740.   J.S.BACH: WIE SICH EIN VATER ERBARMET. CHORALE.

741.   MOZART: IL SERAGLIO. II.

742.   BEETHOVEN: ICH LIEBE DICH.

743.   MOZART: IL SERAGLIO. I.

744.   J.S.BACH: HERR JESU CHRIST, DU HÖCHTES GUT. CHORALE.

745.   MOZART: PIANO SONATA IN A MINOR. I. (K.310)

746.   J.S.BACH: ERHALT' UNS, HERR, BEI DEINEM WORT. CHORALE.

747.   J.HAYDN: STRING QUARTET IN F MINOR. OP.20, NO 5. I.

748.   J.S.BACH: HEUT' TRIUMPHIRET GOTTES SOHN. CHORALE.

749.   VIVALDI: VIOLIN SONATA IN C MAJOR.

750. J.S.BACH: CHRISTUS, DER IST MEIN LEBEN. CHORALE.

751. CORELLI: CONCERTO GROSSO IN G MINOR. OP.6, NO 8.

752. J.S.BACH: JESU, DER DU MEINE SEELE. CHORALE.

753. LULLY: ALCESTE. III.

754. MOZART: „SONATA FACILE" IN C MAJOR. I. (K.545)

174

755. J.S.BACH: BIN ICH GLEICH VON DIR GEWICHEN. CHORALE.

756. J.HAYDN: PIANO SONATA IN G MAJOR. III.

757. MOZART: THE MARRIAGE OF FIGARO. I.

758.   J.S.BACH: SO WAR ICH LEBE. CHORALE.

759.   BEETHOVEN: PIANO SONATA IN E MAJOR. OP.14, NO. 1. I.

760.   HANDEL: SERSE. I.

761.   J.S.BACH: GUTE NACHT, O WESEN. CHORALE.

762. J.HAYDN: STRING QUARTET IN F MINOR. OP.20, NO 5. III.

763. MOZART: COSÌ FAN TUTTE. I.

764. J.S.BACH: O HERZENSANGST, O BANGIGKEIT UND ZAGEN. CHORALE.

765. MOZART: THE MAGIC FLUTE. II.

177

766.   MOZART: PIANO SONATA IN G MAJOR. I. (K.283)

767.   J.S.BACH: ICH DANK' DIR SCHON DURCH DEINEN SOHN. CHORALE.

768. BEETHOVEN: SEHNSUCHT.

769. MOZART: PIANO SONATA IN D MAJOR. III. (K.284)

770. J.S.BACH: LASS, O HERR, DEIN OHR SICH NEIGEN. CHORALE.

771. MOZART: „SONATA FACILE" IN C MAJOR. I. (K.545)

772. J.S.BACH: JESU, DER DU SELBST SO WOHL. CHORALE.

773. BEETHOVEN: PIANO SONATA IN G MAJOR. OP.49, NO 2. I.

774. J.S.BACH: DURCH ADAMS FALL IST GANZ VERDERBT. CHORALE.

775. MOZART: „SONATA FACILE" IN C MAJOR. III. (K.545)

776. CIMAROSA: PIANO SONATA IN G MAJOR.

777. J.S.BACH: HERR JESU CHRIST, ICH SCHREI ZU DIR. CHORALE.

778. BEETHOVEN: PIANO SONATA IN E FLAT MAJOR. OP.31, NO 3. II.

779.   J.S.BACH: JESU, DER DU MEINE SEELE. CHORALE.

780.   LULLY: ALCESTE. V.

781.   J.S.BACH: THE WELL–TEMPERED CLAVIER. I. PRELUDE IN C MAJOR.

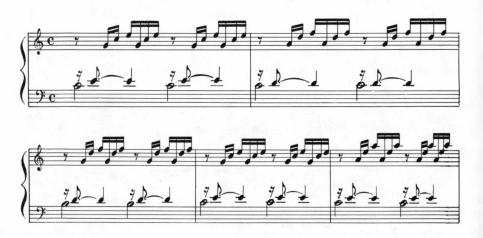

782. HANDEL: DETTINGEN TE DEUM.

783. J.S.BACH: ERKENNE MICH, MEIN HÜTER. CHORALE.

784. LULLY: ALCESTE. PROLOGUE.

785. J.S.BACH: WO SOLL ICH FLIEHEN HIN. CHORALE.

786. LULLY: BELLÉROPHON. I.

787. J.S.BACH: IN MEINES HERZENS GRUNDE. CHORALE.

788. LULLY: PROSERPINE. V.

789. J.S.BACH: DU FRIEDEFÜRST, HERR JESU CHRIST. CHORALE.

790. VIVALDI: THE FOUR SEASONS. OP.8, NO 2.

SIGHT-SINGING
Unison Extracts from the Musical Literature
MATERIAL IN STAFF NOTATION

Melodies in pentatonic and church modes

791. BARTÓK: CONCERTO. I.

792. LISZT: DIE HEILIGE CÄCILIA. LEGENDE. (OR.: 2♯)

793. KODÁLY: TREACHEROUS GLEAM.

794. BRITTEN: PETER GRIMES. II. (OR.: 0)

795. LISZT: DIE HEILIGE CÄCILIA. LEGENDE. (OR.: 5♭)

796. KODÁLY: TWO SONGS. OP.5, NO 1. (OR.: 1♭)

797. MUSSORGSKY: BORIS GODUNOV. II.

798. BARTÓK: MICROCOSM III. NO 70. (OR.: 5♯)

799. FAURÉ: REQUIEM. VII. (OR.: 2♯)

800. BARTÓK: MICROCOSM III. NO 84. (OR.: 2♯)

801. KODÁLY: PEACOCK VARIATIONS. (OR.: 4♯)

802. KODÁLY: VALSETTE. (OR.: 7♭)

803. BARTÓK: SECOND PIANO CONCERTO. I. (OR.: 0)

804. HONEGGER: SONATINA FOR VIOLIN AND CELLO. (OR.: 1♯)

805. MUSSORGSKY: KHOVANSHTCHINA. III. (OR.: 2♯)

806. HONEGGER: JEANNE D'ARC. VIII. (OR.: 3♭)

807. BARTÓK: DANCE SUITE. FINALE. (OR.: 0)

808. CHOPIN: MAZURKA IN C MAJOR. OP.56, NO 2. (OR.: 0)

809. LISZT: CHRISTUS. II.

810. BARTÓK: CONCERTO. V. (OR.: 7♭)

189

811. BARTÓK: PILLOW DANCE.

812. HONEGGER: SONATINA FOR VIOLIN AND CELLO. (OR.: 1♯)

813. COPLAND: QUIET CITY. (OR.: 3♭)

Major and minor melodies

Remaining in the same key signature

814. J.S.BACH: B MINOR MASS. a/ NO 1. KYRIE. (OR.: 2♯)

b/ NO 3. KYRIE.

c/ NO 23. AGNUS. (OR.: 2♭)

815. MOZART: COSÌ FAN TUTTE. I. (OR.: 2♭)

816. HANDEL: TAMERLANO. III. (OR.: 1♭)

817. RAMEAU: DARDANUS. III. (OR.: 2♭)

818. VIVALDI: CELLO SONATA IN B FLAT MAJOR. (OR.: 2♭)

819. VIVALDI: VIOLIN SONATA IN F MINOR. (OR.: 3♭)

820. HANDEL: RODELINDA. III. (OR.: 2♯)

821. J.HAYDN: STRING QUARTET IN G MINOR. OP.20, NO 3. I. (OR.: 2♭)

191

822. VIVALDI: CELLO SONATA IN A MINOR. (OR.: 0)

823. HANDEL: SAMSON. III.

824. HANDEL: TAMERLANO. I. (OR.: 2♯)

825. HANDEL: RODELINDA. III. (OR.: 0)

826. LULLY: PSYCHE. I. (OR.: 3♭)

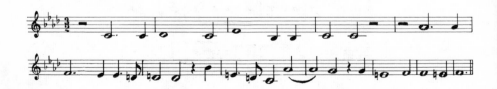

827. HANDEL: SAMSON. III.

828. J.S.BACH: ST.MATTHEW PASSION. I. (OR.: 2♭)

829. HANDEL: SAMSON. I.

830. VIVALDI: VIOLIN SONATA IN D MINOR. (OR.: 1♭)

With "d" change

831. LULLY: ALCESTE. PROLOGUE. (OR.: 3♭)

832. H.PURCELL: SAUL AND THE WITCH AT ENDOR. (OR.: 3♭)

833. HANDEL: SAMSON. I.

834. J.HAYDN: THE CREATION. I. (OR.: 1♭)

835. HANDEL: TAMERLANO. III. (OR.: 2♭)

836.   J.HAYDN: THE SEASONS. III.

837.   VIVALDI: CELLO SONATA IN B FLAT MAJOR. (OR.: 2♭)

838.   ZANETTI: AVEZZATI, MIO CORE. CANTATA. (OR.: 2♭)

839.   VIVALDI: CELLO SONATA IN B FLAT MAJOR. (OR.: 2♭)

840. CORELLI: CONCERTO GROSSO IN F MAJOR. OP.6, NO 2.

Suggested further material: The previously cited Bach Collection
(Chapter VI, page 85), volume I, Nos. 11, 12, 14, 20, 31, 34, 134, 178, 185, 190;
36, 54, 72, 85, 86, 97, 100, 102, 104, 110, 114, 131, 142, 147, 148, 153, 162, 167,
171, 176, 191, 205, 209, 222, 236.

Extracts in solfa notation

The following extracts should be sung only with note names, using the key signatures
of four flats or three sharps, accompanied by beating time.

841. J.S.BACH: NICHT SO TRAURIG, NICHT SO SEHR. CHORALE. (OR.: 3♭)

842. MOZART: COSÌ FAN TUTTE. II. (OR.: 0)

843. CARISSIMI: NON POSSO VIVERE. (OR.: 0)

d' t l si si l si l t m   l t d' t d'r' d'd' t l

844. MOZART: COSÌ FAN TUTTE. I. (OR.: 2♯)

d r r   r m m   m f f   m s f   l s d' d'l f r   s m d   m r d

845. LULLY: PHAÉTON. I. (OR.: 1♭)

m f s   fi   fi si l   si l t   d' r'd't l   l si l l

846. H.PURCELL: HAIL! BRIGHT CECILIA. ODE. (OR.: 1♯)

l t d' si   d'   d't t   t l si l   l t d't l si   l

847. HANDEL: SAMSON. II. (OR.: 2♭)

d'r'm' l   d'r'   d' t s d' t l   d'r'd't l   si m m' m'r'd't

d'm l   l s f m   f l r' r'd't l   m'si l r m   m   l

848. RAMEAU: DARDANUS. III. (OR.: 2♭)

d' d'l   f'   t d'r' si   si m'm't d'd' l l f s   d

849. H.PURCELL: DIDO AND AENEAS. I. (OR.: 3♭)

l si l m   d'   t l t d't si   l si l   m   d'   t l t d't l   si l t!   l

197

850. HANDEL: SAMSON. III. (OR.: 4♭)

m'd' l si m'd' l   m m'd' l d r m si l

851. HANDEL: GIULIO CESARE. I. (OR.: 1♭)

t d' m f d' t f m t l m r r' r't si m t

d' t l m si l m f r t m' l si l l

852. MOZART: COSÌ FAN TUTTE. I. (OR.: 2♯)

s, s, d t, d di r s, s, s, r di r ri m d

Material in Several Parts

853. BYRD: MASS FOR FOUR PARTS. AGNUS.

854. PIER DE LA RUE: MOTET. (OR.: 0)

855. LASSUS: MOTET. (OR.: 1♭)

856. HANDEL: DETTINGEN TE DEUM. (OR.: 1♭)

857. MONTEVERDI: QUAL SI PUÒ DIR MAGGIORE. MADRIGAL. (OR.: 1♭)

858. PALESTRINA: RECORDATA. MOTET. (OR.: 0)

859.   J.S.BACH: FÜHR' AUCH MEIN HERZ UND SINN. CHORALE.

860. LULLY: BELLÉROPHON. II. (OR.: 2♭)

861. J.S.BACH: ALLELUJA! DES SOLLN WIR ALLE. CHORALE.

862. MORLEY: I WILL NO MORE COME TO THEE. (OR.: 0)

863.   J.S.BACH: ERLEUCHT' DOCH UNSERN SINN UND HERZ. CHORALE.

864.   LASSUS: SUPER FLUMINA. MOTET. (OR.: 0)

865. J.S.BACH: ICH BIN'S, ICH SOLLTE BÜSSEN. CHORALE.

866.   LULLY: PHAÉTON. II. (OR.: 2♭)

867.   J.S.BACH: SEELENBRÄUTIGAM. CHORALE.

868. SCHÜTZ: ST.MATTHEW PASSION. (OR.: 2♭)

869.   J.S.BACH: SEID FROH, DIEWEIL. CHORALE.

DEVELOPMENT OF MUSICAL MEMORY
Memorizing and Transposing
a Unison Melody

Quotations 831—840 of the sight-singing material should be memorized as before. (See Chapter VI, page 107 for detailed description.)

Memorizing and Transposing
Two-Part Material

Carry out this complex task as in Chapter VI (see page 108). Transposition of the musical excerpts is no longer an occasional event, but is now an organic part of the memorizing process, just as it was in the case of unison melodies.

The two-part extracts

871.   FARNABY: FANTASIA. (OR.: 0)

872.   J.HAYDN: STRING QUARTET IN C MAJOR. OP.20, NO 2. IV. (OR.: 0)

873. J.HAYDN: PIANO SONATA IN D MAJOR. III. (OR.: 2♯)

874. HANDEL: FUGUE IN G MAJOR. (OR.: 2♯)

875. FESTA: GLORIA. (OR.: 0)

876. J.S.BACH: ENGLISH SUITE IN E MINOR. PASSEPIED I. (OR.: 1♯)

Memorizing Three-Part Material

The musical quotations given below should be memorized as described in the previous chapter (see Chapter VI, page 111).

The three-part extracts

877.   MORLEY: COME, LOVERS FOLLOW ME. (OR.: 0)

878.   MARENZIO: AMATEMI BEN MIO. MADRIGAL. (OR.: 0)

879. BYRD: MASS IN FOUR PARTS. GLORIA.

880. PALESTRINA: VIDE DOMINE. MOTET. (OR.: 0)

881. PALESTRINA: RECORDATA. MOTET. (OR.: 0)

882. PALESTRINA: BONUS EST. MOTET. (OR.: 0)

883. PALESTRINA: CRUCIFIXUS. MOTET. (OR.: 0)

Memorizing and Transposing
Chord Progressions

Carry out this task according to the detailed suggestions given in the previous chapter (Chapter VI, page 115, points 1–8), complete the learning procedure with the transposition of the chord progressions. As conscious transposition has already been practised intensively and for a long time, its use now connected with harmony studies should not cause any problems.

Transposition procedure may start only after performing the memorized chord progression in the original key and singing it with different variations (see Chapter VI, page 115, points 1–8). When transposing the progression to the new key, practise in the same way as when first committing the progression to memory.

Figured bass progressions

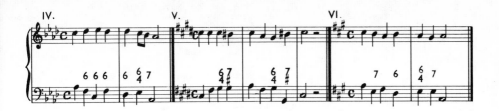

EAR TRAINING
Recognition of Intervals

Interval progressions within the major
and minor tonality

Practise the progressions as described in Chapter VI (see page117) with sequences using only fourth, fifth and sixth intervals.

The intervals of the harmonic minor pentachords

In the harmonic minor key we find diminished and augmented intervals which, when taken out of the tonality, are heard rather as enharmonically equivalent diatonic intervals. (For example, a major third is heard in place of the diminished fourth, or a minor third in place of the augmented second, etc.).

Thus, there are two basic conditions for practising this ear training exercise successfully:

1. The teacher has to plan the succession of intervals in such a way that the diminished or augmented sound of the intervals will be clear and unambiguous to the students.

2. The students must be thoroughly familiar with the intervallic relations within the harmonic minor so that they will not misinterpret the actual interval in terms of its enharmonic equivalent.

For example, if the students hear a minor third and a diminished fifth from the same note upwards, it is not sure that the latter one really has the function of a diminished fifth. If, however, a perfect fifth is heard further on, then the sounding diminished fifth must actually be some type of fourth. Conversely, if a perfect fourth appears among the new intervals, the interval heard as a diminished fifth may not be interpreted as an augmented fourth.

This will become quite clear if we compare the intervals belonging to the pentachords starting from "r" and "t":

The augmented fourth and the diminished fifth correspond enharmonically. Their structural difference (a fifth instead of a fourth and vice versa) will become clear and understandable only by placing them in their tonal context.

A similar problem might be caused by the enharmonically corresponding major third—diminished fourth and minor third—augmented second intervals. Therefore, it is very important to plan the successive order of the intervals belonging to the given pentachord very carefully when putting together a progression for ear training purposes.

The method of practice is otherwise the same as it was in the case of the diatonic pentachords (see Chapter IV, page 342).

The intervals of the first
and second inversion (6, $\frac{6}{4}$) triads

Among the intervallic distances between the notes of these chords we find thirds, fourths, and sixths only. The recognition of interval pairs in relation to a middle note has already been practised (see Chapter IV, page 343), we will therefore now take the bottom or top note as a starting point. On this basis, the following pairs of intervals come into being:

a/ From the 6 chord: 3↑6↑; 6↑3↑; 4↓6↓; 6↓4↓;

b/ from the $\frac{6}{4}$ chord: 4↑6↑; 6↑4↑; 3↓6↓; 6↓3↓.

If we take into consideration the different qualities of the intervals as well (minor 3rd, major 3rd; perfect 4th, augmented 4th, diminished 4th; minor 6th, major 6th), we find that there are many types of variations. The teacher should devise sequences for ear training purposes using interval pairs of different structures, qualities, and directions, in a great variety.

For example, m6↑m3↑ (major 6 chord) — m3↓M6↓ (dim. $\frac{6}{4}$) — m6↓m3↓ (minor $\frac{6}{4}$) — M6↑p4↑ (major $\frac{6}{4}$) — aug.4↓M6↓ (dim. 6) etc.

The procedure of recognition and writing down, then checking, finally singing, should be carried out according to the essentially similar previous interval exercises (for example, Chapter IV, page 343).

224

Interval recognition from "Let Us Sing Correctly"

Use exercises Nos. 71, 73, 74, 75 and 81 for ear training as previously practised (see Chapter III, page 248).

The characteristic intervals of the modes

The modes of minor character can be identified by the second or sixth intervals, the modes of major character by the fourth or seventh intervals. In many instances, both intervals are necessary for precisely determining the specific mode having a major or minor character. For example, a minor triad+minor 6th may occur in both the phrygian and aeolian modes, a major triad+major 7th may appear both in the lydian and ionian modes, etc.

When practising recognition of the modes, however, use those groups of tones in which the minor or major triad is completed by only one characteristic interval. In this way the students will be aware of the similarities existing between the modes.

Consequently, the following groups of tones can be used for recognition exercises: minor triad+major 2nd (aeolian, dorian) — major triad+major 7th (ionian, lydian) — minor triad+minor 6th (aeolian, phrygian) — major triad+aug.4th (lydian) — minor triad+minor 2nd (phrygian) — major triad+perfect 4th (mixolydian, ionian) — minor triad+major 6th (dorian) — major triad+minor 7th (mixolydian).

Procedure for ear training:

1. Recognition.

2. Checking.

3. Singing to deepen conscious knowledge, both with diatonic and comparative names:

225

Chord Recognition

Second inversion seventh ($\frac{4}{3}$) chords

Type recognition

$\frac{4}{3}$ *chords placed within tonality*

Practise both exercises in ways similar to those used for root position seventh chords (see Chapter VI, page 119).

Third inversion seventh ($\frac{4}{2}$) chords

Type recognition

$\frac{4}{2}$ *chords placed within tonality*

Both ways of practice have to be carried out similarly to those used for root position seventh chords (see Chapter VI, page 119).

Seventh chords and its inversions ($\frac{6}{5}$, $\frac{4}{3}$, $\frac{4}{2}$) from a given tone of the major key

Practise in the same manner used for triads (see Chapter VI, page 118).
  For example, the succession $\frac{6}{5}$, $\frac{4}{2}$, 7, $\frac{4}{3}$ with "t" as lowest note, from starting pitch D#:
  1. Recognition.

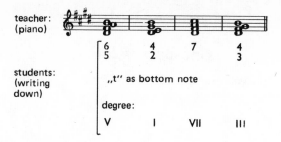

teacher:
(piano)

students:
(writing
down)

„t" as bottom note

degree:

V   I   VII   III

2. Individual and group checking.
3. Singing in broken form: a/ with solfa, b/ with note names.

Chord progressions

Recognition with the help of singing

Practise this exercise using the figured bass progressions found in Chapter VII, page 220, according to the method suggested in Chapter VI (see page 121).

Recognition with the help of inner hearing

The chord progressions of the previous chapter, which were practised for recognition by help of singing, should now be used for dictation purposes (see Chapter VI, page 115).

The basic elements of this task are: a/ establishing the key; b/ putting down the bass and soprano parts with continuous writing; c/ notation of degree numbers + inversions appropriate to the individual chord-sound as framed by the written outer parts.

For example, chord progression No. VI on page 116 should appear as follows:

C minor: I   VI   II⁶   V♮   I

Rhythm Dictation
(Musical material on page 485 of the Supplement)

Practise as in Chapter VI (see page 121).

Melody Dictation

One-part dictation

(Musical material on page 489 of the Supplement)

When choosing a melody for dictation from any group of the given material—pentatonic and modal or major and minor—one fundamental point of view must never be forgotten: as long as orientation within the new "d" system involves any difficulties for the students, we must continue the three-step procedure of memorizing, singing, and writing when giving melodic dictation.

Later we may practise memorizing, performing on an instrument without singing, and then writing.

Finally we may simply memorize and write, omitting the vocal or instrumental middle step.

The new possibilities of melodic dictation described in Chapter VI — memorizing a series of shorter extracts and then writing them down (see page 122, point 2), continuous writing of pentatonic melodies (see page 123) — must play a more and more important role. Continuous-writing dictation may be extended to include themes in modal keys as well, when the students are able to read fluently the melodies of the Pentatonic Music and the sight-singing material in solfa notation of Chapter VII (page 196) with note names in the present given "d" system.

In the case of major and minor melodies, let us not forget to prepare those melodic segments containing altered notes.

Two-part dictation

Concentration on the vertical sounding
(Musical material on page 495 of the Supplement)

Practise this type of dictation as described in Chapter VI (see page 123) but now use two or three excerpts instead of one: after the students have performed the first extract by heart (solfa singing + hand-signs; note name singing + hand-signs; two-part hand-sign performance; singing + piano; see Chapter IV, page 349, point 2) they learn a second extract in the same manner—possibly a third as well—and only then, following all this, may they write them down on paper.

When practising extracts which contain altered notes for which no standardized hand-signs exist, we should omit those steps including hand-signs.

Concentration on the horizontal melodic movement

(Musical material on page 497 of the Supplement)

Practise in the manner described in Chapter VI (see page 124).

Bach Chorale Extracts

Two-part continuous writing

(Musical material on page 500 of the Supplement)

The exercise has to be carried out as described in Chapter VI (see page 125).

Memorizing and writing down the bass of modulating musical material

(Musical material on page 503 of the Wupplement)

The chorale extracts—apart from the last one—contain only one-fifth modulations. Thus we find a re-interpretation of the notes "fi" and "ta" previously practised with hand-signs (see Chapter VII, page 154). Observing, hearing, and interpreting a modulation is an easy task when the altered tone turning to the new key is heard in the bass. But if this tone, however, appears in the soprano or in one of the middle parts, the function of the bass within the new key will be clear and unambiguous only at the cadence.

Suggested procedural steps

1. The teacher gives the key signature of the extract, and then presents the musical material while the students, with the help of their inner hearing, try a/ to follow the bass progression and b/ to find the moment when the modulation—that is, the "d" change, in this case—actually occurs.

2. When the teacher plays the extract on the piano a second time, the students sing the bass part with solfa names, trying to correctly place to "d" change (or "d" changes) as they sing.

3. After realizing successfully the "d" change according to the logic of the musical material, the students establish the new key by the common note they have named.

4. When the extract is played a third time, the students can consciously and easily memorize the bass.

5. One student who knows the bass securely will sing it by memory a/ to solfa, then b/ to note names.

6. The students write down the bass part.

7. As a check, they sing it with note names.

8. The final step is a group performance of the given extract: the teacher plays the four-part musical material on the piano while the students sing the bass progression they have written in their exercise-books, with solfa.

PLANNING SUGGESTION

(See the diagram at the end of the book.)

CHAPTER VIII
(Material in staff notation uses D and D flat as "d")

KODÁLY MATERIAL
Unison Pentatonic Melodies
MATERIAL IN STAFF NOTATION

(333 Reading Exercises)

The set of notes used for note finding practice in staff notation:

New elements

$\frac{7}{4}$ metre: 332

The inner division of the seven-beat bar is here 3+4. As the metrical unit is ♩, let us by all means accompany the singing with the appropriate beating time, which is a combination of the $\frac{6}{4}$ and the subdivided $\frac{4}{2}$ time-beating:

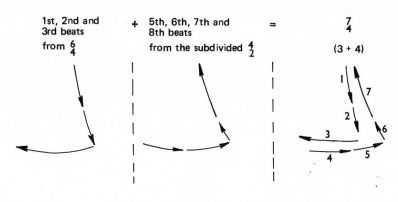

233

Suggested way of practising:

a/ At first sing only bars 4 and 8, together as one continuous unit, in order to become thoroughly familiar with the new time-beating.

b/ Sing the entire melody through in the following manner: to the appropriate beating time, one group of students sing the $\frac{4}{4}$ bars, the other group the $\frac{7}{4}$ bars.

c/ The groups exchange parts.

d/ Everyone sings the entire melody while beating time.

♫ 4↑, ♪ 4↑, ♩. *melodic beginning: 331*

Three possible notes within the pentatonic system can generate two consecutive ascending fourths:

♫ ♪♩.   ♫ ♪♩.   ♫ ♪♩.

l, l, r s   ;   r r s d'   and   m m l r'

Before singing the melody, it is most useful to first practise these melodic patterns, for example, in the following sequence:

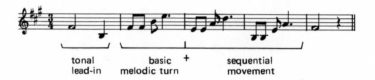

tonal	basic +	sequential
lead-in	melodic turn	movement

Familiar elements

Tripody: 295

Isorhythm: 296, 326

Descending fifth-change with pentatonic sixth: 333

New elements

$\frac{7}{4}$ metre: IV/93

The inner division of the seven-beat bar is here 4+3. The time-beating in principle corresponds to 3+4 beating time (see Chapter VIII, page 233): the four-beat unit stems from the subdivided $\frac{4}{2}$, the three-beat unit from the $\frac{6}{4}$ time-beating:

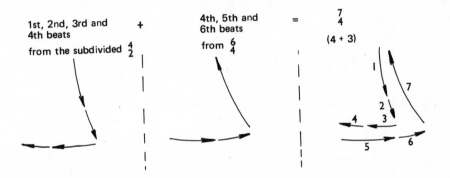

| 1st, 2nd, 3rd and 4th beats | + | 4th, 5th and 6th beats | = | $\frac{7}{4}$ |
| from the subdivided $\frac{4}{2}$ | | from $\frac{6}{4}$ | | (4 + 3) |

Practise first the seven-beat bars and the final bar consecutively with beating time. Sing through the entire melody only when this new seven-beat time-beating is secure. $(\frac{1}{4} = \smile \text{♪})$

Familiar elements

ALTERNATION OF METRES
WITH CONSTANT METRICAL UNITS

$\frac{5}{8}$ (2 + 3) and $\frac{4}{8}$: I/90

Sing a/ with two-part rhythm accompaniment: $\frac{5}{8}$ and $\frac{4}{8}$;

b/ with ostinato: $\frac{5}{8}$ and $\frac{4}{8}$.

$\frac{6}{8}$ and $\frac{5}{8}$ (3 + 2): IV/66

Practise with the ostinato: $\frac{6}{8}$ ♩ ♪♫♫♫ and $\frac{5}{8}$ ♩ ♪♫♫ .

ALTERNATION OF METRES
WITH DIFFERENT METRICAL UNITS

$\frac{2}{4}$ and $\frac{3}{8}$: IV/57

Sing a/ tapping the metrical unit, b/ beating time.

$\frac{3}{4}$ and $\frac{5}{8}$ (2 + 3): IV/62

Again practise tapping the metrical unit and beating time ($\frac{5}{8}$ = ⤵⤦).

$\frac{2}{4}$ and $\frac{6}{8}$: IV/67

Sing a/ with the ostinato: $\frac{2}{4}$ ♪♩ ♪ and $\frac{6}{8}$ ⸜ ♫♩ ⸜ ♫ ; b/ with beating time ($\frac{6}{8}$ = ⤵⤦).

$\frac{2}{4}$ and $\frac{7}{8}$ (3 + 4): IV/89

Practise a/ with the ostinato: $\frac{2}{4}$ ⸜ ♪⸜ ♪and $\frac{7}{8}$ ♩ ♪♫⸜ ♪ b/ beating time in a slow tempo ($\frac{7}{8}$ = ⤵⤦).

When the students are able to sing the $\frac{2}{4}$ + $\frac{7}{8}$ melody accurately and securely, it is worthwhile to accompany the $\frac{7}{8}$ bars with beating time as follows:

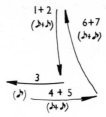

We have thus three quarter-note beats and one eighth-note beat:

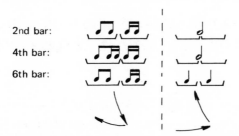

The duration of the second beat is therefore only half that of the other beats. This kind of time-beating better expresses the organic connections within the motivic material of the melody.

$\frac{7}{8}$ (4 + 3) and $\frac{2}{4}$: IV/95

Sing a/ with the ostinato: $\frac{7}{8}$ ♩ ♪ ♪ ♪ ♪ ♫♩ and $\frac{2}{4}$ ♪♩ ♫ ; b/ with beating time. As the eighth-note motion is continuous, we can accompany the $\frac{7}{8}$ bars with time-beating as follows:

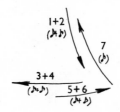

237

Thus we again have three quarter-note beats and one eighth-note beat:

In this time-beating the duration of the first, second, and third beat is double that of the fourth.

Easy melodies for practising note name singing
(333/278,281,290; I/19,39,43, II/8,14,23,37, III/33)

After preparation with hand-signs (see Chapter VIII, page 261), we can use these melodies for note name sight-singing. As staff notation material for this chapter uses D and D♭ as "d", melodies within the s,-l range will use the following set of notes:

We can accompany note name singing with tapping the metrical unit, beating time, or with an ostinato. We may practise in answering form or with alternating inner singing and singing aloud as well.

Two-Part Material

PREPORATORY EXERCISES:
"LET US SING CORRECTLY"

(Nos. 88,89,90,91,92,93)

Sing the exercises in the usual manner. To be able to maintain proper intonation of the intervals now that the rhythm is more active, the teacher should tap aloud, in a slower tempo, than previously the steady ♩ pulse. A preceding intervallic analysis, in the interest of conscious observation, should include all vertical intervals.

For example, the written intervallic analysis of exercise 89:

TWO-PART WORKS

Pentatonic range of notes

ONE-SYSTEM PENTATONIC THEMES

Two-part pentatonic exercises on D "d" are generally written with a key signature of only one sharp since the C♯ ("t") does not occur in this pentatonic system.

Material for sight-singing includes melodies in D♭ "d" as well as in D "d". Therefore, practise note name singing from staff notation in both "d" systems, in both G and F clefs.

a/ With D as "d":

b/ With D♭ as "d":

Bicinia Hungarica IV/150

1. The theme, A⁵ A,⁵ A A, structure, contains the following notes:

final note

Thus we find a "l" pentatonic mode.

2. A secure, rhythmically exact performance of this melody requires great effort. The difficult melodic figures are set to constantly changing metrical pulse which alternates $\frac{3}{4}$ metre and $\frac{6}{8}$ metre.

Suggested way of practice:

a/ Learn the melodic outline of the theme:

b/ Sing the theme in its original form with a two-part rhythmic accompaniment in which the right hand marks the steady ♪ motion and the left hand marks the metrical unit:

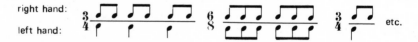

c/ First practise, similarly, all the accompanying material, then the soprano voice and finally the alto voice.

d/ Accompany the two-part performance with metric unit tapping only. If successful, try singing in two parts with the appropriate $\frac{6}{8} + \frac{3}{4}$ time-beating.

240

Suggested further exercises: Bicinia Hungarica IV/153,154,176,172,174.

TWO-SYSTEM PENTATONIC THEMES

Bicinia Hungarica IV/158

1. The set of notes used in this fifth-changing theme:

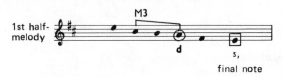

The pentatonic major third of the first half of the melody is placed a fifth lower in the second half. In the complete melody we find two pentatonic systems, in fifth relation, both with "s" as final note. The theme is therefore in a two-system "s" pentatonic mode.

When singing the theme, change the "d" after the cadential figure in bar 8:

241

2. The notes of the accompanying material remain entirely in one pentatonic system:

"D" change occurs therefore only in the alto part:

3. Summary of the complete musical material:

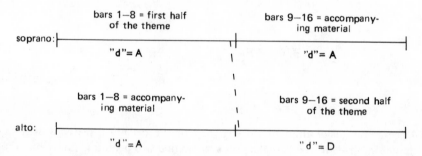

Bicinia Hungarica IV/130

1. The theme is once again in a two-system "s" pentatonic mode with fifth-change:

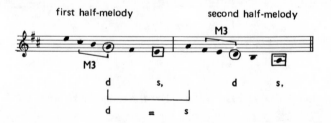

The "d" change occurs, on the first note of the second half of the theme, coinciding with the fifth-change.

The accompanying material remains in the A "d" system throughout. "D" change occurs therefore only in the alto part:

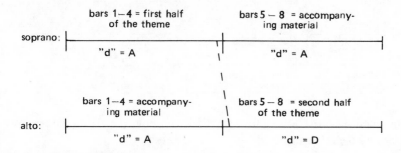

The "d" change occurs thus:

3. The inner division of the $\frac{5}{4}$ metre:

a/ The theme shows a 2+3 division, which is corroborated by the rhythmic notation of the first bar of the accompanying voice.

b/ The inner division of the accompanying material is not uniform. The imitation brings about metrical stress displacement. The melodic turns and their rhythmic patterns lead us to the following interpretation:

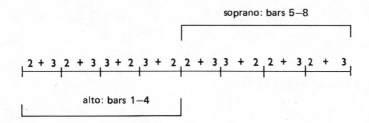

Bicinia Hungarica IV/160

1. The fifth-changing theme is again in a two-system "s" pentatonic mode, as were the preceding two exercises. The accompanying material remains in the A "d" system throughout.

2. The "d" change occurs, for both theme and alto part, in bar 5:

3. The inner division of the $\frac{5}{4}$ metre:

a/ The 3+2 and 2+3 divisions alternate in the motivic material of the theme:

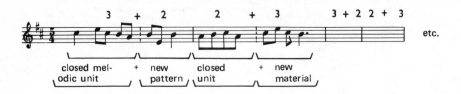

| 3   +   2 | 2   +   3 | 3 + 2 2 + 3 | etc.

closed mel- + new   closed   + new
odic unit   pattern   unit   material

b/ In establishing the beating time for the accompanying material, we can, perhaps, be guided by the following:

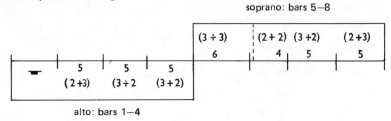

soprano: bars 5—8

alto: bars 1—4

Specifically in bars 5 and 6, the already familiar melodic turns do not fit within the five-beat frame:

bar 5 — 6

Bicinia Hungarica IV/170

1. As in the previous exercises, the fifth-changing theme has a two-system "s" pentatonic mode. Place of "d" change:

bar 8 (soprano) — bar 9 (alto)

s   d = s,

2. The accompanying material remains in the lower pentatonic system throughout. In contrast to the exercises we have sung up to this point, the "d" change now occurs only in the soprano part:

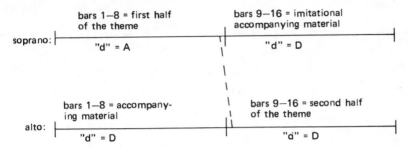

Place of "d" change:

The exercise begins with a different "d" for each part: soprano "d" = A, alto "d" = D. The first alto entrance is therefore rather difficult. As preparation, practise the following:

3. The alternating $\frac{2}{4}$ and $\frac{3}{4}$ metres as notated do not correspond at all times to the metrical pulse. Namely, the syncopated motivic figure of the theme is always an independent figure, starting on a stressed beat and filling one whole bar. If we examine the accompanying material with this fact in mind, the metrical alternation assumes the following shape:

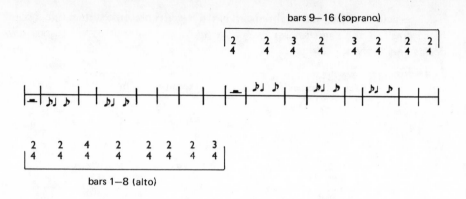

bars 9—16 (soprano)

bars 1—8 (alto)

Suggested further exercise: Bicinia Hungarica I/32

Diatonic range of notes

Bicinia Hungarica II/89

1. In the set of notes of this "l"-ending theme of A A B A, structure, the "f" as
the sixth degree above the keynote does not appear. Since the "t", however, has
a significant role in the opening melodic motion of each line, the tonality of the
theme is aeolian in character.

2. In the third bar of the "A" melodic lines, the sharp dissonance of the minor
second, approched by leap, and its resolution demand careful treatment:

m2 m3   p 5

To ensure really pure intonation of the cadential fifth, the soprano must maintain
the G very firmly in order to prevent the F♯ which follows from becoming too low.

Suggested further exercises: Bicinia Hungarica II/90;
55 Two-Part Exercises/10,13.

246

55 Two-Part Exercises/21

1. The musical material of this four-line theme in aeolian mode shows an A A,^{5} A^5,, A folksong structure. (The fourth line is divided between soprano and alto.) Elements of tonal fifth-change appear in the A^5 variant lines:

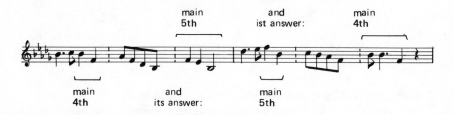

2. The sequence of secondary dominants, commonly found in functional harmony, colour to the accompanying material of lines 3 and 4:

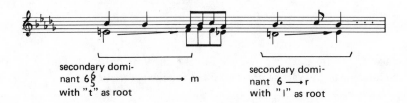

(Secondary dominant; see Chapter VIII, page 277)

3. At the same time, the aeolian character with no leading tone, is maintained through the melodic cadential pattern:

55 Two-Part Exercises/38

1. The theme is a four-bar unit derived from a basic two-bar motif which is then treated sequentially at the lower fourth:

2. The comes is a tonal answer:

(Cf.: Bach, The Well-Tempered Clavier I, Fugue in F♯ minor.)

3. The one difficult melodic turn of the exercise occurs in the mirror inversion of the comes (alto, bars 29—32):

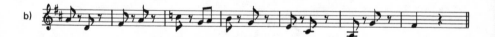

In place of "f" the students may very likely sing "m" or "s", the lower neighbour of the following "l". Practise, therefore, the following variations:

Only after the above variations are sung with very secure intonation may we sing the part in its original form.

4. The theme appears successively in the following keys:

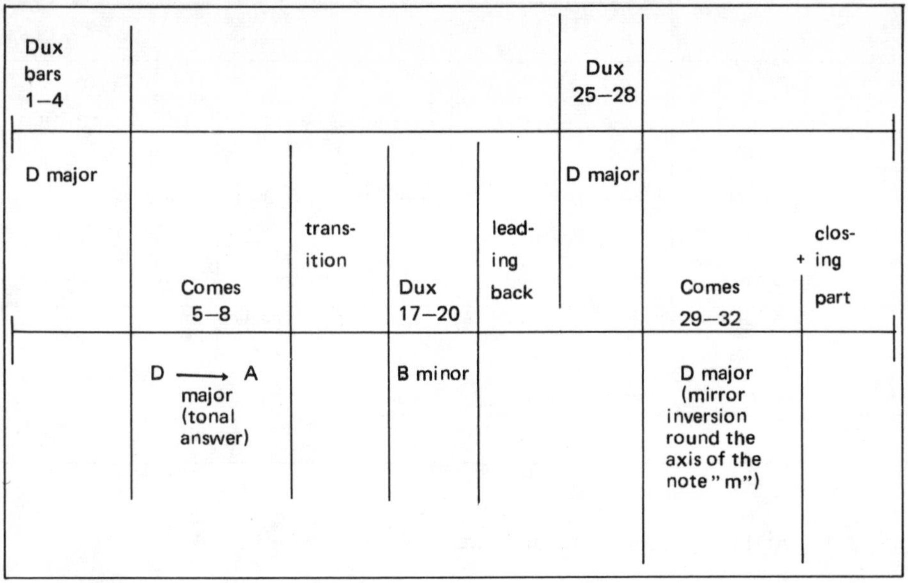

Dux bars 1—4					Dux 25—28		
D major		trans-ition		lead-ing back	D major		clos-ing
	Comes 5—8		Dux 17—20			Comes 29—32	+ ing part
	D ⟶ A major (tonal answer)		B minor			D major (mirror inversion round the axis of the note " m")	

The comes, true to its role, brings us to the key of the dominant. As the theme remains open melodically, and does not even contain the leading tone, a "d" change is not really needed here. Furthermore, the accompanying part does not even contain the leading tone in the key of the dominant. Thus the entire exercise may be sung according to the key signature with D as "d".

Suggested further exercise: 55 Two-Part Exercises/11

Modulating musical material

66 *Two-Part* Exercises/59

1. The four-line theme in folk melody form, has the following structure:

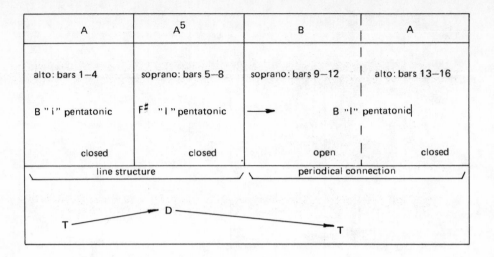

2. The A^5 line appears as a tonal answer:

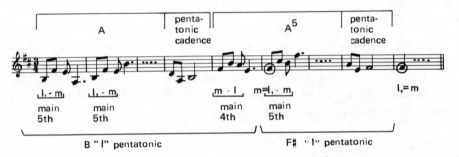

3. The accompaniment to the "A" material of the theme appears at the beginning of each line as a succession of ascending seconds:

4. The accompanying material remains throughout in B aeolian, at times in B melodic minor. It can be sung without "d" change.

1. The theme once again is built on a two-bar basic motif extended sequentially at the lower third:

The second characteristic leap of a seventh, to the leading tone which in turn resolves to the keynote, causes no problem in intonation. The first leap of a seventh, however, being without clear tonal feeling, may cause difficulty. Since the theme will later be heard in a minor variant, practise the following sequences several times:

2. The theme appears successively in the following keys:

Dux bars 1—4					Theme 21—24		Theme 32—25	
D major		trans- ition (with new ma- terial)		trans- ition	F# minor (trans- formed)	lead- ing back	D major	
	Comes 5 – 8		Theme 15—18					clos- ing part
	A major (real answer)		B minor (trans- formed)					

251

The above key plan placed on a pillar of thirds:

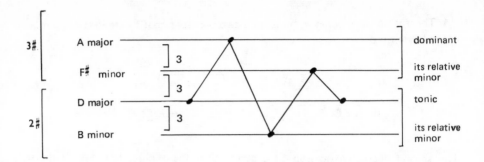

(Cf.: Bach, Two-Part Inventions)

3. Suggested places for "d" change:

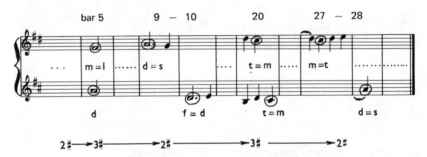

4. Bars 13—14 in the alto accompanying material require extra practice. Here the intonation of the melodic minor tetrachord is liable to become too high because of the E—E♯ chromatic half-step. Prepare the phrase in the following manner:

1. The theme is a sixteen-bar melody in a two-system "s" pentatonic mode with fifth-change:

Its melodic and formal structure:

2. The entire melody is heard only at the beginning of the exercise. The first half of the theme, "s" pentatonic on E, appears once again in the soprano from bar 21 with a two-bar extension:

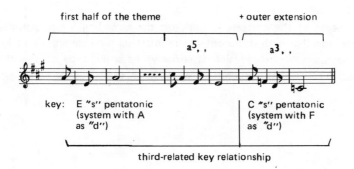

The second half of the theme, "s" pentatonic on A, appears in the alto from bar 41. Developmental-type musical material connects the two separate half-melodies.

3. Suggested places for "d" change:

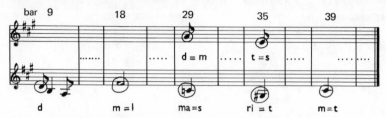

At the end of the piece, as in those exercises of Bicinia Hungarica, Vol. IV based on two-system pentatonic themes (see Chapter VIII, page 241), each part is singing in its own "d" system.

4. An especially interesting stylistic element of the middle section is the repeated a,, motif and its accompaniment. A characteristic chord progression of functional harmony has been placed under the pentatonic melody:

(Cf.: Chapter VIII, page 286, quotations 910, 912)

44 Two-Part Exercises/39

1. The theme of the exercise is built on the ascending major chromatic scale. This theme, together with its accompanying material produce an unusually exciting chord progression. If we examine attentively the sound-type of the chords and the successive roots of the progression we arrive at the following harmonic outline:

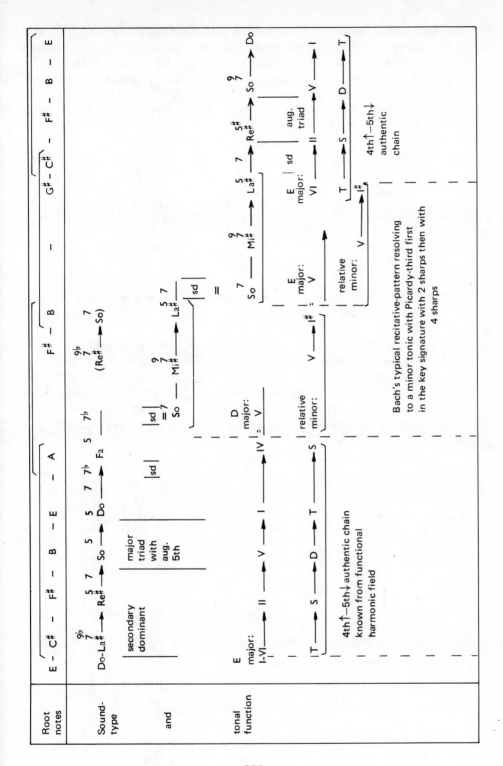

2. A two-voice performance of the exercise will be successful only after we have first thoroughly learned the characteristic melodic contours of the alto part and then have joined them in one continuous melodic arc. To do this we need a plan of "d" changes which will insure the greatest accuracy of intonation without contradicting the logic of the harmonic progression.

Taking these two factors into consideration, the following plan of "d" changes in the alto part is a satisfactory solution:

3. When the students know the alto part securely, we may then attempt a two-part performance. The soprano, as is only logical, should naturally be sung entirely on E "d".

In the last soprano bars preceding the end, the step from the altered leading tone "li" to the diatonic leading tone "t" is indeed difficult. Moreover, the harmonic progression (secondary dominant on II with an augmented fifth leading to V) is also unusual. It is useful to play the harmonic outline of the second half of the exercise for the students several times. Being familiar with the sound of the harmonic movement will then help the students' intonation of this difficult melodic figure when they are ready to sing it:

Suggested further exercises: 55 Two-Part Exercises/15,35; 44 Two-Part Exercises/17; 22 Two-Part Exercises/2.

Three-Part Material

Tricinia/4

1. The tonality is D major. Although the notes "fi" and "ta" occur in the piece, their presence signifies only momentary tonal deviation into the dominant and subdominant key, rather than an actual modulation. There is therefore no reason to change the "d" at any time.

2. If singing of the individual voices and two-part singing is not accompanied by tapping the metrical unit, the students will tend to hurry the chain of syncopations. We may eliminate beating the metrical unit when singing in three parts, as a new tone, in one of the voices, will always mark the first and third eighth of each $\frac{2}{4}$ bar.

3. The only difficulties in intonation are caused by the overlapping entrances at the very beginning and in bars 12—13. Practise, therefore, individually and as a group, the following sequence:

Tricinia/17

The tonality is D♭ major. The musical material is in the relative key of B♭ minor in bars 6—10, but then returns to the original key of D♭ major.

Elements requiring extra practice:

1. The third motif in the mezzo voice contains a diminished third. Practise the following:

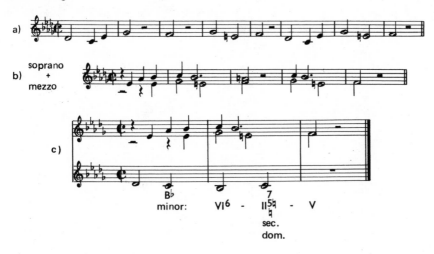

Sing this mezzo phrase together with the soprano melody only when the above three-chord progression can already be heard securely and sung with proper intonation

by the students. If not, the soprano lower changing note A ()

will pull the mezzo note E up to F, and in place of the written chord we will hear the familiar V_4^6 of functional harmony.

2. Soprano, bars 8–11: The seemingly unusual melodic line is derived from the notes of the augmented $\frac{4}{3}$ chord (see Chapter IX, page 389), here decorated with suspensions. All difficulties in these soprano bars will be eliminated if we practise the chord notes in broken form before singing the actual melodic line:

resol-
ution

Augm. $\frac{4}{3}$ sus- melodically upper
pen- changing note,
sion harmonically the
combination of

augm. $\frac{4}{3}$ and augm. $\frac{6}{5}$

chords (see Chapter
IX. page 389)

3. Mezzo, bar 14: In its given surroundings (VI — IV^6 — I_4^6 — $IV^{7\flat}$ — V_2^4 — I^6; see

parallel   diminished

Chapter VIII, pages 277 and Chapter IX, page 389), the F♭ is likely to become lower than necessary. Practise it in the following way:

mezzo:

alto:

The above exercise must be practised until the dominant-fifth of the penultimate bar 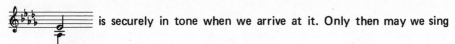 is securely in tone when we arrive at it. Only then may we sing

the original form of the two voices. (We find here once again the familiar chord pattern with elision: the raised IV^{7b} — sometimes elsewhere as a II^6_5 secondary dominant — resolves functionally to the dominant; melodically, however, the progression omits the "s" and moves to "f", that is to the V^4_2. See Chapter VIII, page 252)

4. Mezzo, bar 15: The chromatic step from E^b to E is sometimes higher or lower than necessary. If so, the following F will not fit into the secondary dominant on I. Practise bars 15—17 omitting the mezzo note E and singing the melody of bar 15 in a syncopated version:

Sing the parts in various combinations with the mezzo bar in the above form, in the following order: a/ alto + mezzo (the alto should always end on the D^b in bar 17); b/ soprano + mezzo; c/ alto + mezzo; d/ all three parts.

When the ensemble of the three voices is secure, we may replace the original mezzo melody. If the chromatic step is still unsecure, return again to the syncopated variation.

THEORETICAL INFORMATION AND TECHNICAL EXERCISES
Range of Notes, Hand-Signs

Pentatony

Note name singing to hand-signs

Practise with D and D♭ as "d". (Cf.: Chapter VI, page 41)

Diatony

Note name singing to hand-signs

Use the 2 sharp and 5 flat key signatures for this exercise. (Cf.: Chapter VI, page 41)

Diatony+ alteration

Solfa singing from staff notation

The set of notes used for practising:
  a/ In the G clef:

b/ In the F clef:

When singing, practise first of all the characteristic augmented second, diminished third, augmented fourth and diminished fifth intervals. (Cf.: Chapter VIII, page 272)

Solfa + note name singing in answering form

Practise with 2 sharps or 5 flats as key signature, using melodic patterns including the diminished and augmented intervals. (Cf.: Chapter VI, page 42,; and Chapter VIII, page 272)

Practising change of key from hand-signs

So far (see Chapter VI, page 43 and Chapter VII, page 154) we have practised key changes one fifth apart. Since the musical material of this chapter (Kodály exercises, sight-singing material) will now include more daring modulations and momentary tonal deviations, it is most useful to practise singing more distantly related key progressions.

With the help of those hand-signs which we have used so far (the seven diatonic notes + "fi" and "ta") we can connect the following fifth-related key signatures:

		d	r	m	f	fi	s	l	ta	t	
	7♯	-	-	-	-	f	-	-	-	ta	+7
	6♯	-	-	ta	-	d	-	-	-	f	+6
	5♯	-	-	f	-	s	-	ta	-	d	+5
the function of the common note in the key of arrival	4♯	-	ta	d	-	r	-	f	-	s	+4
	3♯	-	f	s	-	l	ta	d	-	r	+3
	2♯	ta	d	r	-	m	f	s	-	l	+2
	1♯	f	s	l	ta	t	d	r	-	m	+1
set of notes in the key of start extended by the notes "fi" and "ta"		d	r	m	f	fi	s	l	ta	t	0
		d	r	m	f	fi	s	l	ta	t	
	1♭	s	l	t	d	-	r	m	f	fi	−1
	2♭	r	m	fi	s	-	l	t	d	-	−2
	3♭	l	t	-	r	-	m	fi	s	-	−3
the function of the common note in the key of arrival	4♭	m	fi	-	l	-	t	-	r	-	−4
	5♭	t	-	-	m	-	fi	-	l	-	−5
	6♭	fi	-	-	t	-	-	-	m	-	−6
	7♭	-	-	-	fi	-	-	-	t	-	−7

It is evident from the diagram above that a change of key seven fifths apart is very difficult to sing accurately as the f=fi, fi=f, t=ta and ta=t re-interpretations change the role of the melodic leading tones exactly in the opposite direction. Thus, in this chapter we shall practise only key-changes using two keys whose fifth distance is not more than 1—6. We shall sing with solfa, establishing the new key and the name of the common note at the same time.

For example, the succession of C major → E major → B♭ major → C major:

	(+4 fifths)	(−6 fifths)	(+2 fifths)

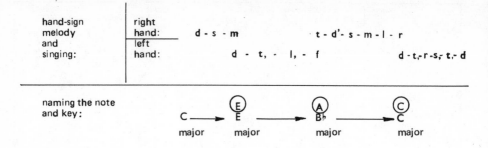

hand-sign melody and singing:	right hand:	d - s - m		t - d' - s - m - l - r
	left hand:		d - t, - l, - f	d - t, r -s, t, d

naming the note and key:

C $\longrightarrow$ (E) E $\longrightarrow$ (A) B♭ $\longrightarrow$ (C) C

major   major   major   major

(Cf.: Chapter VI, page 43)

Keys and Modes

The pentatonic modes with D and D♭ as 'd''

Practise as in the preceding chapters (see Chapter VI, page 44, Chapter VII, page 155).

Two-system pentatony

We come across this tonal system in melodies with a real fifth-change if the notes used in the first melody-unit taking part in the fifth-change already include the characteristic major third of pentatony (or its inversion, the minor sixth). This specific tonal system of folk music origin often appears in Kodály's pedagogical works with many different final notes.

For example:

(See the diagram on page 265)

(Cf.: Chapter VIII, pages 241—246)

264

Exercise	Set of notes		Key
	of the theme		

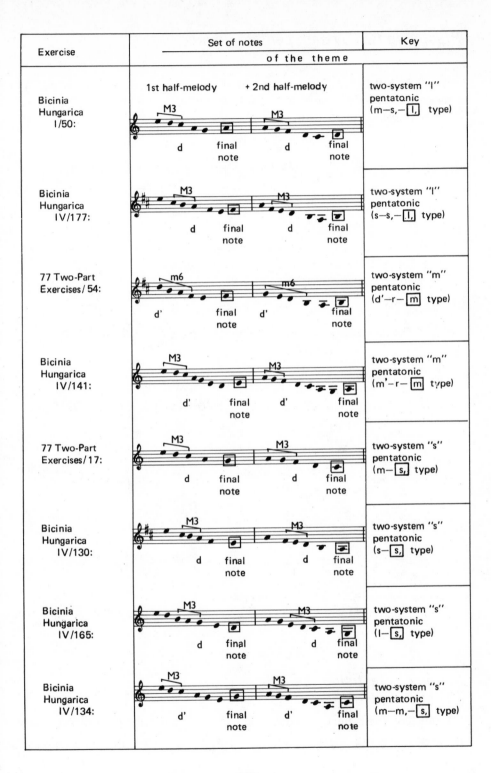

Practising two-system pentatonic modes

1. (M) Sing the smallest range types of the above two-system "l", "m" and "s" pentatonic modes downwards, from the same starting note with solfa + note names. For example, starting from C:

2. (M) Similarly practise the same modes as above but now in such a way that the final note in the second half-melody remains constant. For example, with B as final note:

Major and minor keys with two sharps or five flats

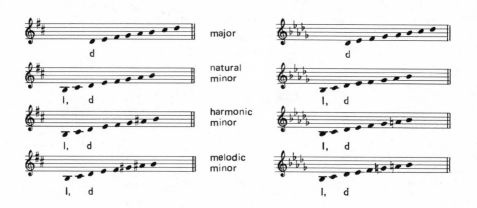

Forms of practising the minor

1. (M) Sing the natural, harmonic, and melodic B minor and B♭ minor keys using the $\frac{7}{4}$ ♩ ♩ ♩ ♩ ⁞ ♩ ♩ (4+3) or $\frac{7}{4}$ ♩ ♩ ⁞ ♩ ♩ ♩ ♩ (3+4) rhythm pattern and

accompany this singing with beating the $\frac{7}{4}$ time appropriate to the combination of the metre.

2. (M) Practise singing these scales also in the faster, $\frac{7}{8}$ metre, beating the $\frac{4}{8}$ group as ♩ + ♩ and the $\frac{3}{8}$ group as ♩ + ♪:

(Cf.: Chapter VIII, page 237)

Sing the succession of the different types of minor, continuously moving in equal eighth notes.

For example, in the case of B minor:

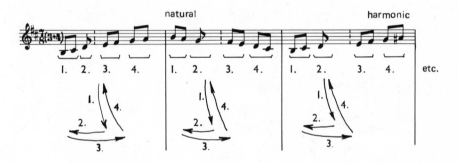

Note finding exercises in major and harmonic minor

Use the range given below for all forms of practice (see Chapter VI, page 46):

Church modes

1. (M) Practise the mixolydian mode moving upwards and downwards on the fifth pillar, as we have already practised the dorian, phrygian and lydian modes (see Chapter VI, page 47 and Chapter VII, page 158).

2. Practise note finding singing within the framework of the modal keys in a previously set order of degree numbers, with solfa; a/ with diatonic names, b/ with comparative names.

For example: the succession of degree numbers is 1 5 3 7 4 6 VII 2 VI 5 1; the order of modes is ionian, phrygian, lydian, aeolian, locrian, dorian, mixolydian; the starting pitch is D.

a/ Singing with diatonic names:

b/ Singing with comparative names:

Transformed singing

In this chapter we shall practise transformed singing with melodies of an octave range or larger, again from memory, with diatonic and comparative solfa names and note names (see Chapter VII, page 159).

Musical quotations for transformed singing

Nos. 972, 974, 975, 976 from the unison sight-singing material and the following themes taken from Kodály exercises:

885.   KODÁLY: 77 TWO–PART EXERCISES. NO 66.

886.   KODÁLY: 77 TWO–PART EXERCISES. NO 67.

887.   KODÁLY: 77 TWO–PART EXERCISES. NO 69.

888.   KODÁLY: 77 TWO–PART EXERCISES. NO 68.

889.   KODÁLY: 44 TWO–PART EXERCISES. NO 10.

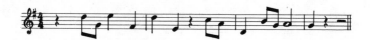

890.   KODÁLY: 77 TWO–PART EXERCISES. NO 73.

891.   KODÁLY: 66 TWO–PART EXERCISES. NO 43.

892.   KODÁLY: 66 TWO–PART EXERCISES. NO 49.

893.   KODÁLY: 66 TWO–PART EXERCISES. NO 50.

894.   KODÁLY: 66 TWO–PART EXERCISES. NO 37.

895.   KODÁLY: 66 TWO–PART EXERCISES. NO 63.

896.   KODÁLY: 44 TWO–PART EXERCISES. NO 1.

897.   KODÁLY: 33 TWO–PART EXERCISES. NO 26.

898.   KODÁLY: 44 TWO–PART EXERCISES. NO 11.

899.   KODÁLY: 55 TWO–PART EXERCISES. NO 32.

900. KODÁLY: 33 TWO-PART EXERCISES. NO 13.

901. KODÁLY: 66 TWO-PART EXERCISES. NO 47.

902. KODÁLY: 33 TWO-PART EXERCISES. NO 20.

Intervals

New forms of practising sixths and sevenths

1. Sing upward or downward sixths with solfa + note names from the given degrees of the major and harmonic minor keys using 2 sharps or 5 flats as key signature. (Cf.: Chapter VI, page 58).

2. (M) Practise the different types of sevenths in B and B♭ minor with solfa + note name singing, both upwards and downwards: a/ minor sevenths upwards, b/ minor sevenths downwards, c/ major sevenths upwards, d/ major sevenths downwards, e/ diminished seventh upwards, f/ diminished seventh downwards.

For example, exercise d/ in B minor:

Singing augmented and diminished intervals

Practise the sequential progressions given below only with solfa, by memory, if possible, starting from any desired pitch.

Augmented second upwards

a) $\frac{3}{4}$ | f l f si l | s t s li t | d' m d' ri' m' ||

b) $\frac{3}{4}$ | l f si l | t s li t | m' d' ri' m' ||

c) $\frac{3}{2}$ | t, m t, d ri m | d f d ra m f | r... | m... | s... | l... ||

Augmented second downwards

a) $\frac{3}{4}$ | t s t lo s | m d m ra d ||

b) $\frac{3}{4}$ | s t lo s | d m ra d ||

c) $\frac{3}{2}$ | d' s d' t lo s | l m l si f m | s... | f... | m... | r... ||

Diminished third

This interval appears mainly in melodic phrases where the dominant or tonic note is surrounded by the upper and lower changing notes. Thus we shall practise singing this interval in such melodic phrases as described above.

Downwards:

a) 4/2   s   lo s fi s lo   fi   s | d   ra d t, d ra   t,   d | m... l,... ‖

b) 3/4   s lo fi s | d ra t, d | m f ri m | l, ta, si, l, ‖

Upwards:

a) 4/2   s   fi s lo s fi   lo   s | d   t, d ra d t,   ra   d | m... l,... ‖

b) 3/4   s fi lo s | d t, ra d | m ri f m | l, si, ta, l, ‖

Augmented fourth upwards

a) 3/4 d s d fi s | r, r r si l | m... f... s... l... ‖

b) 3/4 s d fi s | l r si l | t... d'... r'... m'.. ‖

c) 3/4 f l, ta, m f | s t, d fi s | d' m f t d' |

Augmented fourth downwards

a) 3/4 t m t f m | l r l ma r | s...   m...   r... ‖

b) 3/4 m t f m | r l ma r | d... l, ... s, ... ‖

c) 3/4 m d' t f m | t, s fi d t, | l, f m ta, l, ‖

273

Diminished fifth downwards

a) $\frac{3}{4}$ d's d'fi s | l m l ri m | s... | f... | m... | r... ‖

b) $\frac{3}{4}$ s, d fi,s, | l, r si,l, | t, m li,t, | d... | r... | m... ‖

Diminished fifth upwards

a) $\frac{3}{4}$ t,m t, f m | r s r lo s | m l m ta l | s... | l... ‖

b) $\frac{3}{4}$ m' t f'm' | r' l ma'r' | d' s ra'd' | l... | s... ‖

Combined sequences of fourths and fifths

It is quite a common error, when singing, to exchange fourths and fifths, one for the other. This is why we must include the most diverse variations of intervallic sequences in the course of our practice.

1. a/ **4 + 4** for example in major:

$\frac{2}{4}$ d f f t | d f t | r s s d' | r s d' ‖ etc.

b/ **4 + 4** for example in harmonic minor:

$\frac{2}{4}$ l mm t, | l m t, | si r r l, | si r l, ‖ etc.

2. a/ **5 + 4** for example in harmonic minor:

$\frac{2}{4}$ l, mm l | l, m l | t, f f t | t, f t ‖ etc.

274

b/ $\underrightarrow{5 + 4}$ for example in major:

$\frac{2}{4}$ ♫♫ | ♫♩ | ♫♫ | ♫♩ | etc.

     d' f f d   d' f d   t m m t,   t m t,

3. a/ $\underrightarrow{4 + 5}$ for example in major:

$\frac{2}{4}$ ♫♫ | ♫♩ | ♫♫ | ♫♩ | etc.

     d f f d'   d f d'   r s s r'   r s r'

b/ $\underrightarrow{4 + 5}$ for example in harmonic minor:

$\frac{2}{4}$ ♫♫ | ♫♩ | ♫♫ | ♫♩ | etc.

     l m m l,   l m l,   si r r si,   si r si,

4. a/ $\underrightarrow{5 + 5}$ for example in harmonic minor:

$\frac{2}{4}$ ♫♫ | ♫♩ | ♫♫ | ♫♩ | etc.

     l, m m t   l, m t   t, f f d'   t, f d'

b/ $\underrightarrow{5 + 5}$ for example in major:

$\frac{2}{4}$ ♫♫ | ♫♩ | ♫♫ | ♫♩ | etc.

     d' f f t,   d' f t,   t m m l,   t m l,

5. a/ $\underrightarrow{5 + 4 \qquad 5 + 4}$ for example in major:

$\frac{3}{4}$ ♫♫♩ | ♫♫♩ | etc.

     d s d' f d   r l r's r

b/ $\underrightarrow{5 + 4 \qquad 5 + 4}$ for example in harmonic minor:

$\frac{3}{4}$ ♫♫♩ | ♫♫♩ | etc.

     l r l, m l   si d si, r si

6. a/ $\overset{4+5 \quad 4+5}{\longrightarrow}$ for example in harmonic minor:

$$\frac{3}{4} \; \text{♫♫♩} \; | \; \text{♫♫♩} \; |$$
     l, r l m l,   t, m t m t,   etc.

b/ $\overset{4+5 \quad 4+5}{\longrightarrow}$ for example in major:

$$\frac{3}{4} \; \text{♫♫♩} \; | \; \text{♫♫♩} \; |$$
     d's d f d'   t f t, m t   etc.

Metre

The new compound metre is $\frac{7}{4}$ (and $\frac{7}{8}$). In the musical material of the chapter, two types of inner division appear: 3+4 and 4+3. The time-beating patterns have already been described in connection with the given Kodály material (see Chapter VIII, pages 233—237).

Chords

Revision exercises

Sing the exercises with seventh-chords (in a given tonality) found in the previous chapters (Chapter VI, pages 65—66,, points 1—5, and Chapter VII, pages 167—169, points 1. and 5—7). Practise them in the keys using 2♯ and 5♭ as key signature.

Altered chords within functional harmony

The basic, inner regularity of music in the Baroque and Viennese classical styles, is the functional affinity: tonic → subdominant → dominant → tonic. This authentic functional progression is often coloured by altered leading tones, as well, which connect the chords even more organically. The alterations intensify the inner

276

f/ Dominant seventh in third inversion ($\frac{4}{2}$).

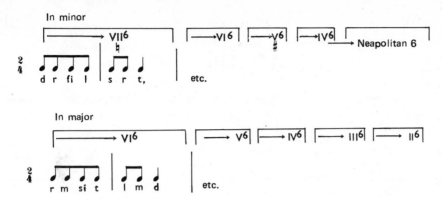

In minor

In major

g/ Diminished first inversion (6) chord. For example in major:

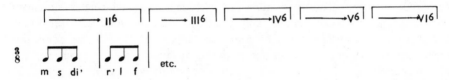

h/ Diminished seventh chord in root position. For example in minor:

i/ Diminished seventh chord in first inversion ($\frac{6}{5}$). For example in major:

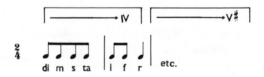

j/ Diminished seventh chord in second inversion ($\frac{4}{3}$). For example in major:

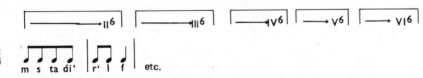

k/ Half-diminished ("ti"–) seventh (only in major):

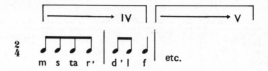

2. Practise the sequences in 1. with solfa + note names, in the keys using 2 sharps or 5 flats.

Secondary dominants in chain-like succession

In Viennese classicism there is a frequently occuring chord progression in which the resolution of the secondary dominant of V^7 type becomes a secondary dominant again, thus the consonant relative tonic chord will be heard only later, sometimes after a long chain-like progression. This continuous succession of secondary dominants is characteristic mainly of the major key, usually as the chain of root position seventh chords or $\frac{6}{5} - \frac{4}{2}$ chords (the $7 - \frac{4}{3}$ sequence is relatively rare).

Singing exercises

1. Practise the following chord progressions in major, broken in ⌒↘ direction, with solfa, from various starting notes:

a) $\underbrace{\text{VII}^{\frac{7}{5\sharp}}_{\sharp} - \text{III}^{7}_{\sharp} - \text{VI}^{7}_{\sharp} - \text{II}^{7}_{\sharp}}_{\text{secondary dominants}} - V^7 - I$

b) $\underbrace{\text{VII}^{\frac{7}{5\sharp}}_{\sharp} - \text{III}^{\frac{6\sharp}{4}}_{3} - \text{VI}^{7}_{\sharp} - \text{II}^{\frac{6\sharp}{4}}_{3}}_{\text{secondary dominants}} - V^7 - I$

c) $\underbrace{\text{III}^{6}_{5\sharp} - \text{VI}^{\frac{4\sharp}{2}} - \text{II}^{6}_{5\sharp}}_{\text{secondary dominants}} - V^{\frac{4}{2}} - I^6$

d) $\underbrace{\text{VI}^{6}_{5\sharp} - \text{II}^{\frac{4\sharp}{2}} - V^{6}_{5}}_{\text{sec. dom.}} - \underbrace{\text{I}^{\frac{4}{2}}_{\flat}}_{\text{sd}} - \text{IV}^6$

282

For example, series b/:

9/8 ♩♩♩ ♩♩♩ ♩ ♪ | ♩♩♩ ♩♩♩ ♩ ♪ | etc.

t, ri fi l fi ri t,   t, r m si m r t,

VII#⁷₅# -   III⁶#₃ -

2. Sing the sequences in 1. in an upward direction only.
For example, the succession in c/:

4/4 ♩ ♩ ♩ ♩ | ♩ ♩ ♩ ♩ | etc.

si, t, r m   s, l, di m   etc.

III⁶₅# - VI²⁴# -

Harmonic analysis

The following quotations all contain one or more secondary dominants. When interpreting these chord patterns and writing an analysis we must always look in two directions: we consider the role of the chords in both the original key and in the key to which the secondary dominant arrives.

For example, quotation No. 903:

				sec. dom.		s.d.	

main D
key: major: I - IV, - II# - V - III# - VI ...

momentary tonal   (A   (B
devitation: major : V - l) minor: V# - l)

If the secondary dominant brings about only a momentary tonal deviation without a modulation, practise singing the chord progressions with solfa (see Chapter III, pages 214—216 and Chapter VII, page 170) based on the position of the chord within the main key.

For example, sing the above-mentioned chord progression as follows:

I ——→ IV   - II# ——→ V - III# ——→ VI -._...
      sec. dom.   s.d.

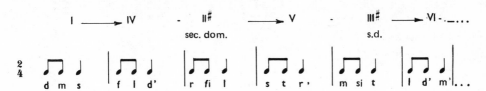

2/4 ♪♪♩ | ♪♪♩ | ♪♪♩ | ♪♪♩ | ♪♪♩ | ♪♪♩ |

d m s   f l d'   r fi l   s t r'   m si t   l d'm'...

283

Musical quotations for harmonic analysis

903.   BEETHOVEN: BAGATELLE IN D MAJOR. OP.119, NO 3.

904.   J.S.BACH: DAS WALT' GOTT VATER UND GOTT SOHN. CHORALE.

905.   MOZART: THE MARRIAGE OF FIGARO. I.

906. J.S.BACH: ICH RIEF DEM HERRN IN MEINER NOTH. CHORALE.

907. BEETHOVEN: PIANO SONATA IN G MAJOR. OP.14, NO 2. II.

908. MOZART: THE MARRIAGE OF FIGARO. I.

909. MOZART: IL SERAGLIO. I.

910. BEETHOVEN: LIED.

911. VIVALDI: BASSOON CONCERTO (,,LA NOTTE" IN B FLAT MAJOR. OP.45, NO 8.

912. MOZART: IL SERAGLIO. III.

913. J.S.BACH: SEID FROH, DIEWEIL. CHORALE.

914. MOZART: THE MARRIAGE OF FIGARO. II.

915. BEETHOVEN: BAGATELLE IN A MAJOR. OP.33, NO 4.

916. J.S.BACH: ERMUNTRE DICH, MEIN SCHWACHER GEIST. CHORALE.

917. VIVALDI: FLUTE CONCERTO IN D MAJOR. OP.10, NO 3.

918. MOZART: THE MARRIAGE OF FIGARO. I.

919. J.HAYDN: STRING QUARTET IN E FLAT MAJOR. OP.20, NO 1. IV.

920.   BEETHOVEN: BAGATELLE IN A MAJOR. OP.33, NO 4.

921.   J.S.BACH: FREUET EUCH, IHR CHRISTEN ALLE. CHORALE.

922.   MOZART: PIANO SONATA IN C MAJOR. III. (K.309)

923.   J.S.BACH: EIN KIND GEBORN ZU BETHLEHEM. CHORALE.

924. BEETHOVEN: PIANO SONATA IN C SHARP MINOR. OP.27, NO 2. III.

925. J.HAYDN: THE CREATION. II.

926. MOZART: PIANO SONATA IN B FLAT MAJOR. I. (K.333)

927. J.HAYDN: PIANO SONATA IN E FLAT MAJOR. I.

928. BEETHOVEN: PIANO SONATA IN C MINOR. OP.10, NO 1. III.

929. J.S.BACH: WER WEISS WIE NAHE MIR MEIN ENDE! CHORALE.

930. BEETHOVEN: PIANO CONCERTO IN G MAJOR. II.

931. HANDEL: SARABAND.

932.   MOZART: THE MARRIAGE OF FIGARO. II.

933.   J.S.BACH: KOMM, O TOD, DU SCHLAFES BRUDER. CHORALE.

934.   J.S.BACH: ICH DANK' DIR, GOTT, FÜR ALL' WOHLTHAT. CHORALE.

935.   J.S.BACH: VALET WILL ICH DIR GEBEN. CHORALE.

936.   MOZART: PIANO SONATA IN A MINOR. III. (K.310)

937. J.S.BACH: VATER UNSER IM HIMMELREICH. CHORALE.

938. MOZART: THE MAGIC FLUTE. II.

939. MOZART: PIANO SONATA IN F. MAJOR. I. (K.332)

940. MOZART: THE MAGIC FLUTE. I.

941. MOZART: PIANO SONATA IN C MAJOR. I. (K.308)

942. VIVALDI: THE FOUR SEASONS. OP.8, NO 3.

943.   MOZART: PIANO SONATA IN E FLAT MAJOR. II. (K.282)

944.   MOZART: IL SERAGLIO. I.

945.   J.HAYDN: PIANO SONATA IN D MAJOR. II.

946.   MOZART: PIANO SONATA IN E FLAT MAJOR. II. (K.282)

947.   MOZART: PIANO SONATA IN C MAJOR. II. (K.330)

948.   BEETHOVEN: PIANO CONCERTO IN G MAJOR. I.

949.   MOZART: PIANO SONATA IN G MAJOR. III. (K.283)

950.   J.HAYDN: PIANO SONATA IN C SHARP MINOR. I.

951.   MOZART: PIANO SONATA IN G MAJOR. III. (K.283)

952. MOZART: IL SERAGLIO. II.

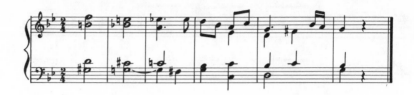

953. MOZART: IL SERAGLIO. II.

954. MOZART: PIANO SONATA IN F MAJOR. I: (K. 533)

955. MOZART: PIANO SONATA IN F MAJOR. I. (K.280)

956.   MOZART: PIANO SONATA IN F MAJOR. I. (K.332)

SIGHT-SINGING
Unison Extracts from the Musical Literature
MATERIAL IN STAFF NOTATION

Melodies in pentatonic and church modes

957.   KODÁLY: RHYMED SONG FOR CHILDREN. (OR.: 0)

958.   GLAZUNOV: VIOLIN CONCERTO IN A MINOR. OP.82

859.   KODÁLY: CELLO SONATA. OP.4. II. (OR.: 0)

960.   DEBUSSY: PROSES LYRIQUES. NO 4. (OR.: 5♯)

961.   BRITTEN: PETER GRIMES. I.

962. WAGNER: DAS RHEINGOLD. IV. (OR.: 6♭)

963. BARTÓK: BLUEBEARD'S CASTLE. (OR.: 0)

964. VAUGHAN WILLIAMS: ON WENLOCK EDGE. NO 5. (OR.: 1♯)

965. KODÁLY: PEACOCK VARIATIONS. (OR.: 1♭)

966. DVOŘÁK: STRING QUARTET IN F MAJOR. OP.96, I. (OR.: 1♭)

967. KODÁLY: PEACOCK VARIATIONS. (OR.: 1♭)

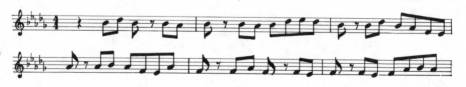

968. DVOŘÁK: STRING QUARTET IN F MAJOR. OP.96, III. (OR.: 1♭)

969. DVOŘÁK: SONATINA IN G MAJOR. OP.100. III. (OR.: 1♯)

970. WAGNER: SIEGFRIED. II. (OR.: 3♯)

971. BARTÓK: MICROCOSM. II. NO 61. (OR.: 1♯)

972. BARTÓK: DANCE SUITE. I. (OR.: 2♭)

973. KODÁLY: PSALMUS HUNGARICUS. (OR.: 0)

974. BARTÓK: MICROCOSM. II. NO 53. (OR.: 0)

975. KODÁLY: CELLO SONATA. OP.4. I. (OR.: 4 ♯)

976. BARTÓK: HUNGARIAN PICTURES. NO 2.

Major and minor melodies

Remaining in the same key signature

977. MOZART: IL SERAGLIO. I: (OR.: 2♭)

978. HANDEL: AH! MIO COR.

979. J.S.BACH: BRANDENBURG CONCERTO. NO 1. II. (OR.: 0)

980. MOZART: COSÌ FAN TUTTE. I: (OR.: 1♭)

981. HANDEL: TAMERLANO. I. (OR.: 1♯)

982. HANDEL: SAUL. I. (OR.: 1♯)

983. VIVALDI: CELLO SONATA IN B FLAT MAJOR. (OR.: 2♭)

984. HANDEL: TAMERLANO. I. (OR.: 3♯)

985. MOZART: THE MAGIC FLUTE. I. (OR.: 0)

986. VIVALDI: CELLO SONATA IN B FLAT MAJOR. (OR.: 2♭)

987. MOZART: IL SERAGLIO. II. (OR.: 2♭)

988. HANDEL: TAMERLANO. III. (OR.: 2♭)

989. CORELLI: VIOLIN SONATA IN B FLAT MAJOR. OP.5. (OR.: 2♭)

990. D'ASTORGA: IN QUESTO CORE. (OR.: 1♯)

991. HANDEL: RODELINDA. III.

992. HANDEL: TAMERLANO. I.

307

With "d" change

993. CORELLI: VIOLIN SONATA IN D MAJOR. OP.5.

994. LULLY: PROSERPINE. I. (OR.: 0)

995. CORELLI: VIOLIN SONATA IN B FLAT MAJOR. OP.5. (OR.: 2♭)

996. HANDEL: GIULIO CESARE. II. (OR.: 3♯)

997. J.HAYDN: THE SEASONS. IV.

998. VIVALDI: VIOLIN SONATA IN F MINOR. (OR.: 4♭)

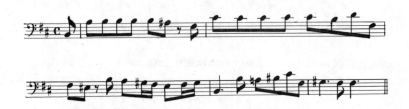

999. VIVALDI: CELLO SONATA IN E MINOR. (OR.: 1♯)

1000. J.S.BACH: ST.MATTHEW PASSION. I.

*Suggested further material:*Bach Collection I/6,9,23,135,157; 52,63,75, 83,84,89,90,92,98,105,108,119,120, 126,140,146,149,155,172,179,189,192,199,200, 204,212,220,221,226,234,235,240, 241.

EXTRACTS IN SOLFA NOTATION

The following extracts should be sung with note names, using key signatures of 2 sharps or 5 flats, with beating time.

1001. CALDARA: ALMA DEL CORE. (OR.: 1♯)

s m f   s f m r d   l f s m f   r d r   r m f   s   f m r   m f m r d   d

1002. CORELLI: CONCERTO GROSSO IN D MAJOR. OP.6, NO 7. (OR.: 2♯)

s f   m f s   f m   r   s f m l t, d   r r   d

1003. J.S.BACH: ERMUNTRE DICH, MEIN SCHWACHER GEIST. CHORALE. (OR.: 1♯):

d d r   m f s   s s fi   s   m   f m   r   d t,   d

r r m   f   f m   r m   r   m m m   f   s l   l si si

l   t   d'   m   f   m   r r s l   s f   m r   d

1004. HANDEL: JUDAS MACCABAEUS. I. (OR.: 1♭)

l, d m l   d' f f   m m   f m r d t,   l, si l d' t l   si m   d t, l,

310

1005. HANDEL: MESSIAH. I. (OR.: 1♭)

m | si l si l t d'si | l f m ri md i r t, | d l, si, l, f r si l | m m l,

1006. CORELLI: VIOLIN SONATA IN D MAJOR. OP.5. (OR.: 2♯)

d l, f m r d l, m l d' t l si | l m f m

l r m m m m l s f m r s, d m

l, r m f t, m f s d f s l s f m r m f r d

1007. LULLY: ALCESTE. V. (OR.: 2♭)

f m m m l l t si fi m r d t, d l, f f m m m r r r r t, d dt, l,

1008. H.PURCELL: THE HISTORY OF DIOCLESIAN. (OR.: 1♯)

s r m f s m l m f m r d r t, d l, d m l m l fi si l t l l

1009. LULLY: ALCESTE. V. (OR.: 2♭)

r m f m m m l t si t, d d r r m f m m l fi si l t l l

311

1010. LULLY: PHAÉTON. I. (OR.: 1♭)

d r m d l, m m l l s fi t si fi m

d' t d' l s fm r s s l f m m r d d

1011. H.PURCELL: KING ARTHUR. V. (OR.: 2♭)

m s d' s l s l t l s m mfs r mr d t, l, t,d r t,

r t, m d f r m m mfsl s di r rmfmr r

s m d m fmrmrd r s, s, dt,l, f fmr s sfm rd d

1012. J.HAYDN: THE CREATION. III. (OR.: 1♭)

s t, d f m l s s fi f m l s t, d

312

Material in Several Parts

1013. LASSUS: BEATUS VIR. MOTET. (OR.: 0)

1014. J.S.BACH: THE WELL-TEMPERED CLAVIER. II. PRELUDE IN B MINOR.

1015. LASSUS: QUEMADMODUM DESIDERAT. (OR.: 0)

1016. J.S.BACH: THRE–PART INVENTION IN D MAJOR.

1017. HANDEL: DETTINGEN TE DEUM. NO 9. (OR.: 2♭)

1018. J.S.BACH: THE ART OF FUGUE. CONTRAPUNCTUS III. (OR.: 1♭)

1019. LULLY: PROSERPINE. II. (OR.: 0)

1020. HASSLER: GAGLIARDA. (OR.: 1♭)

1021. J.S.BACH: BEFIEHL DU DEINE WEGE. CHORALE.

1022. LULLY: ISIS. III. (OR.: 1♭)

1023. J.S.BACH: AUF, MEIN HERZ! DES HERREN TAG. CHORALE.

1024. LULLY: PROSERPINE. I. (OR.: 1♭)

1025. J.S.BACH: JESUM LASS' ICH NICHT VON MIR. CHORALE.

1026. SCANDELLI: BONGIORNO MADONNA. (OR.: 1♭)

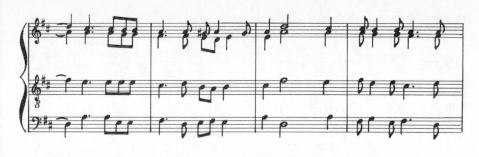

1027. J.S.BACH: NUN KOMM, DER HEIDEN HEILAND. CHORALE.

323

326

DEVELOPMENT OF MUSICAL MEMORY
Memorizing and Transposing
Two-Part Material

We find modulations in the extracts below: the musical material arrives from the tonic key to the dominant key. Before memorizing, it is necessary to establish the point at which we shall change "d" because an improper interpretation may disturb the students' later work.

Practise memorizing and transposing as before (see Chapter VI, page 108).

The two-part extracts

1029. H.PURCELL: SONATA IN C MAJOR. NO VI. (OR.: 0)

1030. J.S.BACH: THE WELL–TEMPERED CLAVIER. I. FUGUE IN G MINOR. (OR.: 2♭)

1031. BEETHOVEN: ORGAN FUGUE IN D MAJOR.

1032. J.S.BACH: THE WELL–TEMPERED CLAVIER. II. FUGUE IN C MINOR.

1033. HANDEL: PIANO SUITE IN F MINOR. ALLEGRO. (OR.: 4♭)

1034. HANDEL: FUGUE IN A MINOR. (OR.: 0)

Memorizing and Transposing
Three-Part Material

Practise memorizing as previously (see Chapter VI, page 111). When the students have faultlessly performed and written down the memorized musical quotations, extend the exercise to include transposition as well.

In the course of transposing, continue to follow the above steps applying each element within the frame of the new key.

The three-part extracts

1035. J.S.BACH: THE WELL-TEMPERED CLAVIER. I. FUGUE IN E FLAT MINOR. (OR.: 6♭)

1036. PALESTRINA: DEPOSUIT. MOTET. (OR.: 0)

1037. HANDEL: FUGUE IN C MAJOR. (OR.: 0)

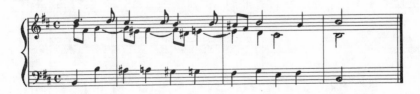

1038. MONTEVERDI: O, ROSSIGNUOL. MADRIGAL. (OR.: 1♭)

1039. HANDEL: DETTINGEN TE DEUM. NO 5.

1040. BEETHOVEN: MASS IN C MAJOR. OP.86. GLORIA. (OR.: 0)

Memorizing and Transposing
Chord Progressions

Modulations occur in the chord progressions Nos. XXI–XXIV: in three cases between relative major-minor keys, and once leading to the dominant key (No XXI). During the preparatory analysis, the teacher has to make sure that the students understand clearly the common chord of the two keys as well as the possible "d"-change.

In all other respects the practice procedure is similar to that in Chapter VII (see page 220).

Figured bass progressions

Memorizing Chorale Extracts

The four-part Bach chorales may be successfully memorized and retained only if the vertical sounding and the linear melody movement form an organic musical unity in our memory. During the learning process, the most important task is to make conscious the harmonic sounding of the four parts. This harmonic outline will later be reduced to individual voice components and finally the sound of the whole chord will be heard again and recorded in the inner hearing.

Memorizing chorales requires initially much time, patience, and great concentration. Regular practice in this area, however, is indispensable, because it plays an important role in establishing conscious, harmonic hearing.

Suggested way of memorizing

1. Analysis: key, degree number, inversion of chord, alien colouring notes (passing note, changing note, suspension, anticipation).
2. Memorizing the bass part a/ with solfa, b/ with degree numbers, c/ with note names.
3. Memorizing the soprano part a/ with solfa, b/ with note names.
4. Performing soprano and bass on the piano, playing both parts and singing a/ the bass to solfa then to degree numbers, b/ the soprano to solfa, at the same time.
5. Memorizing the complete musical material with the help of the elements already made conscious (chord progression, outer parts).
6. Four-part performance on the piano singing the bass part at the same time a/ with degree numbers, b/ with solfa.

Chorale extracts

1042. MACH'S MIT MIR, GOTT, NACH DEINER GÜT'.

1043. BEFIEHL DU DEINE WEGE.

1044. SO WANDELT FROH AUF GOTTES WEGEN.

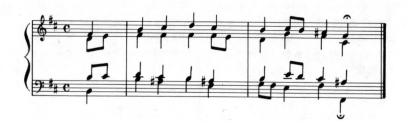

1045. STÄRK MICH MIT DEINEM FREUDENGEIST.

336

1046. BEFIEHL DU DEINE WEGE.

1047. LASS, O HERR, DEIN OHR SICH NEIGEN. (OR.: 2♭)

1048. GOTT DER VATER WOHN' UNS BEI.

1049. EINS IST NOTH, ACH HERR, DIES EINE.

1050. HERZLIEBSTER JESU, WAS HAST DU VERBROCHEN.

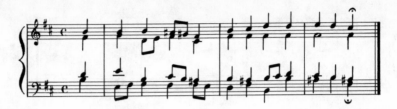

1051. SO WANDELT FROH AUF GOTTES WEGEN.

EAR TRAINING
Recognition of Intervals

Interval progressions within the major and minor tonality

Practise as in Chapter VI (see page 117) but now with the combination of fourths, fifths, sixths and sevenths.

The intervals of the harmonic minor hexachords

Structure the ear-training exercise according to the principles established for the practice of pentachords (see Chapter VII, page 223).

The interval types of pentatony from a given note

The teacher plays the pentatonic interval types remaining within the range of an octave (see Chapter VII, page 166) in any order from the same lower starting note upwards or the same upper starting note downwards, while the students write down the size and quality of the successive intervals. After checking, practise singing with interval names + note names, to reinforce conscious knowledge.

For example, the succession of M6, p4, m7, M2, p5, m3, m6, M3 downwards from the note A:

1. Recognition.

teacher:
(piano)

students:
(writing
down)

M6　　　p4　　　m7　　　etc.

2. Individual, then group checking by naming the intervals.

3. Singing, to reinforce conscious knowledge.

major 6   A—C   perfect 4   A—E

(Cf.: Recognition of Intervals; Chapter II, page 158)

Pairs of intervals not derived from the triads

The teacher, playing first a middle tone, sounds two tones, one above, one below
the sounding of which is different from that of a triad and its inversions but which
does not reach the range of a perfect octave.

The students have already practised the recognition of the interval pairs of the
triads and their inversions (see Chapter III, page 250 and Chapter IV, page 343).
The present task is to be solved similarly except that singing for the purpose
of conscious knowledge should be realized with interval names + note names instead
of solfa.

For example, practising the succession $\frac{\uparrow m2\ \uparrow m6\ \uparrow M2}{\downarrow M6'\ \downarrow m3'\ \downarrow a4/d5/}$:

1. Recognition.

teacher:
(piano)

students:
(writing $\frac{m2}{M6}$ $\frac{m6}{m3}$ $\frac{M2}{a4\ (d5)}$
down)

2. Individual, then group checking by naming the interval types.

3. Singing, starting from the middle tone, to reinforce conscious knowledge:

piano   singing   piano   singing

given   m2   M6   G - A♭ - G - B♭   give   m6   m3
tone   the note

340

Interval successions independent of tonality

The teacher plays a varied succession of intervals, in broken form either upwards or downwards, remaining within the range of a sixth and using all tones of the twelve-note system. The students note the size and quality of the intervals, indicating their direction as well. After checking, the correct solution is written on the blackboard —identification of intervals with possible enharmonic equivalents are agreed upon together—and the students sing the succession from the blackboard with note names, using various pitches as starting notes.

For example:

1. Recognition.

2. Individual, then group checking.

3. Writing the intervals, as already identified, on the blackboard (p5↑, etc.).

4. Singing the intervals from the blackboard with note names a/ as a succession beginning on the original starting note, then b/ transposed.

Chord Recognition

Seventh chords and its inversions ($\frac{6}{5}$, $\frac{4}{3}$, $\frac{4}{2}$) from a given tone of the minor key

Practise as in Chapter VII (see page 226) but now in harmonic minor. Do not forget the leading tone "si".

Secondary dominants in major and minor tonality

After giving the tonic note of the major or harmonic minor key, the teacher plays secondary dominants of different degree, type and inversion within the chosen key (see Chapter VIII, page 278—279), , then plays their resolution according to the functional logic (ibid). The students write down the degree number and inversion of the secondary dominant and its resolution within the given tonality. They also write down the type of the secondary dominant.

As in other similar ear-training exercises, the students sing the "d" or "l" tonic note before each new chord pattern to help them relate the next chord pattern to the given tonic.

After checking, practise singing to reinforce conscious knowledge with solfa only.

For example, the chord patterns $VI_3^{\overset{6\#}{4}} - II^6; V^{6\#} - VI; II_{\#}^{\overset{6\#}{5}} - III^6$ in B♭ major:

1. Recognition.

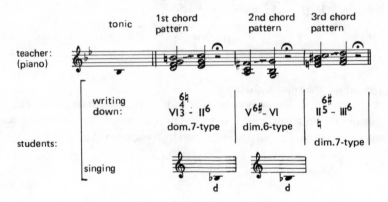

2. Individual, then group checking, naming the type, degree number and inversion of the secondary dominant.

3. Singing to reinforce conscious knowledge, with solfa, after giving the tonic note.

Chord progressions

Recognition with the help of singing

Practise the figured bass sequences of Chapter VIII (see page 333) as described in Chapter VI (see page 121). The students have to recognize the altered chords heard in the sequence not only by naming them with degree numbers and establishing their inversion, but also by their sound-type; for example, secondary dominant of dominant seventh type, diminished seventh chord, half-diminished seventh chord.

Recognition with the help of inner hearing

Use the figured bass sequences in Chapter VII (see page 220) for this purpose according to the steps described on page 227 of Chapter VII.

Chord analysis of quotations taken from musical literature by ear

The teacher chooses a quotation from the material found in Chapter VI (see pages 67—76) for the purpose of harmonic analysis and plays it several times on the piano. The students a/ follow the bass line by ear, b/ listen for the total simultaneous sound and the tonal function of the chords by ear, c/ on the basis of their conscious aural experiences to this point, try to write down the degree number and inversion of the chords.
   Group checking is done as the quotation is played once more.

Rhythm Dictation

(Musical material on page 505 of the Supplement)

Practise as in Chapter VI (see page 121).

Kodály: 24 Little Canons

Sing canons 7, 11, 13 and 14 according to Chapter VI which describes new ways of practice (see page 122), this time using D or D$^\flat$ as "d".

Melody Dictation
One-part dictation
(Musical material on page 509 of the Supplement)

Practise according to the principles summarized in Chapter VII (see page 228). Use continuous writing when dictating major and minor melodies as well.

Two-part dictation

Concentration on the vertical sounding
(Musical material on page 515 of the Supplement)

Dictation should be carried out as in Chapter VII (see page 228).

Concentration on the horizontal melodic movement
(Musical material on page 517 of the Supplement)

We can find excerpts of varying length among the quotations. The shorter extracts should be written out according to previous practice — that is by memorizing first (see Chapter VI, page 124). When dictating longer extracts, however, a better solution, preparing the students for future tasks, is possible: after having memorized, sung, and written down the lower part, the students should use continuous-writing to take down the upper part above the completed notation of the lower part.

When writing down the lower part the students must pay attention to the rhythmic notation since there must be a clear correspondance between the two parts even though they were not written down at the same time.

Two- and three-part canons
(Musical material on page 521 of the Supplement)

Practise the canons in the following way:
1. The students memorize the melody of the canon by ear.
2. After singing from memory with solfa, then with note names, a volunteer tries

an individual performance in two parts: a/ singing the first part and playing the second part on the piano; b/ playing the first part on the piano and singing the second part.

3. Three-part performance at this stage should be carried out by two students: one performs the first and second parts according to solution 2.b/ above, the other sings the third part.

Bach Chorale Extracts

Two-part continuous writing completed by figured bass notation

(Musical material on page 523 of the Supplement)

The students have already come across a similar exercise when notating chord progressions (see: Recognition with the help of inner hearing, Chapter VII, page 227 and Chapter VIII, page 343). The notation of chorale extracts is made somewhat more difficult only by the appearance of occasional colouring notes (passing note, changing note, suspension, anticipation).

Two-part continuous writing of modulating musical material

(Musical material on page 525 of the Supplement)

In the previous chapters we employed continuous writing in connection with only those chorale extracts which remained within the given key signature system. However, modulating chorale extracts have already appeared in the ear training material of Chapter VII (see page 229), but were used only for the purpose of taking down the bass part. The present form of practice presents a double task: the students have to write down with two-part continuous writing, notating both the bass and soprano parts, chorale extracts in which there is a modulation which brings about a "d" change.

PLANNING SUGGESTION

(See the diagram at the end of the book)

CHAPTER IX

(Material in staff notation uses G and G flat as "d")

KODÁLY MATERIAL
Unison Pentatonic Melodies
MATERIAL IN STAFF NOTATION

The set of notes used for note finding practice from staff notation:

Suggested exercises: 333 Reading Exercises/303–308, 315–317.

MATERIAL IN SOLFA NOTATION

Melodies for practising more difficult musical elements
(Pentatonic Music I, IV)

$\frac{5}{8}$ *metre*

    a/ 3+2 inner division : IV/26, 28
    b/ 2+3 and 3+2 inner division : I/98

Alternation of metres with different metrical units

$\frac{2}{4}$ and $\frac{6}{8}$: IV/27

Melodies for practising note name singing

(333 Reading Exercises/300—302; Pentatonic Music IV/12, 119—123, 125, 126)

After preparation with hand-sign exercises (see Chapter IX, page 375), practise the melodies similarly as in Chapter VIII (see page 238). Note name singing in this chapter will naturally use G and G♭ as "d".

Two-Part Material
PREPARATORY EXERCISES:
"LET US SING CORRECTLY"
(Nos. 94, 95, 98, 101, 103)

Practise singing as in Chapter VIII.

TWO-PART WORKS
Pentatonic range of notes
TWO-SYSTEM PENTATONIC THEME

77 Two-Part Exercises/54

1. The notes used in the $A^5 A_?^5 A A$, theme:

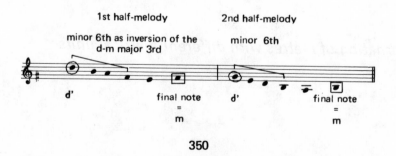

The melody is built on two different pentatonic systems, both with final note "m". Thus it is in a two-system "m" pentatonic mode. (Cf.: Two-system pentatonic themes, Chapter VIII, page 239.)

The "d" change should occur in bar 5 of the theme:

2. The set of notes used in the accompanying material:

The accompanying material remains in the same "d" system throughout:

	bars 1–8 = 1st half of the theme	bars 9–18 = accompanying material
soprano:	"d" = D	"d" = D

	bars 1–8 = accompanying material	bars 9–16 = 2nd half of the theme
alto:	"d" = D	"d" = G

Thus the only "d" change occurs in the alto part when it takes over the second half of the theme from the soprano at the point of fifth-change in bar 5:

3. The entrance of the soprano as accompanying voice in bar 5 may be prepared with the following melodic sequence:

This preparation is most necessary as the G, following the F♯ final note of the first half-melody, attracts so much attention, that it may become difficult for the soprano to continue in the former D="d" tonality.

BITONALITY IN THE TWO-PART MATERIAL

Bicinia Hungarica II/72

1. The "l" pentatonic theme with fifth change is heard in the soprano. Lines 1 and 3 appear in a tonal fifth-changing relation, lines 2 and 4 in a real fifth-changing relation:

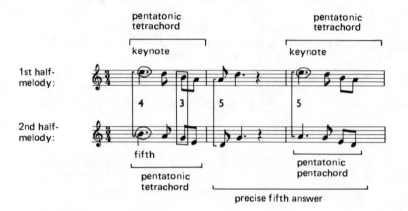

The initial keynote "l" is answered by "m" in line 3, the consequence of which is the appearance of the pentatonic third (m–d), the inversion of the well-known pentatonic sixth (d'–m; see Chapter VI, page 28). The fourth line, however, begins on "r", an exact fifth-answer to "l".

2. The alto presents the same theme in canon at the fifth below, but continues with a real fifth-change in its own part (lines 3 and 4):

3. Thus two "l" pentatonic modes in fifth relation to each other ("l" pentatonic on E and on A) are heard simultaneously in the two-part material:

Range including altered notes

Bicinia Hungarica III/113

1. The 17th century theme appears in the eight-note set of tones characteristic of Gregorian music (seven diatonic notes + "ta"). The three-line theme closes first in G ionian (bar 7), then in the relative D mixolydian, and finally in E aeolian, also a relative mode. The last cadential phrase, coloured by "ta", lends a phrygian character to the final "l"-ending mode:

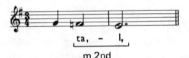

The text having 3 verses, the theme (soprano) and its accompaniment (alto) are heard three times in the course of the composition, the first and second times with the same musical material, the third time in a variant form. Thus the piece has the form of a variant strophic song.

2. The accompanying material of the alto goes beyond the framework of the eight-note system at the mixolydian cadence of the first and second verses only ("fi" + "ri" altered notes, bar 13). At all other times it remains within the diatonic system coloured by "ta", as does the theme itself.

Suggested further exercise: 55 Two-Part Exercises/16

Fifteen Two-Part Exercises/7

1. The exercise is in four eight-bar sections, the fourth section a recapitulation of the first:

number of bars	1 – 8	9 – 16	17 – 24	25 – 32
soprano	Theme D dorian	Counter-point A dorian	leading back with the waving notes t-ta and f-fi	Theme D dorian
alto	Counter-point D dorian	Theme A dorian		Counter-point D dorian
key relation-ship	Tonic	Dominant	⟶	Tonic

2. The various stylistic elements are immediately apparent from the formal outline:

a/ The dorian tonality of the theme and the waving notes t–ta and f–fi in the material leading back to the return are typically Renaissance elements.

b/ The exchange of theme and counterpoint between the parts (the so-called double-counterpoint), the unbroken, on-going melodic line, and the successive tonic — dominant appearances of the theme are all Baroque characteristics.

c/ The uniform eight-bar length of each section and the T — D — T order of keys are characteristic of the Viennese classical style.

3. These stylistic elements determine positively the place and the reason for the "d" changes: the Baroque modulation demands "d" change, the Renaissance waving notes speak against it.

Suggested places for "d" change:

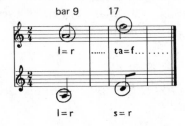

354

Bicinia Hungarica I/59

1. The composition is in three sections:

A	B	C + coda
bars 1 — 5	bars 6 — 17	bars 18 — 28
set of notes with 1♯ as key signature	set of notes without key signature	set of notes with 3♯ as key signature
	(with the waving notes f-fi and s-si)	(with waving notes t-ta)
B phrygian:	A minor:	A major:
closed	open	closed

2. We find many stylistic elements in the musical material which are reminiscent of the modal style (Cf.: Chapter VI, page 36):

a/ The A B C continuation form presenting new material in each section.

b/ The opening phrygian melody and its cadence.

c/ The waving notes f–fi and t–ta of the second (B) section.

d/ The appearance of "ta" to form a perfect fifth in place of the would-be diminished fifth in section C (key signature of 3 sharps):

e/ The two-voiced melodic cadence in phrygian mode preceding the coda:

355

3. Suggested places for "d" change:

55 Two-Part Exercises /34

1. In the first half of this fugue-like exercise we hear the theme in melodic minor (soprano, bars 1—4), its tonal answer (alto, bars 5—8), the theme, somewhat varied, in mirror-inversion (alto, bars 9—12; soprano, bars 13—16), and a transformation (soprano, bars 17—20):

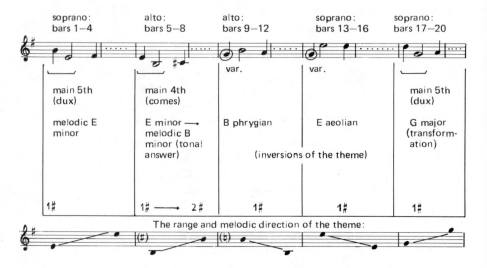

2. New thematic material with a descending melodic line appears in bar 20:

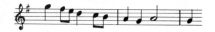

356

The answering soprano-alto exchange which follows creates a nine-bar organically related sequential pattern:

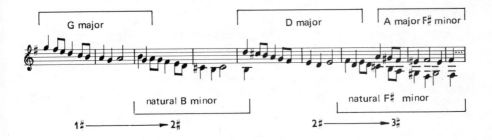

3. In the final eight-bar recapitulation the original dux appears again, first in melodic B minor then in E minor.

4. Suggested places for "d" change:

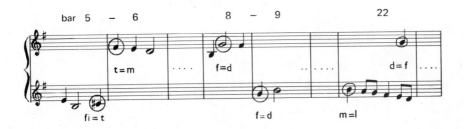

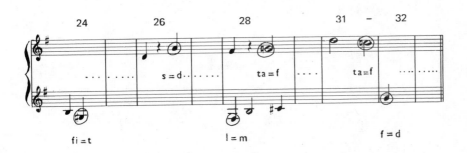

Fifteen Two-Part Exercises/12

1. The formal structure of the exercise:

Theme (T) + counterpoint (Cp) presented in both parts	middle section with varied and transformed theme and counterpoint							pseudo | real recapitulation + coda	
tonic→ dominant ——→	tonic ——→		relative major→		subdominant→		tonic		
Cp bars 1–5	Theme 5–9		Cp., 12–16		Theme, 18–22		Cp., 23–27	Cp/bar 1 27	Theme ,,, 28–31
A minor	E minor	trans-ition 3 bars	A minor	trans-ition 2 bars	C major transf.	trans-ition 1 bar	D minor	A minor	A minor + coda
Theme 1–5	Cp 5–9		Theme 12–16		Cp,, 18–22		Theme ,, 23–27	T/bar 1 27	Cp ,,,, 28–31
A minor	E minor		A minor		C major transf.		D minor	A minor	A minor

Order of keys placed on the pillar of thirds:

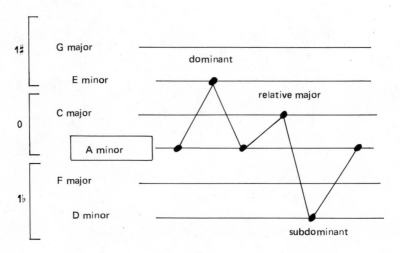

2. Suggested places for "d" change:

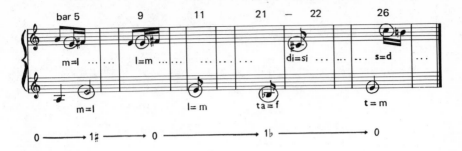

66 Two-Part Exercises/49

1. The order of keys of the theme and its tonal answer take an unusually interesting form.

a/ dux (bars 1—4) = E aeolian:

b/ comes (bars 5—8) = E aeolian → B aeolian (+1 fifth modulation):

c/ dux (bars 12—15) = G mixolydian:

d/comes (bars 16—19) = D mixolydian → A dorian (change of modes from the starting tonality to the fifth higher relative mode):

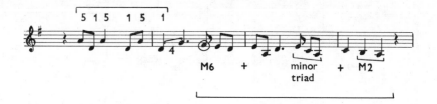

e/ dux (bars 23—26) = the original, E aeolian form of the theme.

2. The stylistic elements of the key relationships:

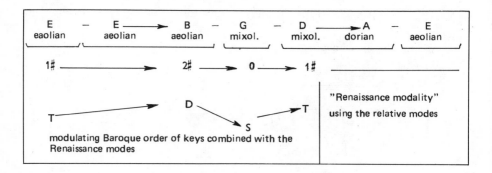

(Cf.: Chapter VII, page 139)

3. The "d" changes:

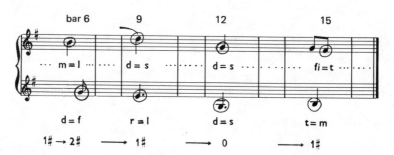

4. The only difficult melodic section is that which leads back to the final entrance of the theme (bars 20—23). Suggestion for practice:

a) Soprano:

s

Once the students can securely sing and hear the main tones of the above sequences, they will be able to sing the original melodic line more easily.

33 Two-Part Exercises/1

This eight-bar little composition arrives at a new tonality in almost every measure with such light and gentle melodic movement that we hardly even notice.

Suggested places for "d" change:

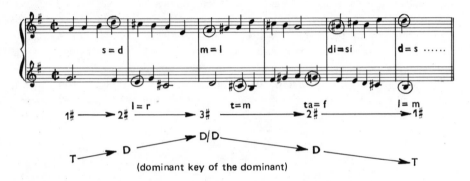

(dominant key of the dominant)

44 Two-Part Exercises/13

1. The typical Baroque stylistic elements in the melodic structure of the theme (Handel) are:

a/ The opening motif in itself determines the key by featuring the significant notes of the tonality.

b/ If we examine the musical events, we see that each stress-group of melodic material, especially in the second half of the melody, is extremely condensed.

The structure of the theme:

361

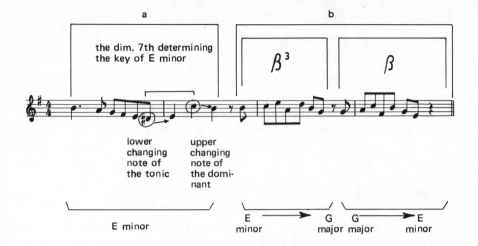

The "b" section of the melody presents many new elements:

a/ Starting on an upbeat, the beginning is unstressed; b/ due to the continuous eighth-note motion, the material is essential more active than in section "a"; c/ the sequential progression of the closed one-bar motifs and the major-minor change of key create independent formal units within the half-melody.

2. The D—T and T—D correspondence in the relation of dux and tonal-answer comes is not found in the successive melodic intervals, but rather in the structurally prominent melodic notes:

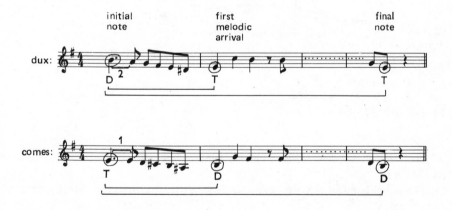

(Cf.: 66 Two-Part Exercises/44, Chapter VII, page 142)

3. The theme appears successively in the following keys:

Dux (a+b) 1—4			Dux (a+b) 12—15	Theme phrase „b" 16—17	Cp 18—19			Dux (a+b) 26—29
E minor		trans-ition	E minor	A minor	D minor	trans-ition		E minor +
	Comes (a+b) 5—8			Cp 16—17	Theme phrase „b" 18—19		Dux (a+b) 22—25	coda
E → B minor (tonal answer)				A minor	D minor		A minor	
			double counterpoint					
1# ——→ 2# ———————→ 1# ——→ 0 ——→ 1# ——→ 0 —————————→ 1#								

The theme is here treated uniquely, remaining throughout in minor with no trans-formed variant. The Baroque (plagal) order of keys is thus quite clear:

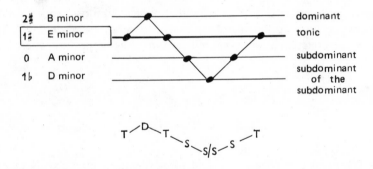

4. Suggested places for "d" change:

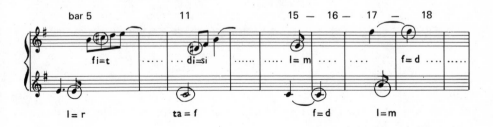

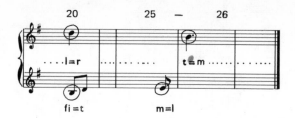

33 Two-Part Exercises/27

1. The theme is based on a one-bar melodic unit which descends sequentially by major seconds forming a four-bar closed melody:

Element "α", with melodic movement of major character, is heard in bar 2 as a real sequence beginning a major second lower, its tonality changed as the keynote C replaces the keynote D as "d". Bar 3 begins again as a real sequence but shifts, as a variant occurs, into the key of the cadential pattern based on D "I". Thus the following interpretation of the theme will help to insure proper intonation:

2. In a very unique manner, we find hidden in the melody, as melodic pillars, the principle notes of the Baroque sequence in natural minor:

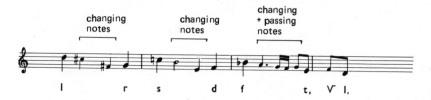

3. We hear the theme five times in course of the exercise. The third appearance is as a mirror inversion:

364

Theme bars 1–4		Theme in mirror inv. 9–12		Theme 17–20	
D major / minor				D major / minor	
					+ coda D minor
	Theme 4–7		Theme 14–17		
	A major / minor		G major / minor		

The consecutive appearances of the theme in its original form follow the Baroque (plagal) order of keys despite its double (maggiore-minore) tonality:

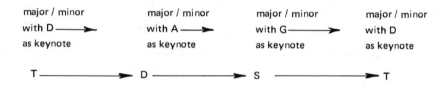

major / minor with D ⟶ as keynote	major / minor with A ⟶ as keynote	major / minor with G ⟶ as keynote	major / minor with D as keynote

T ⟶ D ⟶ S ⟶ T

4. Suggested places for "d" change:

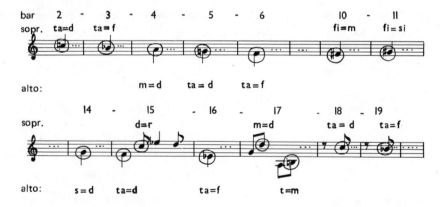

22 Two-Part Exercises/4

1. The theme in its internal structure, is closely related to that of the previous exercise (33/27). Melodically, we find again an initial motif continued as a descending sequence. Now, however, rhythmic variation creates displacement of stress relations:

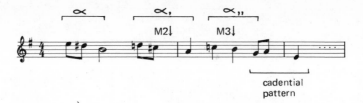

The basic difference between the two themes is that the three-note melodic sequence in this exercise does not bring about a change of key. Its characteristically Baroque chromatic tetrachord belongs to a tonality which has a minor third only above its keynote. The tonality thus remains unchanged. The melodic set of notes:

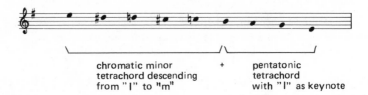

The essence of the opening melodic pattern is a minor 2nd + major 3rd progression:

This figure is each time placed one major second lower and each time with a different rhythmic structure. Thus, as the melody continues, the starting tones of the melodic figures do not coincide with the metric accents.

2. The comes presents a tonal answer:

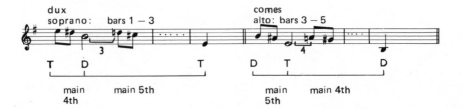

Even though the main notes of the comes (D—T—D progression) do not correspond intervallically to the main notes of the dux (T—D—T progression) we find the same descending order in both chromatic minor tetrachords.

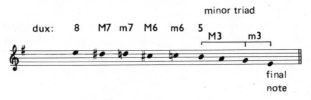

366

The modulation from E minor to B minor occuring in the course of the comes, is not sufficiently convincing as the "t", which would require an additional accidental belonging to the new tonality of the dominant key in which we have arrived, is not present in the tones of the theme. Lest this uncertainty of key not cause any intonational problems in the tonal answer, practise the dux and comes successively with the melodic variation ♩ ♫ | ♩ 𝄾 replacing the pentatonic cadential ♩ ♫ | ♩ 𝄾 figure: m   d   t,   l,   m   d   r   l,

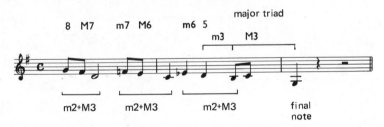

The theme with its original pentatonic cadential figure should be sung only when the students can clearly hear that the keynotes of dux and comes are both "l".

3. The theme appears transformed to major in bars 9—11 and bars 13—15. This is evident from the broken major triad of the cadential figure. Here again the chromatic tetrachord is built into the melodic progression:

The only deviation from the original minor theme is the major third of the cadential tonic chord. (Were we to replace the B by a B♭, we would hear the original minor theme in G.)

4. The theme is heard as a mirror inversion in bars 18—20. More precisely it is the exact mirror inversion of the theme transformed to major:

5. The theme appears successively in the following keys:

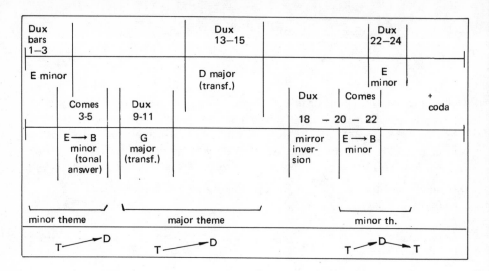

Dux bars 1–3			Dux 13–15		Dux 22–24	
E minor			D major (transf.)		E minor	
	Comes 3-5	Dux 9-11		Dux — Comes 18 — 20 — 22		+ coda
	E → B minor (tonal answer)	G major (transf.)		mirror inver-sion	E → B minor	
minor theme			major theme		minor th.	
T —→ D			T —→ D		T —→ D ←— T	

6. Suggested places for "d" change:

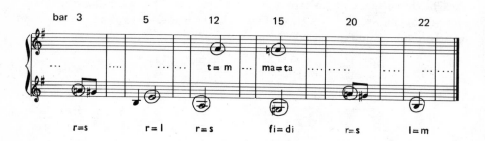

Suggested further exercises: Fifteen Two-Part Exercises/9; 44 Two-Part Exercises/14; 33 Two-Part Exercises/13,26,28; 22 Two-Part Exercises/11.

Three-Part Material

Tricinia/7

1. We meet here a structure reminiscent of Bach's three-part inventions. The composition begins not with the theme, but rather with the contrapuntal-type accompanying voice. The theme, entering later, fits naturally into the given tonal frame. As the work continues, the theme and counterpoint appear each time in two different voices and many times in double counterpoint form.

2. Again we find a tonal answer in the dux-comes relation of the first two appearances of the theme:

3. The formal structure of the composition:

(See the diagram on page 370)

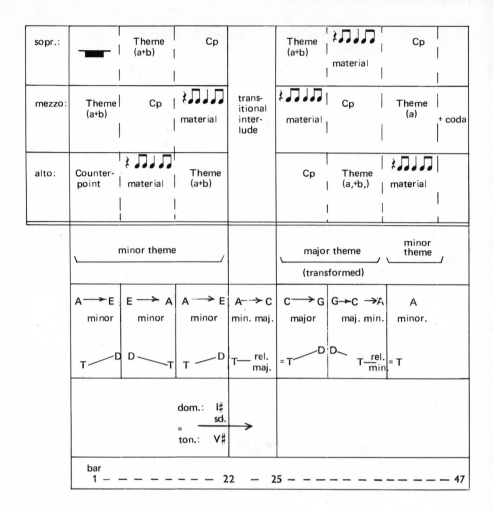

sopr.:	<image: black rectangle>	Theme (a+b)	Cp		Theme (a+b) ♩♪♩♪ material	Cp
mezzo:	Theme (a+b)	Cp	♩♪♩♪ material	trans-itional inter-lude	♩♪♩♪ material	Cp	Theme (a) + coda
alto:	Counter-point	♩♪♩♪ material	Theme (a+b)		Cp	Theme (a,+b,)	♩♪♩♪ material

minor theme				major theme		minor theme
(transformed)						
A→E minor	E→A minor	A→E minor	A→C min. maj.	C→G major	G→C maj. min.	A minor.
T—D	D—T	T—D	T— rel. maj.	=T—D	D T— rel. min.	=T
		dom.: I♯ sd. = ton.: V♯ →				
bar 1 — — — — — — 22 — 25 — — — — — — — — — 47						

(Cf.: Bach, Three-Part Invention in F major, No 8.)

4. Suggested places for "d" change:

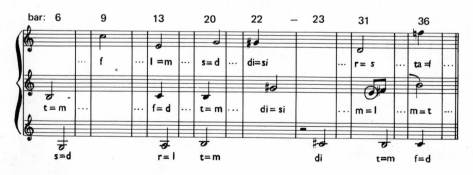

bar: 6	9	13	20	22 — 23	31	36
...f	...l =m ...	s=d ...	di=si ...		...r = s ...	ta =f ...
t = m ...	...f=d	t=m ...	di= si		...m=l	...m=t ...
s=d	r=l	t=m	di	t=m	f=d	

370

1. If we wish to be true to the character of the work, we may have it performed tastefully by a woodwind and voice ensemble. The soprano part, decorated in an eastern manner, may be played by a clarinet (or perhaps oboe or flute), and the lower two voices sung by the students in two groups.

2. The alto theme moves within a phrygian hexachord, but with a major third:

Above this, the mezzo sings a rhythmically and melodically contrasting counterpart in the form of a one-bar ostinato:

3. Examining the entire composition, we find that the theme is simply a melodic ostinato, the organically linked repetitions of which establish the large form:

Section I				Section II				Section III		
Theme + ostinato with B as keynote			2-bar trans- ition	Theme + ostinato with E as keynote		2-bar cadence in A minor	8-bar lead- ing back	Theme + ostinato with B as keynote		4-bar coda
1.	2.	3.		1.	2.			1.	2.	
bars				bars				bars		
1—4	5—8	9—12		15—18	19—22			33—36	37—40	

4. In sections I and III, the soprano presents the theme, decorated with changing notes, in a rhythmically animated variant.

In this richly flowing material, the length of the theme is varied almost at random: the four-bar (tetrapodic) melody being condensed into three bars, two bars, even into one bar. The simultaneous sounding of the theme and its variants gives the entire musical material an extremely tense and dynamic quality.

5. The "d" changes:

l = m ···· l = r ··· ···

di = si ··· f = ta ···

r = l l = r

Tricinia/25

1. The principal tones s—m—d—l, , appearing in the accented part of the bars, create the melodic outline of the theme:

The first three bars feature the major triad, while in bar 4 the melody closes on the main fifth of the relative minor. Thus the key does not remain constant throughout: beginning and continuing in major, it then ends in the relative minor.

2. The theme, heard four times, is sharply varied in its third and fourth presentations. The most essential melodic element, however, re-appears again in each case:

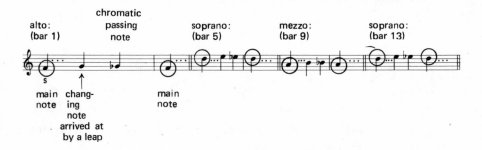

alto: chromatic soprano: mezzo: soprano:
(bar 1) passing (bar 5) (bar 9) (bar 13)
note

main chang- main
note ing note
note
arrived at
by a leap

3. Formal structure:

372

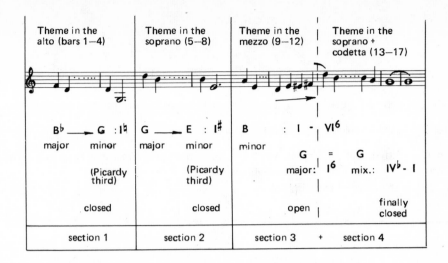

Theme in the alto (bars 1—4)	Theme in the soprano (5—8)	Theme in the mezzo (9—12)	Theme in the soprano + codetta (13—17)
B♭ → G : I♮ major minor	G → E : I♯ major minor	B : I - VI⁶ minor	
(Picardy third)	(Picardy third)	G = G major: I⁶ mix.: IV♭- I	
closed	closed	open	finally closed
section 1	section 2	section 3 +	section 4

4. Suggested places for "d" change:

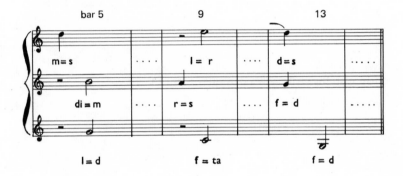

Suggested further works: Tricinia/10, 5.

Melody with Piano Accompaniment

Epigrams/6

1. The melody, which appears in a two-section form, grows out of the organic development of one basic motif. The most essential element of the motivic material is the syncopa which creates an organic musical unit within each two-bar segment.

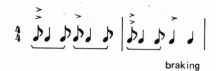

braking

The syncopated figure, starting on the main accent, and the braking rhythmic pattern heard on the secondary accent, change place () in the second half of the melody. The consequence of this is a rhythmic pulse of contrasting character in the motivic material.

2. Key structure of the composition:

1st formal unit			2nd formal unit		
D major	(B minor) ⟶	F# minor	E minor ⟶	(B minor) ⟶	D major
2# ⟶		3#	1# ⟶	2#	
		closed			closed

We find once again the well-known Baroque order of keys:

3. Suggested places for "d" change:

bar 4	8	15

t = m   d = r   m = l

Suggested further work: Epigrams/2

374

THEORETICAL INFORMATION AND THECHNICAL EXERCISES
Range of Notes, Hand-Signs

Pentatony

Note name singing to hand-signs

Practise with G and G♭ as "d". (Cf.: Chapter VI, page 41)

Diatony

Note name singing to hand-signs

Use the 1 sharp and 6 flat key signatures for this exercise. (Cf.: Chapter VI, page 41)

Diatony + alteration

Solfa singing from staff notation

The set of notes used for practising:
  a/ in the G clef:

b/ in the F clef:

Practise singing first the characteristic diminished fourth, augmented fifth, augmented sixth and diminished seventh intervals. (Cf.: Chapter IX, page 383)

Solfa – note name singing in answering form

Practise with 1 sharp or 6 flats as key signature (Cf.: Chapter VI, page 42) using the most difficult melodic patterns possible.

Singing to hand-signs with change of key

1. Practise the succession of keys at the distance of 1—6 fifths from each other using note names (Cf.: Chapter VII, page 154, Chapter VIII, page 262).
2. Sing also the seven-fifth change of key but only with solfa (see Chapter VIII, page 263).

For example, the progression of A major → A♭ major → A major:

d- s- l- f   ta - l - ta - l - s - m - s - t - d'
      fi - s - fi - s - l - fi - s - f - m - s - d'- t

A → (D)(A♭) ————————————————— (G) A
major   major   major

Keys and Modes

The pentatonic modes

With G and G♭ as "d"

Practise as in the previous chapters (for example, Chapter VI, page 44).

Combined singing exercises

1. Sing the same pentatonic mode from the notes of a given pentatonic system, in ⌒ direction, with solfa, in a continuous sequence.

For example, the "m" pentatonic mode from the pentatonic set of notes using G as "d":

a) starting notes:

b) preparatory exercise:

m s m   m s m   m ...   m ...   m ...   m ...   m ....   m .....   m ....

c) scale singing:

m s l d'r'm'r'd'l s m   m ...   m ...   m ...   m ...

2. Practise the exercise 1. in the opposite (⌣) direction.

For example, the "r" pentatonic mode from the pentatonic set of notes using F as "d":

a) starting notes:

b) preparatory exercise:

r d r   r d r   r ...   r ...   r ...   r ...   r ...   r ...   r ...

c) scale singing:

r'd' l s m r   m s l d' r'   r' ...   r' ...   r' ...   r' ...

Major and minor keys with one sharp or six flats

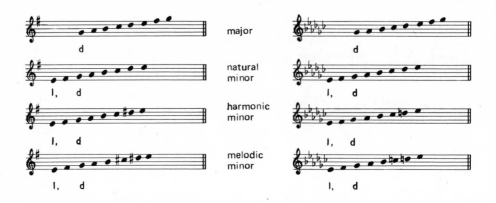

major

d

natural
minor

l,   d

harmonic
minor

l,   d

melodic
minor

l,   d

Forms of practising the minor

1. (M) Sing the natural, harmonic, and melodic E minor and E♭ minor keys in even ♪ metrical units and accompany this singing with the duple time-beating of the $\frac{5}{8}$ metre divided as 3+2.

For example, the different types of E minor:

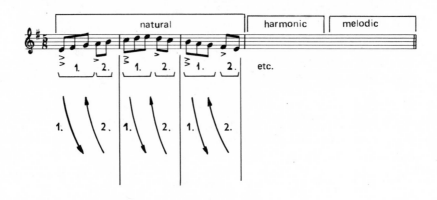

| natural | harmonic | melodic |

1. 2.   1. 2.   1. 2.   etc.

1.   2.   1.   2.   1.   2.

2. (M) Practise the above singing exercise accompanied by the duple time-beating of the $\frac{5}{8}$ metre divided as 2+3.

3. Combine the two kinds of $\frac{5}{8}$ time (3+2 and 2+3):

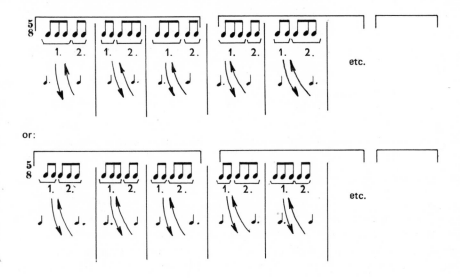

or:

Note finding exercises in major and harmonic minor

For all kinds of practice, use the following set of notes:

(Cf.: Chapter VI, page 46)

Church modes

1. (M) As with the other modes, sing also the locrian mode moving in sequence according to the fifth pillar. (See for example Chapter VI, page 47)

2. Practise note-finding singing from degree numbers now with note names.

For example, the degree numbers in order 1 4 7 3 VI 2 5 8 in the modes with C as keynote:

(Cf.: Chapter VIII, page 268)

Transformed singing

Transformation has been so far practised with diatonic melodies remaining in the same key. This chapter goes one step further in both respects. In some of the melodies we come across a change of diatonic church modes, in other cases the musical material sounds in the harmonic minor or the melodic minor system instead of diatony.

Themes changing mode

As Renaissance modality is present in the melodies below, transformed singing should be practised only with diatonic solfa names and with note names.

1052. KODÁLY: 66 TWO–PART EXERCISES. NO 49.

The melody starts in D mixolydian and ends in the relative A dorian. (See Chapter IX, page 359 for detailed analysis.) If we sing it, for example, beginning in the locrian mode, from B as starting note, it will sound as follows:

1053. KODÁLY: 66 TWO–PART EXERCISES. NO 44.

The melody unit touches the modes C aeolian → G phrygian → F dorian → C aeolian. (See Chapter VII, page 142 for detailed analysis.) If we sing it, for example, from A as starting note, beginning in the dorian mode, the modes will change as follows:

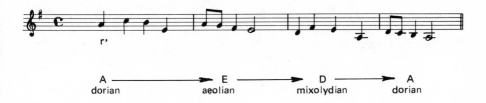

1054. KODÁLY: 77 TWO–PART EXERCISES. NO 59.

The theme starts in the mode with "l" as keynote and ends in the mode with "m" as keynote:

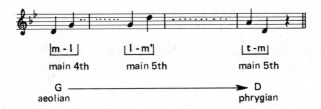

(Cf.: 66 Two-Part Exercises/44)
The melody starts again from D but now in the lydian mode:

Themes sounding in the harmonic and melodic minor system

Transformed singing of the melodies below should be practised within the framework of a given "d" system.

1055. KODÁLY: 22 TWO-PART EXERCISES. NO 5.

The principal structural tones:

The theme appears in the harmonic minor system using C as "d". Transformed singing will be carried out as follows:

1056. KODÁLY: 22 TWO-PART EXERCISES. NO 15.

This form of the theme appears last in the exercise. Its set of notes agrees exactly with the notes belonging to the melodic minor system using A as "d":

When singing with solfa we hear the final note "d" as the most natural melodic ending.

Transformation of the melody, for example, in the system with G as "d":

Diatonic themes remaining in the same tonality

Transform Nos. 1118, 1119 and 1125 from the sight-singing material in already familiar manner (see Chapter VII, page 159).

Intervals

New diminished and augmented intervals

Sing the following series as in Chapter VIII, with solfa only, starting on any desired pitch.

Diminished fourth

Downwards:

l, d si, l,   t, r li, t,   r f di r   m s ri m

Upwards:

d l,si, d l,   r t, li, r t,   f r di f r   s m ri s m

Augmented fifth

Upwards:

d l d si l   r t r li t   f r'f di'r'   s m's ri'm'

Augmented sixth

Upwards:

l' l ta si'l'   s' s lo fi's'   m' m f ri'm'   d' d ra t d'

Downwards:

l l' si'ta l   s s'fi'lo s   m m' ri'f m   d d't ra d

383

Diminished seventh

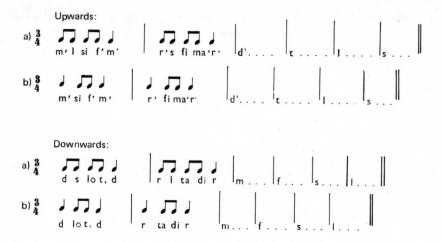

Upwards:

a) ¾   m' l si f' m' | r' s fi ma'r' | d'.... t ....l .... s ...

b) ¾   m' si f' m' | r' fi ma'r' | d'.... t ....l .... s ...

Downwards:

a) ¾   d s lo t, d | r l ta di r | m ... f ... s ... l ...

b) ¾   d lot, d | r ta di r | m... f... s.... l...

General revision exercises
with interval types of diatony

1. (M) Practise the interval types that occur within the set of notes used in the major key and remain within the framework of an octave (see Chapter II, page 130). Sing the intervals from the same starting note upwards and downwards with all the diatonic solfa possibilities: a/ starting with the smallest, b/ starting with the largest.

For example, in downward direction, starting with the largest from the pitch of B:

M7	m7	M6

etc.

t - d,   d - r.   m - s

m - f,   r - m.   r - f.

          f - s,   t - r

          s - l,   l - d

          l - t,

2. Sing each type of interval only once but starting always with a new solfa name:
a/ in increasing order, b/ in decreasing order, c/ in a previously set order.

For example, sing the succession of m3, dim5, m2, m7, p4, M7, p5, M2, m6, aug4, M6, M3 upwards, starting on D:

l₁-d t₋f m-f   r-d' m-l   d-t   l₁-m   f-s   m-d' f-t   r-t   d-m

3. Practise exercises in 2. above with note names as well.

Practising pairs of intervals changing direction

Sing the following interval progressions from any pitch, starting with all diatonic solfa names. (Use only fi, di, si, ri, li and ta, ma, lo, ra as alterations; see Chapter II, pages 114—115.)

Interval successions for practice:

1.

a)
m2	M2	m3	M3
m2	M2	m3	M3

b)
m2	M2	m3	M3
m2	M2	m3	M3

c)
M3	m3	M2	m2
M3	m3	M2	m2

d)
M3	m3	M2	m2
M3	m3	M2	m2

2.

a)
p4	a4	p5
p4	a4	p5

b)
p4	a4	p5
p4	a4	p5

c)
p5	d5	p4
p5	d5	p4

d)
p5	d5	p4
p5	d5	p4

3.

   a) ↑ m3 / ↓ m6   b) ↑ m6 / ↓ m3   c) ↑ m6 / ↓ m3   d) ↑ m3 / ↓ m6

4.

   a) ↑ M3 / ↓ M6   b) ↑ M3 / ↓ M6   c) ↑ M6 / ↓ M3   d) ↑ M3 / ↓ M6

5.

   a) ↑ m2 / ↓ m7   b) ↑ m2 / ↓ m7   c) ↑ m7 / ↓ m2   d) ↑ m2 / ↓ m7

6.

   a) ↑ M2 / ↓ M7   b) ↑ M7 / ↓ M2   c) ↑ M7 / ↓ M2   d) ↑ M2 / ↓ M7

The shorter sequences should be sung individually, one per student, but the longer ones have to be divided among several students.

For example, sequence 3.a/ performed by one person:

l - d' - l - di	m - s - m - si,
t - r' - t - ri	f - lo - f - l,
d - ma - d - m,	s - ta - s - t,
r - f - r - fi,	

or sequence 1.b/ performed by several students:

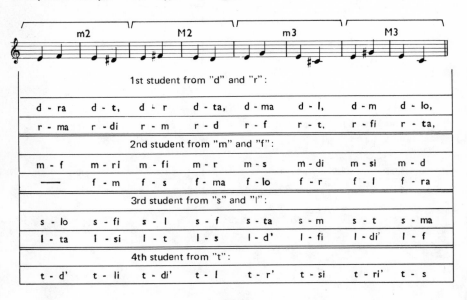

1st student from "d" and "r":							
d - ra	d - t,	d - r	d - ta,	d - ma	d - l,	d - m	d - lo,
r - ma	r - di	r - m	r - d	r - f	r - t,	r - fi	r - ta,
2nd student from "m" and "f":							
m - f	m - ri	m - fi	m - r	m - s	m - di	m - si	m - d
——	f - m	f - s	f - ma	f - lo	f - r	f - l	f - ra
3rd student from "s" and "l":							
s - lo	s - fi	s - l	s - f	s - ta	s - m	s - t	s - ma
l - ta	l - si	l - t	l - s	l - d'	l - fi	l - di'	l - f
4th student from "t":							
t - d'	t - li	t - di'	t - l	t - r'	t - si	t - ri'	t - s

Chords

Parallel chords in major

There is an important group of secondary dominants having an upward leading tone of which resolves to the V degree of the key. These secondary dominants originate in each case from chords of subdominant function — degree II or IV.

In the major key we also meet altered subdominant chords which contain a downward leading tone to the dominant: the  alteration instead of . This flatted note appears as the third of the IV degree, or as the fifth of the II degree and lends the given subdominant the colour of the parallel minor key.

Another characteristic altered chord in major is the VI degree taken from the parallel minor, used mainly in the chord pattern of the deceptive cadence (V → VI).

The most frequent parallel chords

Ways of practising

1. (M) Sing the above five chords with solfa, maintaining a constant given "d".

2. Choose one of these altered chords and sing it with solfa at different pitches, after sounding the tonic note "d".

3. Practise the exercises as described in 1. and 2. with solfa + note name singing in the major keys using 1—7 sharps and flats as key signature.

For example, exercise under 1. in A major:

tonic	IV degree	II degree	VI degree
	f - lo - d' lo - d'- f'	lo - d'- r'- f' d - r - f - lo	lo - d'- ma
	D - F - A F - A - D	F - A - B - D A - B - D - F	F - A - C

387

or exercise in 2. using the II^4_3 chord:

tonic | II^4_3 | tonic | II^4_3 | tonic
(piano) | (singing) | (piano) | (singing) | (piano)

D | lo, d r f | F | lo, d r f | E
major: | B♭ D E G | major: | D♭ F G B♭ | major:

Neapolitan sixth-chord

This is a characteristic altered chord of the minor key: the first inversion chord of the major triad built on the flatted second degree.
For example, in A minor:

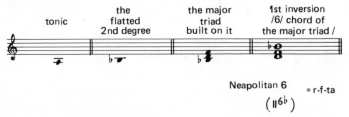

tonic | the flatted 2nd degree | the major triad built on it | 1st inversion /6/ chord of the major triad /

Neapolitan 6   = r-f-ta
($II^{6♭}$)

Suggested way of practising

Sing the Neapolitan 6-chord after sounding various tonic notes given on the piano
a/ with solfa, b/ with solfa + note names in the minor keys with 1—7 sharps or flats as key signature.
For example, exercise a/:

tonic | Neapolitan⁶ | tonic | Neapolitan⁶
(piano) | (singing) | (piano) | (singing)

G minor: | r - f - ta | B minor: | r - f - ta

Chords with augmented sixth

This is the most dynamic group of the altered subdominants as it contains both upward and downward leading tones moving to the dominant:

388

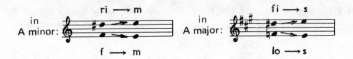

The two leading tones together bring about an augmented sixth interval, the extra-ordinary tension of which is resolved only when arriving at the dominant octave. There are three chords appearing within this augmented sixth range corresponding to each other in the parallel tonalities:

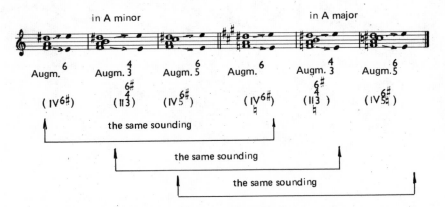

(The above-mentioned chords with the augmented sixth interval are known also as follows: Augmented 6-chord = Italian Sixth; Augmented $\frac{4}{3}$-chord = French Sixth; Augmented $\frac{6}{5}$-chord = German Sixth.)

Singing exercises

1. (M) Practise the outline-tones, then the three types of chords with solfa, both in the minor and major keys, after playing the tonic note:

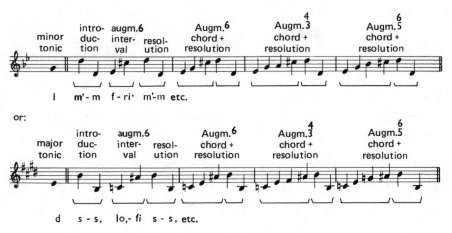

389

2. (M) Sing sequence 1. in the parallel (minore + maggiore) keys a/ first with note names and b/ only later with solfa.

For example, in the keys D minor — D major:

a/ With note names:

A - A   B♭- G♯- A - A   B♭- D - G♯- A - A   B♭- D - E - G♯- A - A   B♭- D - F - G♯- A - A

b/ With solfa:

in minor: m - m,   f, - ri   m - m,   f, - l, - ri   m - m,
in major: s - s,   lo, - fi   s - s,   lo, - d - fi   s - s,

Ninth-chords

Within functional harmony, the dominant seventh chord is often extended to a five-note chord: to the three consecutively built thirds one more is added. The fifth member of the chord is placed at a distance of a ninth from the root. Chords structured in this way are called ninth-chords. The dominant ninth in minor contains a minor ninth, in major a major ninth. In major, however, we often find the dominant with a minor ninth.

A minor: $V_{\sharp 7}^{9}$ C major: V_{7}^{9} or $V_{7}^{9\flat}$

The dominant ninth-chord contains three notes that require resolution: the leading tone resolves upwards, the seventh and ninth resolve downwards:

$V_{\sharp 7}^{9} \rightarrow I$

390

Thus the ninth chord most naturally resolves to the root position triad a fourth higher. Composers often use this chord pattern not only as the V—I progression of the original key, but as a secondary dominant → relative tonic relationship as well. The secondary dominant ninth-chord generally is found in root position. It comes into being by alteration, as do other secondary dominant chords (see Chapter VIII, page 277), and causes a momentary tonal deviation.

Ninth-chords in major

a) as main dominant:

b) as secondary dominant:

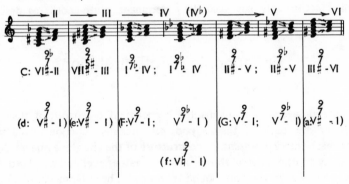

Ninth-chords in minor

a) as main dominant:

b) as secondary dominant.

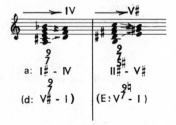

Ways of practising

1. (M) Sing the ninth-chords with their resolutions both in major and minor: a/ with solfa, b/ with solfa + note names in the keys with 1—7 sharps and flats as key signature.

For example, in minor, to solfa:

or in D major with solfa + note names:

s,-t;r-f - l   s-m-d   s,-t,-r-f-lo   s-m-d   l,-di-m-s-t   l-f-r

A-C♯E-G-B   A-F♯-D   A-C♯E-G-B♭   A-F♯-D   B-D♯F♯A-C   B-G-E

2. (M) Practise only the secondary dominant ninth-chords as described in 1.

Enharmonic re-interpretations

The diminished seventh and augmented $\frac{6}{5}$ chords, if taken out of their tonal surroundings, on the basis of their sound, can actually function in many different capacities: each interval present in the structure of the chord may be enharmonically substituted by another interval thus producing another, well-known chord with a new structure, even though the same sound is retained. The enharmonic re-interpretation is made convincing and authentic by the resolution of the chord in its new role.

Re-interpretation of the diminished seventh chord

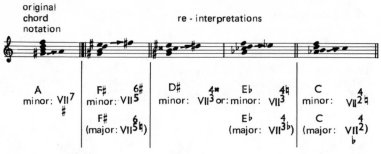

A similar enharmonic re-interpretation often occurs in the case of altered diminished seventh chords. (See Chapter VIII, pages 278 –279)

Re-interpretation of the augmented $\frac{6}{5}$ chord and the dominant seventh chord

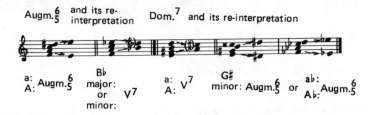

As with the dominant seventh, any secondary dominant may be re-interpreted. (See Chapter VIII, page 278–279)

Harmonic analysis

Practise as previously.

Musical quotations for harmonic analysis

1057. J.HAYDN: PIANO SONATA IN B FLAT MAJOR. I.

1058. J.S.BACH: O GROSSE LIEB', O LIEB'. CHORALE.

1059. J.HAYDN: PIANO SONATA IN F MAJOR. II.

1060. J.HAYDN: PIANO SONATA IN B FLAT MAJOR. II.

1061. MOZART: PIANO SONATA IN B FLAT MAJOR. II. (K.333)

1062. J.S.BACH: FRÖHLICH SOLL MEIN HERZE SPRINGEN. CHORALE.

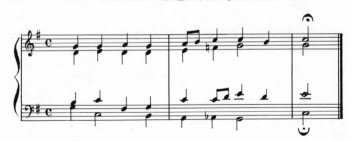

1063. MOZART: THE MAGIC FLUTE. II.

1064. MOZART: PIANO SONATA IN C MAJOR. III. (K.309)

1065. BEETHOVEN: PIANO SONATA IN G MAJOR. OP.14, NO 2. II.

1066. J.HAYDN: PIANO SONATA IN F MAJOR. I.

1067. J.S.BACH: LEIT' UNS MIT DEINER RECHTEN HAND. CHORALE.

397

1068. MOZART: IL SERAGLIO. III.

1069. MOZART: PIANO SONATA IN F MAJOR. III. (K.332)

1070. MOZART: THE MARRIAGE OF FIGARO. OVERTURE.

1071. BEETHOVEN: BAGATELLE IN A MINOR. OP.119, NO 9.

1072. MOZART: THE MAGIC FLUTE. II.

1073. MOZART: IL SERAGLIO. I.

1074. MOZART: THE MAGIC FLUTE. II.

1075. J.S.BACH: ACH GOTT, VOM HIMMEL SIEH' DAREIN. CHORALE.

1076. MOZART: PIANO SONATA IN F MAJOR. II. (K.280)

1077. BEETHOVEN: PIANO SONATA IN C SHARP MINOR. OP.27, NO 2. I.

1080. BEETHOVEN: PIANO SONATA IN F MINOR. OP.57. I.

1081. BEETHOVEN: PIANO SONATA IN C MAJOR. OP.53. I.

1082. MOZART: THE MAGIC FLUTE. II.

1083. J.S.BACH: LIEBSTER IMMANUEL, HERZOG DER FROMMEN. CHORALE.

1084. BEETHOVEN: PIANO SONATA IN C MINOR. OP.13. III.

1085. MOZART: PIANO SONATA IN D MAJOR. III. (K.284)

1086. J.HAYDN: PIANO SONATA IN F MAJOR. II.

1087. MOZART: THE MARRIAGE OF FIGARO. II.

1088. MOZART: IL SERAGLIO. II.

1089. J.S.BACH: ICH HAB' MEIN' SACH' GOTT HEIMGESTELLT. CHORALE.

1090. J.HAYDN: THE CREATION. II.

1091. BEETHOVEN: PIANO SONATA IN G MAJOR. OP.31, NO 1. I.

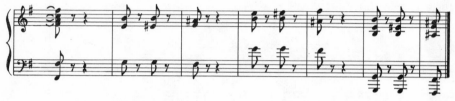

1092. MOZART: IL SERAGLIO. II.

1093. HANDEL: SERSE. II.

1094. BEETHOVEN: PIANO SONATA IN C MINOR. OP.53, I.

1095. J.S.BACH: BEFIEHL DU DEINE WEGE. CHORALE.

1096. MOZART: THE MAGIC FLUTE. II.

1097. MOZART: IL SERAGLIO. II.

1098. BEETHOVEN: PIANO SONATA IN C MINOR. OP. 13. II.

1099. BEETHOVEN: PIANO SONATA IN C MINOR. OP. 10, NO 1. III.

1100. J.S.BACH: WER NUR DEN LIEBEN GOTT LÄSST WALTEN. CHORALE.

1101. BEETHOVEN: PIANO SONATA IN G MAJOR. OP.14, NO 2. I.

1102. BEETHOVEN: PIANO SONATA IN E FLAT MAJOR. OP.7. II.

1103. BEETHOVEN: 32 VARIATIONS IN C MINOR.

1104. BEETHOVEN: PIANO SONATA IN F MINOR. OP.57. II.

1105. BEETHOVEN: PIANO CONCERTO IN C MINOR. OP.37. III.

1106. MOZART: IL SERAGLIO. II.

1107. MOZART: THE MAGIC FLUTE. II.

1108. J.HAYDN: PIANO SONATA IN F MAJOR. I.

411

1109. J.HAYDN: PIANO SONATA IN A FLAT MAJOR. I.

1110. J.HAYDN: PIANO SONATA IN G MAJOR. I.

1111. MOZART: PIANO SONATA IN C MAJOR. I. (K.279)

1112. MOZART: IL SERAGLIO. III.

SIGHT-SINGING

Unison Extracts from the Musical Literature

MATERIAL IN STAFF NOTATION

Melodies in pentatonic and church modes

1113. DEBUSSY: NUAGES. (OR.: 6♯)

1114. WAGNER: SIEGFRIED. II.
    a/ (OR.: 4♯)

    b/

1115. WAGNER: THE FLYING DUTCHMAN. II. (OR.: 2♭)

415

1116. BARTÓK: MICROCOSM V. NO 125.

1117. KODÁLY: TWO SONGS. OP.5, NO 2.

1118. MUSSORGSKY: BORIS GODUNOV. II. (OR.: 2♯)

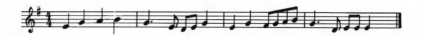

1119. BARTÓK: SECOND PIANO CONCERTO. I. (OR.: 1♭)

1120. HONEGGER: JEANNE D'ARC. VIII. (OR.: 0)

1121. BARTÓK: MICROCOSM. III. NO 77. (OR.: 1♭)

1122. BARTÓK: DON'T LEAVE ME.

1123. BARTÓK: BLUEBEARD'S CASTLE (OR.: 1♭)

1124. BARTÓK: 44 DUOS. NO 30.

1125. KODÁLY: MAROSSZÉK DANCES.

Major and minor melodies

Remaining in the same key signature

1126. HANDEL: MESSIAH. SINFONY.

1127. HANDEL: RODELINDA. I.

1128. J.S.BACH: THE ART OF FUGUE. (OR.: 1♭)

1129. LULLY: PSYCHE. II. (OR.: 2♭)

1130. J.HAYDN: FAREWELL SYMPHONY. NO 45, IN F SHARP MINOR. IV. (OR.: 3♯)

1131. J.HAYDN: THE SEASONS. III.

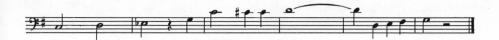

1132. LULLY: PSYCHE. PROLOGUE. (OR.: 0)

1133. HANDEL: TAMERLANO. I.

1134. MONTEVERDI: THE CORONATION OF POPPEA. II. (OR.: 2♭)

1135. HANDEL: TAMERLANO. II. (OR.: 0)

1136. MOZART: IL SERAGLIO. I. (OR.: 1♭)

1137. LULLY: PSYCHE. V. (OR.: 1♭)

1138. LULLY: PHAÉTON. II. (OR.: 3♭)

1139. HANDEL: TAMERLANO. I. (OR.: 2♯)

1140. VIVALDI: CELLO SONATA IN F MAJOR. (OR.: 2♭)

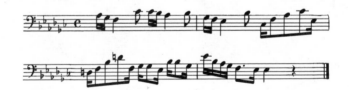

With "d" change

1141. J.HAYDN: STRING QUARTET IN C MAJOR. OP.76, NO 3.

1142. HANDEL: GIULIO CESARE. III. (OR.: 4♯)

1143. LULLY: PROSERPINE. PROLOGUE. (OR.: 1♭)

1144. HANDEL: TAMERLANO. II. (OR.: 0)

1145. CORELLI: VIOLIN SONATA IN B FLAT MAJOR. OP.5. (OR.: 1♭)

1146. LULLY: BELLÉROPHON. II. (OR.: 1♭)

421

1147. VIVALDI: CELLO SONATA IN E MINOR. (OR.: 1♯)

1148. LULLY: PSYCHE. III. (OR.: 1♭)

1149. BEETHOVEN: FIDELIO. I. (OR.: 0)

Suggested further material: Bach Collection I/13,30,32,33,36,154; 35,37,
44,49,50,51,53,57,59,66,67,78,80,106, 107,109,111,113,117,122,123,124,130,159,
161,166,168,180,186,187,196,207,208, 214,217,224,228,229,230,233,238.

EXTRACTS IN SOLFA NOTATION

The following extracts should be sung with note names, using the key signatures of one sharp or six flats, accompanied by beating time.

1150. HANDEL: SAMSON. II. (OR.: 2♯)

l, d t, l, t, m, l, r d t, d t, l, t, d r m r d r s, d r t, d

1151. HANDEL: SAUL. I. (OR.: 2♭)

m l, t, d r m d r m f m r t, d r m t, d l, r t, m m, l,

1152. H. PURCELL: THE HISTORY OF DIOCLESIAN. (OR.: 0)

m l, m f m l, t, si, m l, t, d d t, t, l, l,

1153. HANDEL: SAMSON. II. (OR.: 2♭)

d d d d m r d s, d m r d s, d m, f, s, d, d l, f, r, s, d,

1154. J.S.BACH: WACH' AUF, MEIN HERZ. CHORALE. (OR.: 2♭)

d d t, l, t, d r d d d r t, l, s, d t, t,

d d r m r r m f m r m r d d r r d d

1155. CORELLI: VIOLIN SONATA IN C MAJOR. OP.5. (OR.: 0)

m l, f si, l, t, d r t,m,m m l,r r d t, d t, l,

1156. H.PURCELL: HAIL! BRIGHT CECILIA. ODE. (OR.: 1♭)

d l, t, si, t,l, t,d r d t,d l, t, m, m l, t, d m, si, l, t, t, l, l,

1157. LULLY: PSYCHE. V. (OR.: 1♭)

m m r r d t, l,si, fi,m, d t, t, l, l,

1158. HANDEL: SERSE. I. (OR.: 1♯)

l, f m f f f m r d t,d d d l,ta, ta, l, si,l, t, si, f m r d t, l, l,

1159. RAMEAU: DARDANUS. II. (OR.: 0)

m r d t, l, r t, d l, si,l, t, d m, f, s, l, t, d l, r t, r r s d m

l, f f m r m f m m f m r d t, l, m m d d d t, t, t, t, d t, l,l, si, l,

1160. D.SCARLATTI: QUAL FARFALLETTA. (OR.: 0)

d t, m m, l, si, t, l, d t, d t, m m, l, si, l, t, d

r t, si, r f, m, m d t, l, t, l, si, l,

1161. HANDEL: DETTINGEN TE DEUM. (OR.: 2♯)

m, d ml,l,si,si, r si,m m, s, s,s,f,r r r r rfmr d t,l,si, l, l,

Material in Several Parts

1162. MORLEY: COME, LOVERS, FOLLOW ME. (OR.: 0)

1164. J.S.BACH: THREE–PART INVENTION IN D MINOR. (OR.:1♭)

1165. BANCHIERI: TRE VILLANELLE VEZZOSE E BELLE.(OR.: 1♭)

1166. J.S.BACH: NUN FREUT EUCH, LIEBEN CHRISTEN G'MEIN. CHORALE.

1168. J.S.BACH: NUN LASST UNS GOTT, DEM HERREN. CHORALE.

1169. BYRD: MASS FOR FOUR PARTS. SANCTUS. (OR.: 0)

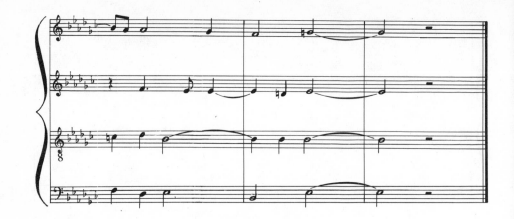

1170. J.S.BACH: UNS IST EIN KINDLEIN HEUT' GEBOR'N. CHORALE.

1171. LULLY: PHAÉTON. IV. (OR.: 2♭)

1172. J.S.BACH: NUN PREISET ALLE GOTTES BARMHERZIGKEIT. CHORALE.

1173. LULLY: PHAÉTON. IV. (OR.: 2♭)

1174. J.S.BACH: WAS GOTT THUT, DAS IST WOHLGETHAN. CHORALE.

1175. J.S.BACH: SINGT DEM HERREN EIN NEUES LIED. CHORALE.

438

439

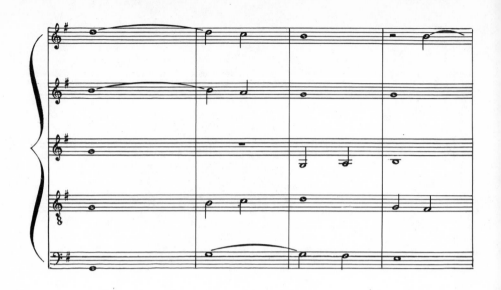

DEVELOPMENT OF MUSICAL MEMORY
Memorizing and Transposing
Two-Part Material

Practise the modulating excerpts as in Chapter VIII (see page 329).

The two-part extracts

1177. H.PURCELL: SONATA VII.

1178. J.S.BACH: THE ART OF FUGUE. (OR.: 1♭)

1179. J.S.BACH: ENGLISH SUITE IN E MINOR. PASSEPIED. I. (OR.: 0)

1180. HANDEL: THE MESSIAH. II. (OR.: 4♭)

1181. J.S.BACH: ENGLISH SUITE IN E MINOR. PRÉLUDE. (OR.: 1♯)

1182. HANDEL: FUGUE IN C MINOR. (OR.: 3♭)

1183. D.SCARLATTI: „SONATA" IN A MINOR. (OR.: 0)

Memorizing and Transposing
Three-Part Material

The following excerpts contain modulating musical material. As with the two-part quotations, it is again advisable to discuss "d" changes before the students begin individual work. The learning procedure is the same as previously (see Chapter VIII, page 331).

447

The three-part extracts

1184. MOZART: PIANO FUGUE IN G MINOR. (K.401)

1185. J.S.BACH: THE WELL–TAMPERED CLAVIER. II. FUGUE IN G SHARP MINOR.

1186. BEETHOVEN: MASS IN C MAJOR. OP.86. CREDO. (OR.: 0)

1187. BEETHOVEN: STRING QUARTET IN C SHARP MINOR. OP. 131. I.

1188. BOYCE: VOLUNTARY. (FOR ORGAN.) (OR.: 0)

1189. MOZART: REQUIEM. KYRIE.

1190. J.HAYDN: STRING QUARTET IN F MINOR. OP.20, NO 5. IV.

Memorizing and Transposing
Chord Progressions

In the figured bass successions given below, we find altered chords as well. When analysing the extracts, the sound-type and the resulting functional role of the altered chord must first be clearly understood by the students. They must also know to which group the altered chords belong: secondary dominant, chord with augmented sixth, chord taken from the parallel minor, etc.

The learning procedure is similar to that of Chapter VIII (see page 333).

Figured bass progressions

453

Memorizing Chorale Extracts

Practise and study as in Chapter VIII (see page 335).

1191. ALLEIN GOTT IN DER HÖH' SEI EHR'.

1192. ALLES IST AN GOTTES SEGEN.

1193. DU GROSSER SCHMERZENSMANN.

1194. GUTE NACHT, O WESEN.

1195. KOMM, HEILIGER GEIST, HERRE GOTT.

1196. HEUT' SCHLEUSST ER WIEDER AUF DIE TÜR.

1197. NUN LASST UNS GOTT, DEM HERREN.

1198. ICH STEH' AN DEINER KRIPPEN HIER.

1199. WAS GOTT THUT, DAS IST WOHLGETHAN.

1200. WER GOTT VERTRAUT, HAT WOHLGEBAUT.

EAR TRAINING
Recognition of Intervals

Pairs of intervals not derived from the triads

This type of interval recognition has already been practised in Chapter VIII (see page 340). Practise it now in the same way but shorten the sounding duration of the intervals.

Interval successions independent of tonality

We have already met this kind of ear-training exercise, as well, in Chapter VIII (see page 341). At that time, only intervals up to a sixth were used. In this chapter we include the seventh and ninth intervals in the series as well. The working procedure is the same.

The interval types of diatony from a given note

The teacher plays types of intervals smaller than an octave occuring within the major key in any order desired, starting upwards from a given note or downwards from a given note while the students write down the size and quality of the intervals. After checking, singing to re-inforce conscious knowledge is practised using interval names and note names. (Cf.: Chapter VIII, page 339, The interval types of pentatony from a given note.)

Diminished and augmented intervals

In the interval-singing exercises of Chapters VIII and IX all diminished and augmented intervals which appear in the melodic world of functional harmony were used (see Chapter VIII, page 272 and Chapter IX, page 383). Now, the recognition of the same intervals will be practised with the help of various types resolutions.

In the ear-training exercises, the students will hear pairs of intervals in which the first interval always has a diminished or augmented quality, and the second interval follows as a diatonic melodic resolution. Though the sound of the augmented or diminished interval agrees with the sound of another, enharmonically equivalent diatonic interval in all cases, its diminished or augmented function becomes apparent by the melodic movement as it resolves.

In the course of the ear-training exercise, the students have to establish the kinds of pairs of intervals they hear and sing them, after checking, with note names. The first task is to recognize the interval type of resolution. The students should compare the preceding diminished or augmented interval to this one.

There will be two types of resolution: either with two or one leading tones. In either case, the interval may have two possible resolutions.

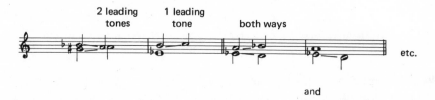

The working procedure is similar to that used in other exercises with intervals: 1. Recognition; 2. Checking; 3. Singing to re-inforce conscious knowledge.

The last stage, for example, sounds as follows in case of the above first two pairs of intervals:

Chord Recognition

Seventh chord and its inversions ($\frac{6}{5}, \frac{4}{3}, \frac{4}{2}$) from a given tone of the harmonic minor key

Continue practising as begun in Chapter VIII (see page 341).

Ninth chords within the major and minor tonality

After sounding the tonic note of the major or harmonic minor tonality the teacher plays root position ninth chords of different degrees within the chosen key giving also their functional resolution (see Chapter IX, page 390). The students write down the degree number of the ninth chord and its resolution and also establish the sound-type of the given ninth chord (i.e. whether it has a minor or a major ninth). The further procedure for the ear-training exercise is the same as that of the secondary dominant (see Chapter VIII, page 342).

For example, the successions $I^{7\flat}_{9}$–IV; $VII^{5\sharp}_{7}{}^{9}_{\sharp}$– III; $V^{7}{}^{9}$ – I in D major:

1. Recognition.

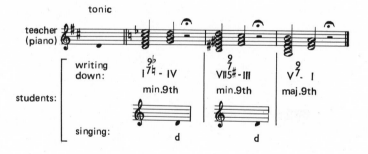

2. Checking.
3. Singing to re-inforce conscious knowledge.

Characteristic altered subdominant chords

While the teacher plays the different altered subdominant chords, as found in context of functional harmony, within an authentic cadence, the students a/ write down the name of the altered chord, b/ determine its degree number and inversion, c/ mark its altered tones with the appropriate accidentals. After checking, they sing the written chords with solfa then with note names.

The authentic cadence which contains the different altered subdominant chords should be that cadence type which is extended by the I^{6}_{4} chord: I^{8} * — altered subdominant — I^{6}_{4} — V — I. The framework remains the same, only the subdominant chord will change.

The altered subdominant chords that can be placed into this chord progression are the following:

a/ in minor:

sec. dom.	dim. 7	Neap. 6	Augm.6	Augm. $\frac{6}{5}$	Augm. $\frac{4}{3}$
$II\#^{\frac{6}{5}}_{\#}$ $II\#^{6}_{\#}$	$IV\#^{7}_{\#}$	II^{6b}	$IV^{6\#}$	$IV^{6\#}_{5}$	$II3^{\frac{6\#}{4}}$

b/ in major:

sec. dom.	dim. 7	half-dim.7	dim. 6	parallel chord	Augm. 6	Augm. $\frac{6}{5}$	Augm. $\frac{4}{3}$
$II^{\frac{6}{5}}_{\#}$ $II^{6}_{\#}$	$IV^{7b}_{\#}$	$IV^{7}_{\#}$	$IV^{6\#}$	IV^{b} IV^{6}_{b} $II3^{4}_{b}$	$IV^{6\#}_{b}$	$IV^{\frac{6\#}{5b}}$	$II3^{\frac{6\#}{4}}_{b}$

(See Chapter VIII, pages 276—282, and Chapter IX, pages 387—393)

---

* Four-part structure with root doubled in soprano.

Chord progressions

Recognition with the help of singing

Practise the figured bass progressions in Chapter IX (see page 451) as described on page 121 of Chapter VI. When identifying the chords, it is very important again to name the altered chords according to their sound-type as well (parallel chord; Neapolitan 6; Augmented 6-chord, etc.).

Recognition with the help of inner hearing

Use the figured bass progressions in Chapter VIII (see page 333) for this purpose, as described on page 227 of Chapter VII. The accidentals used when marking the degree numbers of altered chords should be written very accurately.

Chord analysis of quotations taken from the musical literature by ear

Choose appropriate quotations from the harmonic analysis material of Chapter VII (see page 170). Practise ear training as described in Chapter VIII (see page 343).

Rhythm Dictation

(Musical material on page 529 of the Supplement)

Melody Dictation

One-part dictation

(Musical material on page 533 of the Supplement)

Give the dictations according to the principles described in Chapters VII and VIII (see pages 228 and 344), always trying to adapt the given exercise in as many ways as possible to deepen and expand the level of skill.

Two-part dictation

Concentration on the vertical sounding

(Musical material on page 539 of the Supplement)

Practise as in Chapter VII (see page 228).

Concentration on the horizontal melodic movement

(Musical material on page 542 of the Supplement)

When dictating shorter excerpts, the working procedure containing the stages memorizing + singing + two-part performance + writing should be applied (see Chapter VI, page 124). The notation of longer extracts, however, should be done as two-part continuous writing.

The last quotations include more definite tonal deviations and even modulations. It is absolutely necessary to discuss the keys which are touched during the tonal deviation and the key of arrival of the modulation before starting to write down the quotations. The discussion should of course be based on the heard musical material. If the melody has a sequential structure, the students may sketch in some principle outline-tones which may be of help in following the momentary tonal deviations in the course of the melody.

Two- and three-part canons

(Musical material on page 546 of the Supplement)

Practise as described in Chapter VIII (see page 344). We can, however, add one more technique to the presentation of three-part canons: after two persons have performed the canon successfully, one person should perform in three parts, playing the first part on the piano, singing the second part with solfa and playing the third part on the piano again.

Bach Chorale Extracts

Two-part continuous writing of modulating
musical material completed by figured bass notation

(Musical material on page 548 of the Supplement)

The first stage of this task is the notation of the bass and the soprano parts with continuous writing as was practised in Chapter VIII (see page 345).

The next step is the notation of the chords. Since there is a modulation taking place in the musical material, there are minimally two—but possibly more—tonalities occuring in the single quotations. The two tonalities are linked by a diatonic or an altered common chord which plays a double role in the given succession: it is heard as a specific chord in the starting key, but, then becomes a chord performing a new role in the key of arrival. We must carry out the notation of these pivotal chords in such a way that their double role should be apparent from the notation.

For example, in the case of quotation No 1521:

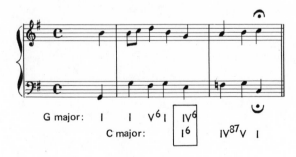

Suggested method for ear training

1. Write down the bass and soprano parts with continuous writing.
2. Check the written parts.
3. Discuss and notate the change of key after another hearing.
4. Write down the degree numbers and inversions, as well as mark the altered notes during subsequent hearings.
5. Group checking.

Two-part continuous writing
of modulating musical material

(Musical material on page 551 of the Supplement)

Dictate the material as in Chapter VIII (see page 345)

PLANNING SUGGESTION

(See the diagram at the end of the book)

SUPPLEMENT

MUSICAL MATERIAL
FOR EAR-TRAINING EXERCISES

CHAPTER VI

(See "Ear Training" and "Planning Suggestion" on pages 117—126.)

Rhythm Dictation

1201. MOZART: „SONATA FACILE" IN C MAJOR. III. (K.545)

1202. J.HAYDN: PIANO SONATA IN G MAJOR. III.

1203. BEETHOVEN: PIANO SONATA IN G MAJOR. OP.31, NO 1. I.

1204. MOZART: THE MAGIC FLUTE. II.

1205. HANDEL: RODELINDA. II.

1206. HANDEL: RODELINDA. I.

1207. J.S.BACH: TWO–PART INVENTION IN D MAJOR.

1208. MOZART: PIANO SONATA IN F MAJOR. I. (K.280)

1209. RAMEAU: DARDANUS. PROLOGUE.

1210. MOZART: PIANO SONATA IN D MAJOR. II. (K.284)

1211. MOZART: PIANO SONATA IN B FLAT MAJOR. I. (K.570)

1212. RAMEAU: DARDANUS. IV.

1213. HANDEL: SAMSON. I.

1214. HANDEL: SAMSON. II.

469

1215. MOZART: PIANO SONATA IN B FLAT MAJOR. III. (K.333)

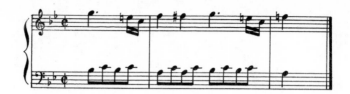

1216. MOZART: IL SERAGLIO. III.

1217. MOZART: RONDO IN F MAJOR. (K.494)

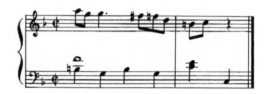

1218. MOZART: PIANO SONATA IN D MAJOR. III. (K.284)

Melody Dictation

One-part dictation

Melodies in pentatonic and church modes

1219. KODÁLY: CHILDREN'S DANCES. NO 6. (OR.: 1♭)

1220. BARTÓK: FOR CHILDREN. III. NO 9. (OR.: 2♭)

1221. KODÁLY: CHILDREN'S DANCES. NO 8. (OR.: 1♭)

1222. KODÁLY: CHILDREN'S DANCES. NO 7. (OR.: 1♭)

1223. BARTÓK: FIFTEEN HUNGARIAN PEASANT SONGS. NO 6. (OR.: 1♭)

1224. BARTÓK: 44 DUOS. NO 19.

1225. KODÁLY: CHILDREN'S DANCES. NO 11. (OR.: 1♯)

1226. BARTÓK: I SHOULDN'T HAVE SEEN YOU. CHORUS.

1227. CHOPIN: RONDEAU À LA MAZUR. OP.5. (OR.: 1♭)

1228. BARTÓK: MICROCOSM VI. NO 149.

Major and minor melodies

1229. HANDEL: SAMSON. I. (OR.: 3♯)

1230. J.S.BACH: THE WELL–TEMPERED CLAVIER. II. FUGUE IN E FLAT MAJOR.

1231. J.HAYDN: PIANO SONATA IN E FLAT MAJOR. III.

1232. BEETHOVEN: MOLLYS ABSCHIED. (OR.: 1#)

1233. J.HAYDN: MINUETTO IN G MAJOR. (OR.: 2♭)

1234. MOZART: THE MAGIC FLUTE. II. (OR.: 0)

1235. J.HAYDN: PIANO SONATA IN E FLAT MAJOR. III.

1236. MOZART: FUGUE FOR TWO PIANOS IN C MINOR. (K.426)

1237. MOZART: IL SERAGLIO. II. (OR.: 2♭)

1238. J.HAYDN: PIANO SONATA IN E MAJOR. III.

1239. MOZART: RONDO. (K.15ʰʰ) (OR.: 4♭)

Two-part dictation

Concentration on the vertical sounding

1240. MOZART: ALLEGRO. (OR.: 1♭)

1241. LASSUS: MOTET. (OR.: 1♭)

1242. MOZART: 12 DUOS. NO 1. (K.487) (OR.: 1♯)

477

1243. HANDEL: MENUET. (OR.: 1♭)

1244. LASSUS: QUI VULT VENIRE. MOTET. (OR.: 1♭)

1245. HANDEL: PIANO SUITE IN G MINOR. ALLEGRO. (OR.: 2♭)

1246. L.MOZART: BOURRÉE. (OR.: 1♭)

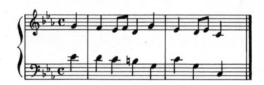

1247. LASSUS: QUI VULT VENIRE. MOTET. (OR.: 1♭)

1248. MOZART: MENUET. (K.1) (OR.: 0)

1249. LASSUS: SERVE BONE. MOTET. (OR.: 0)

1250. MOZART: MENUET. (K.1) (OR.: 1♯)

Concentration on the horizontal melodic movement

1251. MOZART: MENUET. (K.1) (OR.: 1♯)

1252. VIVALDI: VIOLIN SONATA IN D MINOR. (OR.: 1♭)

1253. HANDEL: FUGUE IN C MAJOR. (OR.: 0)

1254. LASSUS: MOTET. (OR.: 0)

1255. D.SCARLATTI: „SONATA" IN A MINOR. (OR.: 0)

1256. CLAUDE LE JEUNE: MA MIGNONNE. (OR.: 1♭)

1257. HANDEL: PIANO SUITE IN F MINOR. ALLEMANDE. (OR.: 4♭)

1258. J.S.BACH: THE WELL-TEMPERED CLAVIER. I. FUGUE IN A MAJOR. (OR.: 3♯)

Bach Chorale Extracts
Two-part continuous writing

1259. HERR, ICH DENK' AN JENE ZEIT.

1260. WOHL DEM, DER SICH AUF SEINEN GOTT.

1261. HERR, ICH DENK' AN JENE ZEIT.

1262. MEINEN JESUM LASS' ICH NICHT.

1263. ES IST DAS HEIL UNS KOMMEN HER.

1264. JESUM LASS ICH NICHT VON MIR.

1265. NICHT SO TRAURIG, NICHT SO SEHR.

1266. JESUM LASS ICH NICHT VON MIR.

1267. DA HERR CHRIST ZU TISCHE SASS.

1268. GIEB, DASS ICH THU' MIT FLEISS.

1269. WACHET AUF, RUFT UNS DIE STIMME.

1270. WIE SCHÖN LEUCHTET DER MORGENSTERN.

Memorizing and writing down the bass

1271. AUF, MEIN HERZ!

1272. O MENSCH, BEWEIN' DEIN SÜNDE GROSS.

1273. SCHWING' DICH AUF ZU DEINEM GOTT. (OR.: 1♭)

1274. IN MEINES HERZENS GRUNDE.

CHAPTER VII

(See "Ear Training" and "Planning Suggestion" on pages 223–230.)

Rhythm Dictation

1275. J.S.BACH: ST.MATTHEW PASSION. I.

1276. BEETHOVEN: STRING QUARTET IN E MINOR. OP.59, NO 2. I.

1277. MOZART: PIANO SONATA IN F MAJOR. III. (K.332)

1278. MOZART: PIANO SONATA IN D MAJOR. III. (K.284)

1279. HANDEL: SAMSON. I.

1280. HANDEL: SAMSON. I.

1281. VIVALDI: VIOLIN SONATA IN D MINOR.

1282. MOZART: PIANO SONATA IN B FLAT MAJOR. III. (K.570)

1283. HANDEL: SAMSON. I.

1284. HANDEL: RODELINDA. II.

1285. J.S.BACH: TWO-PART INVENTION IN E MAJOR.

1286. J.S.BACH: GOLDBERG-VARIATIONS. NO 4.

1287. HANDEL: SAMSON. I.

1288. HANDEL: RODELINDA. I.

1289. MOZART: IL SERAGLIO. III.

1290. MOZART: PIANO SONATA IN D MAJOR. III. (K.284)

1291. CACCINI: UDITE AMANTI.

1292. MOZART: RONDO IN F MAJOR. (K.494)

Melody Dictation

One-part dictation

Melodies in pentatonic and church modes

1293. KODÁLY: CHILDREN'S DANCES. NO 12. (OR.: 1♭)

1294. BARTÓK: 44 DUOS. NO 20. (OR.: 1♯)

1295. KODÁLY: CHILDREN'S DANCES. NO 10. (OR.: 1♯)

1296. BARTÓK: 44 DUOS. NO 37.

1297. BARTÓK: MICROCOSM. IV. NO 105. (OR.: 1♯)

1298. BARTÓK: FOR CHILDREN. III. NO 20. (OR.: 0)

1299. KODÁLY: CHILDREN'S DANCES. NO 4. (OR.: 1♭)

1300. BARTÓK: THIRD PIANO CONCERTO. III. (OR.: 5♯)

1301. CHOPIN: MAZURKA. OP.41, NO 1.

1302. BARTÓK: CONCERTO. V. (OR.: 7♭)

491

Major and minor melodies

1303. MOZART: COSÌ FAN TUTTE. II. (OR.: 2♯)

1304. HANDEL: FLUTE SONATA IN E MINOR. MENUET. (OR.: 0)

1305. BEETHOVEN: SEHNSUCHT. (OR.: 0)

1306. J.S.BACH: THE WELL-TEMPERED CLAVIER. I. FUGUE IN C SHARP MAJOR.
(OR.: 7♯)

1307. HANDEL: SAMSON. II. (OR.: 0)

1308. J.S.BACH: THE WELL-TEMPERED CLAVIER. II. FUGUE IN F SHARP MAJOR. (OR.: 6♯)

1309. MOZART: PIANO SONATA IN E FLAT MAJOR. I. (K.282) (OR.: 3♭)

1310. HANDEL: FLUTE SONATA IN E MINOR. ALLEGRO. (OR.: 1♯)

1311. HANDEL: JUDAS MACCABAEUS. I. (OR.: 0)

493

1312. J.S.BACH: THE WELL–TEMPERED CLAVIER. I. FUGUE IN F MINOR.

1313. J.S.BACH: BRANDENBURG CONCERTO. NO 1. II. (OR.: 1♭)

1314. HANDEL: FLUTE SONATA IN A MINOR. I. (OR.: 0)

1315. J.S.BACH: THE WELL–TEMPERED CLAVIER. I. FUGUE IN F SHARP MINOR.

Two-part dictation

Concentration on the vertical sounding

1316. TÜRK: ALLEGRO. (OR.: 2♯)

1317. MOZART: 12 DUOS. NO 5. (K.487) (OR.: 2♯)

1318. MOZART: 12 DUOS. NO 6. (K.487) (OR.: 2♯)

1319. MOZART: ALLEGRO. (OR.: 1♭)

1320. MOZART: CONTRADANCE. (K.587) (OR.: 0)

1321. LASSUS: MOTET. (OR.: 0)

1322. MOZART: MENUET. (OR.: 2♭)

1323. H.PURCELL: MENUET. (OR.: 1♭)

1324. CIMAROSA: SONATA IN G MINOR. (OR.: 2♭)

1325. BEETHOVEN: SONATINA IN G MAJOR. (OR.: 2♯)

1326. MOZART: ALLEGRO. (OR.: 2♭)

Concentration on the horizontal melodic movement

1327. J.S.BACH: THREE–PART INVENTION IN A MAJOR.

1328. TELEMANN: GAVOTTE. (OR.: 0)

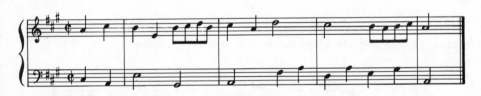

1329. HANDEL: FUGUE IN C MAJOR. (OR.: 0)

1330. J.S.BACH: ENGLISH SUITE IN A MAJOR. BOURRÉE. I.

1331. BEETHOVEN: 15 VARIATIONS IN E FLAT MAJOR. OP.35. (OR.: 3♭)

1332. MOZART: PIANO SONATA IN C MAJOR. I. (K.309) (OR.: 0)

1333. HANDEL: ISRAEL IN EGYPT. I. (OR.: 0)

1334. J.S.BACH: ENGLISH SUITE IN F MAJOR. MENUETTO. I. (OR.: 1♭)

1335. H.PURCELL: SONATA I. (OR.: 2♭)

1336. J.S.BACH: THREE-PART INVENTION IN C MINOR. (OR.: 3♭)

1337. HANDEL: PIANO SUITE IN G MINOR. ALLEGRO. (OR.: 2♭)

1338. J.S.BACH: SCHWINGT FREUDIG EUCH EMPOR. CANTATA. NO 36. (OR.: 2♯)

Bach Chorale Extracts

Two-part continuous writing

1339. O GROSSE LIEB', O LIEB'. (OR.: 2♭)

1340. WIE SICH EIN VATER ERBARMET.

1341. WIE WUNDERBARLICH IST DOCH DIESE STRAFE! (OR.: 2♯)

1342. WER NUR DEN LIEBEN GOTT LÄSST WALTEN. (OR.: 0)

1343. O GROSSE LIEB', O LIEB'. (OR.: 2♭)

1344. WER NUR DEN LIEBEN GOTT LÄSST WALTEN. (OR.: 0)

1345. WAS FRAG' ICH NACH DER WELT.

1346. O WELT, SIEH' HIER DEIN LEBEN.

1347. SEELENBRÄUTIGAM.

501

1348. SEID FROH, DIEWEIL.

1349. EIN KIND GEBORN ZU BETHLEHEM. (OR.: 0)

Memorizing and writing down the bass of modulating
musical material

1350. GOTTLOB, ES GEHT NUNMEHR ZU ENDE.

1351. ALS JESUS CHRISTUS IN DER NACHT.

1352. ER NAHM ALLES WOHL IN ACHT.

1353. WENN ICH IN ANGST UND NOTH.

1354. ICH BIN JA, HERR, IN DEINER MACHT.

1355. DEIN WILL' GESCHEH', HERR GOTT.

1356. DER ZEITLICHEN EHR' WILL ICH GERN ENTBEHR'N.

1357. CHRISTE, DU BEISTAND DEINER KREUZGEMEINDE.

CHAPTER VIII

(See "Ear Training" and "Planning Suggestion" on pages 339–346.)

Rhythm Dictation

1358. MOZART: PIANO SONATA IN D MAJOR. I. (K.284)

1359. VIVALDI: SINFONIA FOR STRINGS IN C MAJOR.

1360. MOZART: PIANO SONATA IN D MAJOR. I. (K.284)

1361. HANDEL: SAMSON. III.

1362. HANDEL: SAMSON. II.

1363. MOZART: THE MAGIC FLUTE. II.

1364. MOZART: PIANO SONATA IN C MAJOR. III. (K.309)

1365. MOZART: PIANO SONATA IN C MAJOR. III. (K.330)

1366. MOZART: PIANO SONATA IN D MAJOR. III. (K.576)

1367. MOZART: PIANO SONATA IN D MAJOR. III. (K.576)

1368. MOZART: PIANO SONATA IN C MAJOR. II. (K.309)

1369. MOZART: PIANO SONATA IN D MAJOR. II. (K.284)

1370. HANDEL: SAMSON. I.

1371. A.SCARLATTI: IO DISSI.

1372. HANDEL: SAMSON. I.

1373. A.SCARLATTI: IO DISSI.

1374. J.S.BACH: TWO-PART INVENTION IN E MAJOR.

1375. M.A.ROSSI: ANDANTINO ED ALLEGRO.

1376. MOZART: ALLEGRETTO. (K.15ª)

508

Melody Dictation
One-part dictation

Melodies in pentatonic and church modes

1378. PUCCINI: TURANDOT. II. (OR.: 1♭)

1379. KODÁLY: CHILDREN'S DANCES. NO 3. (OR.: 1♭)

1380. DVOŘÁK: SONATINA IN G MAJOR. OP.100. I. (OR.: 1♯)

1381. BARTÓK: FIFTEEN HUNGARIAN PEASANT SONGS. NO 8. (OR.: 1♭)

1382. KODÁLY: CHILDREN'S DANCES. NO 2. (OR.: 1♭)

1383. BARTÓK: MICROCOSM VI. NO 151. (OR.: 0)

1384. BARTÓK: DIVERTIMENTO. III. (OR.: 7♭)

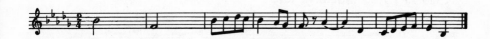

1385. CHOPIN: MAZURKA IN C MAJOR. OP. 24, NO 2. (OR.: 0)

1386. BARTÓK: SECOND SUITE. IV. (OR.: 3♭)

Major and minor melodies

1387. MOZART: COSÌ FAN TUTTE. I. (OR.: 1♯)

1388. MOZART: IL SERAGLIO. III. (OR.: 1♭)

1389. BEETHOVEN: PIANO SONATA IN A MAJOR. OP.101, III. (OR.: 0)

1390. MOZART: COSÌ FAN TUTTE. II. (OR.: 1 ♯)

1391. H.PURCELL: I ATTEMPT FROM LOVE'S SICKNESS TO FLY. (OR.: 1 ♯)

1392. MOZART: PIANO SONATA IN G MAJOR. III. (K.283)

1393. MOZART: THE MAGIC FLUTE. I. (OR.: 3♭)

1394. HANDEL: JUDAS MACCABAEUS. II. (OR.: 1♭)

1395. J.HAYDN: PIANO SONATA IN F MAJOR. III. (OR.: 1♭)

1396. MOZART: PIANO SONATA IN D MAJOR. III.(K.284)

1397. J.S.BACH: THE WELL-TEMPERED CLAVIER. I. FUGUE IN B MINOR.

Two-part dictation

Concentration on the vertical sounding

1398. J.S.BACH: MENUET. (OR.: 1♯)

1399. HANDEL: MENUET. (OR.: 1♭)

1400. J.S.BACH: MENUET. (OR.: 1♯).

515

1401. L.MOZART: MENUET. (OR.: 1♭)

1402. J.S.BACH: TWO-PART INVENTION IN C MAJOR. (OR.: 1♭)

1403. D.SCARLATTI: SONATA IN E MINOR. (OR.: 1♯)

1404. J.S.BACH: THE WELL-TEMPERED CLAVIER. II. PRELUDE IN B FLAT MINOR.

1405. J.S.BACH: TWO-PART INVENTION IN D MAJOR. (OR.: 3♯)

1406. BEETHOVEN: 6 EASY VARIATIONS IN F MAJOR. NO V. (OR.: 1♭)

1407. CHR. FR. BACH: MENUET.

1408. J.S.BACH: ENGLISH SUITE IN F MAJOR. GIGUE. (OR.: 1♭)

1409. J.S.BACH: ENGLISH SUITE IN A MINOR. PRELUDE. (OR.: 0)

Concentration on the horizontal melodic movement

1410. J.S.BACH: THE WELL–TEMPERED CLAVIER. II. PRELUDE IN B MINOR.

1411. BEETHOVEN: PIANO SONATA IN C MINOR. OP.13. III. (OR.: 4♭)

1412. MOZART: 12 DUOS. NO 11. (K.487) (OR.: 1♯)

1413. FESTA: GLORIA. (OR.: 1♭)

1414. J.HAYDN: PIANO SONATA IN A MAJOR. MENUET I. (OR.: 3♯)

1415. HANDEL: FLUTE SONATA IN B MINOR. ALLEGRO.

1416. J.S.BACH: THE WELL−TEMPERED CLAVIER. II. PRELUDE IN E MINOR. (OR.: 1♯)

1417. BEETHOVEN: 8 VARIATIONS IN F MAJOR. NO VIII. (OR.: 1♭)

1418. SWEELINCK: FANTASIA. (OR.: 1♭)

1419. JOSQUIN DES PRÉS: AVE MARIA. (OR.: 1♭)

1420. BEETHOVEN: STRING QUARTET IN C SHARP MINOR. OP.131. IV. (OR.: 3♯)

1421. H.PURCELL: SONATA X. (OR.: 3♯)

Two- and three-part canons

1422. FROM THE 18TH CENTURY.

1423. CHERUBINI

1424. HUNGARIAN FOLK-SONG CANON.

1425. CALDARA

1426. CALDARA

1427. ENGLISH CANON.

1428. CALDARA

1429. CALDARA

Bach Chorale Extracts

Two-part continuous writing
completed by figured bass notation

1430. FÜR DEINEN THRON TRET' ICH HIERMIT.

1431. AUF, MEIN HERZ!

1432. LOBT GOTT, IHR CHRISTEN ALLZUGLEICH.

1433. WAS MEIN GOTT WILL', DAS G'SCHEH' ALLZEIT.

1434. FÜR DEINEN THRON TRET' ICH HIERMIT.

1435. STÄRK' MICH MIT DEINEM FREUDENGEIST.

1436. NUN KOMM, DER HEIDEN HEILAND.

1437. DAS WORT SIE SOLLEN LASSEN STAHN.

1438. NUN KOMM, DER HEIDEN HEILAND.

1439. ALLE MENSCHEN MÜSSEN STERBEN.

1440. EINS IST NOTH, ACH HERR, DIES EINE.

1441. LIEBSTER IMMANUEL, HERZOG DER FROMMEN.

Two-part continuous writing of modulating musical material

1442. LOB SEI GOTT, DEM VATER.

1443. BEFIEHL DU DEINE WEGE.

1444. O HERRE GOTT, DEIN GÖTTLICH WORT.

1445. CHRISTUS, DER UNS SELIG MACHT.

1446. ACH GOTT UND HERR.

1447. ICH DANK' DIR, LIEBER HERRE.

CHAPTER IX

(See "Ear Training" and "Planning Suggestion" on pages 457—464.)

Rhythm Dictation

1448. MOZART: PIANO SONATA IN C MAJOR. II. (K.309)

1449. MOZART: PIANO SONATA IN D MAJOR. II. (K.576)

1450. MOZART: PIANO SONATA IN C MAJOR. II. (K.309)

1451. MOZART: PIANO SONATA IN D MAJOR. II. (K.284)

1452. MOZART: PIANO SONATA IN C MAJOR. II. (K.309)

1453. MOZART: THE MAGIC FLUTE. II.

1454. MOZART: PIANO SONATA IN C MAJOR. III. (K.309)

1455. MOZART: PIANO SONATA IN D MAJOR. III. (K.576)

1456. J.HAYDN: PIANO SONATA IN F MAJOR. I.

1457. MOZART: PIANO SONATA IN C MAJOR. I. (K.330)

1458. HANDEL: SAMSON. I.

1459. MOZART: PIANO SONATA IN B FLAT MAJOR. II. (K.281)

1460. J.S.BACH: TWO–PART INVENTION IN E MAJOR.

1461. A.SCARLATTI: IO DISSI.

1462. HANDEL: SERSE. I.

1463. A.SCARLATTI: IO DISSI.

1464. HANDEL: RODELINDA. I.

1465. M.A.ROSSI: ANDANTINO ED ALLEGRO.

1466. J.S.BACH: GOLDBERG VARIATIONS. NO 7.

1467. MOZART: PIANO SONATA IN A MAJOR. I. (K.331)

Melody Dictation

One-part dictation

Melodies in pentatonic and church modes

1468. KODÁLY: CHILDREN'S DANCES. NO 12. (OR.: 1♭)

1469. BARTÓK: FIFTEEN HUNGARIAN PEASANT SONGS. NO 2. (OR.: 0)

1470. BARTÓK: 44 DUOS. NO 6.

1471. RIMSKY-KORSAKOV: SADKO. IV.

1472. BARTÓK: 44 DUOS. NO 31. (OR.: 1♭)

1473. BARTÓK: MICROCOSM. IV. NO 100. (OR.: 0)

1474. BARTÓK: FOR CHILDREN. III. NO 17.

1475. BARTÓK: 44 DUOS. NO 33. (OR.: 1♭)

Major and minor melodies

1476. J.S.BACH: ENGLISH SUITE IN E MINOR. SARABANDE.

1477. MOZART: WALTZ. (K.536/2)

1478. H.PURCELL: SONATA I. (OR.: 2♭)

1479. J.S.BACH: ENGLISH SUITE IN E MINOR. GIGUE.

1480. MOZART: THE MARRIAGE OF FIGARO. II. (OR.: 2♭)

1481. J.S.BACH: THE WELL–TEMPERED CLAVIER. II. FUGUE IN E MINOR.

1482. J. HAYDN: PIANO SONATA IN E MINOR. III.

1483. J.S.BACH: THE MUSICAL OFFERING. CANON IN 4 PARTS. (OR.: 2♭)

1484. J.HAYDN: DRUM-ROLL SYMPHONY IN E FLAT MAJOR. NO 103. II. (OR.: 3♭)

1485. HANDEL: FLUTE SONATA IN A MINOR. I. (OR.: 0)

Two-part dictation

Concentration on the vertical sounding

1486. MOZART: PRESTO. (K.15¹¹) (OR.: 1♭)

1487. MOZART: MENUET. (K.1) (OR.: 0)

1488. MOZART: CONTRADANCE. (K.267/3) (OR.: 3♯)

1489. J.S.BACH: ENGLISH SUITE IN G MINOR. GAVOTTE I. (OR.: 2♭)

1490. J.S.BACH: THE WELL–TEMPERED CLAVIER. II. PRELUDE IN E MINOR.

1491. MENUET FROM THE 18TH CENTURY. (OR.: 0)

1492. J.S.BACH: ENGLISH SUITE IN G MINOR. GAVOTTE I. (OR.: 1♭)

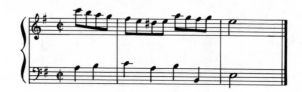

540

1493. MOZART: MENUET I. (K.6) (OR.: 0)

1494. MOZART: RONDO. (K.15^{hh}) (OR.: 1♭)

1495. J.S.BACH: ENGLISH SUITE IN F MAJOR. MENUET I. (OR.: 1♭)

1496. MOZART: 12 DUOS. NO 6. (K.487)

1497. BEETHOVEN: PIANO SONATA IN C MAJOR. OP.2, NO 3. III. (OR.: 0)

541

Concentration on the horizontal melodic movement

1498. MOZART: THE MAGIC FLUTE. II. (OR.: 0)

1499. MOZART: 12 DUOS. NO 2. (K.487) (OR.: 2♯)

1500. HANDEL: ISRAEL IN EGYPT. II. (OR.: 0)

1501. LASSUS: QUI VULT VENIRE. MOTET. (OR.: 1♭)

1502. J.S.BACH: CANTATA. NO 36. (OR.: 2♯)

1503. J.S.BACH: THREE-PART INVENTION IN D MAJOR. (OR.: 2♯)

1504. J.HAYDN: SURPRISE SYMPHONY IN G MAJOR. NO 94. I.

1505. J.S.BACH: ENGLISH SUITE IN A MAJOR. BOURRÉE II. (OR.: 1♭)

1506. J.S.BACH: ENGLISH SUITE IN A MAJOR. BOURRÉE II.

1507. MOZART: 12 DUOS. NO 6. (K.487) (OR.: 0)

1508. J.S.BACH: ENGLISH SUITE IN A MINOR. GIGUE.

1509. BEETHOVEN: PIANO SONATA IN B FLAT MAJOR. OP.106. I. (OR.: 3♭)

1510. J.S.BACH: ENGLISH SUITE IN A MINOR. GIGUE.

1511. HANDEL: PIANO SUITE IN E MINOR. GIGUE.

545

Two- and three-part canons

1512. SARTORIUS

1513. CHERUBINI

1514. CHERUBINI

1515. CALDARA

1516. PALESTRINA

1517. CALDARA

1518. PRAETORIUS

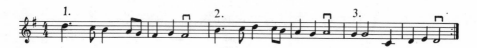

1519. CALDARA

1520. MOZART

547

Bach Chorale Extracts

Two-part continuous writing of modulating musical material completed by figured bass notation

1521. UNS IST EIN KINDLEIN HEUT' GEBOR'N.

1522. ERMUNTRE DICH, MEIN SCHWACHER GEIST.

1523. ICH HAB IN GOTTES HERZ UND SINN.

1524. DRUM WILL ICH, WEIL ICH LEBE.

1525. NUN PREISET ALLE GOTTES BARMHERZIGKEIT.

1526. GUTE NACHT, O WESEN.

1527. DIE NACHT IST KOMMEN.

1528. LOBT GOTT, IHR CHRISTEN ALLZUGLEICH.

1529. ES IST DAS HEIL UNS KOMMEN HER.

1530. DAS ALTE JAHR VERGANGEN IST.

1531. KOMM, O TOD, DU SCHLAFES BRUDER.

1532. UND OBGLEICH ALLE TEUFEL.

Two-part continuous writing of modulating
musical material

1533. ER NAHM ALLES WOHL IN ACHT.

1534. SOLL'S JA SO SEIN.

1535. FRÖHLICH SOLL MEIN HERZE SPRINGEN.

1536. ES STEH'N VOR GOTTES THRONE.

1537. ES WOLL' UNS GOTT GENÄDIG SEIN.

1538. ES IST GENUG; SO NIMM, HERR, MEINEN GEIST.

ACKNOWLEDGMENTS

The following copyright musical examples are included by kind permissions of the Publishers as shown:

BOOSEY AND HAWKES MUSIC PUBLISHERS LTD., LONDON:

(a) For all countries of the world: *Example or Page Nos.*
    Concerto for Orchestra: Bartók
      Movement I (bars 1—6) . . . .   Ex. 791
      Movement V (bars 201—211) . . . .   Ex. 810
                                    1302

    Divertimento: Bartók
      (bars 184—191) . . . .   Ex. 1384

    Don't leave me: Bartók
      (bars 1—12) . . . .   Ex. 1122

    Microcosm: Bartók

Volume I,	No 2.b.	(bars 1—8)	Ex. 571
Volume I,	No 7.	(bars 1—14)	Ex. 579
Volume I,	No 10.	(bars 1—4)	Ex. 565
Volume I,	No 15.	(bars 1—3)	Ex. 569
Volume I,	No 17.	(bars 13—16)	Ex. 570
Volume I,	No 24.	(bars 17—23)	Ex. 577
Volume II,	No 37.	(bars 1—3)	Ex. 573
Volume II,	No 43.a.	(bars 1—2)	Ex. 586
Volume II,	No 50.	(bars 16—18)	Ex. 587
Volume II,	No 53.	(bars 1—8)	Ex. 974
Volume II,	No 55.	(bars 2—9)	Ex. 585
Volume II,	No 55.	(bars 9—16)	Ex. 589
Volume II,	No 61.	(bars 4—15)	Ex. 971
Volume II,	No 62.	(bars 1—12)	Ex. 560
Volume II,	No 63.	(bars 12—16)	Ex. 590

Volume II, No 66   (bars 13—17,19—23) . . . . . .   Ex. 644
Volume III, No 70   (bars 1—8) . . . .   Ex. 798
Volume III, No 77   (bars 1—18) . . . .   Ex. 1121
Volume III, No 84   (bars 4—11) . . . .   Ex. 800
Volume III, No 87   (bars 21—23) . . . .   Ex. 568
Volume III, No 90   (bars 1—4) . . . .   Ex. 588
Volume III, No 94   (bars 1—5) . . . .   Ex. 729
Volume IV, No 100   (bars 1—10) . . . .   Ex. 1473
Volume IV, No 101   (bars 1—5) . . . .   Ex. 564
Volume IV, No 105   (bars 1—9) . . . .   Ex. 1297
Volume V, No 125   (bars 3—9) . . . .   Ex. 1116
Volume VI, No 149   (bars 4—7) . . . .   Ex. 1228
Volume VI, No 151   (bars 1—4) . . . .   Ex. 1383

Second Suite: Bartók
   Movement IV (bars 27—30) . . . .   Ex. 648
   Movement IV (6 bars) . . . .   Ex. 1386

3rd Piano Concerto: Bartók
   Movement III (bars 253—261) . . . .   Ex. 1300

Peter Grimes: Britten
   Act I   (2 bars) . . . .   Ex. 961
   Act II (2 bars) . . . .   Ex. 794
   Act III (3 bars) . . . .   Ex. 638

Quiet City: Copland
   (13 bars) . . . .   Ex. 813

Children's Dances: Kodály
   No 2 (bars 1—8) . . . .   Ex. 1382
   No 3 (bars 1—8) . . . .   Ex. 1379
   No 4 (bars 1—8) . . . .   Ex. 1299
   No 6 (bars 16—27) . . . .   Ex. 1219
   No 7 (bars 1—8) . . . .   Ex. 1222
   No 8 (bars 9—12) . . . .   Ex. 1221
   No 10 (bars 1—8) . . . .   Ex. 1295
   No 11 (bars 1—8) . . . .   Ex. 1225
   No 12 (bars 1—8) . . . .   Ex. 1468
   No 12 (bars 17—20) . . . .   Ex. 1293

Two Songs: Kodály
  No 1 (3 bars) . . . . Ex. 796
  No 2 (16 bars) . . . . Ex. 1117

Le Sacre du Printemps: Stravinsky
  (5 bars) . . . . Ex. 567

On Wenlock Edge: Vaughan Williams
  No 5. (4 bars) . . . . Ex. 964

(b) For all countries of the world except Hungary:

Let Us Sing Correctly: Kodály
  No 89 . . . . p. 239

Fifteen Two-Part Exercises: Kodály
  No 13 (bars 1—5) . . . . Ex. 730
  No 14 (bars 1—4) . . . . Ex. 735
  No 14 (bars 1—4, 5—8) . . . . p.   37

Peacock Variations: Kodály
  (bars 32—39) . . . . Ex. 801
  (bars 137—140) . . . . Ex. 641
  (bars 253—263) . . . . Ex. 967
  (bars 408—415, 424—431) . . . . Ex. 965

Rhymed Song for Children (Hippity Hoppity): Kodály
  (bars 5—8) . . . . Ex. 957

Treacherous Gleam (False Spring): Kodály
  (bars 6—9) . . . . Ex. 793
  (bars 26—33) . . . . Ex. 635

(c) For all countries of the world except Hungary, Roumania, Czechoslovakia, Poland,
  Bulgaria, the German People's Republic and Albania (for these countries: Editio
  Musica Budapest):

Bicinia Hungarica: Kodály
  Volume II   No 66. (bars 2—4) . . . . p. 40
  Volume III No 114. (bars 3—5) . . . . p. 32
  Volume IV   No 137. (bars 1—4) . . . . p. 29

77 Two-Part Exercises: Kodály

No 59 (bars 1—4) . . . . Ex. 1054
No 66 (bars 21—24) . . . . Ex. 885
No 67 (bars 1—3) . . . . Ex. 886
No 68 (bars 1—4) . . . . Ex. 888
No 69 (bars 1—4) . . . . Ex. 887
No 73 (bars 1—3) . . . . Ex. 890

66 Two-Part Exercises: Kodály

No 23 (bars 1—4,9—12,5—8,13—24) . . . . p. 33
No 25 (bars 1—4) . . . . Ex. 734
No 27 (bars 7—8) . . . . Ex. 719
No 28 (bars 1—4) . . . . Ex. 580
No 37 (bars 1—5) . . . . Ex. 894
No 40 (bars 1—5) . . . . p. 137
No 43 (bars 1—4) . . . . Ex. 891
No 44 (bars 1—2) . . . . Ex. 720
No 44 (bars 20—23) . . . . Ex. 1053
No 44 (bars 15—17) . . . . p. 145
No 47 (bars 1—7) . . . . Ex. 901
No 49 (bars 1—4) . . . . Ex. 892
No 49 (bars 1—4,12—15,5—8,16—19) . . . . p. 359
No 49 (bars 16—19) . . . . Ex. 1052
No 50 (bars 1—3) . . . . Ex. 893
No 51 (bars 1—4) . . . . p. 33
No 59 (bars 1—3) . . . . p. 250
No 61 (bars 1—8,9—16,27—30) . . . . p. 253
No 63 (bars 1—4) . . . . Ex. 895

55 Two-Part Exercise: Kodály

No 5 (bars 2—7) . . . . p. 134
No 20 (bars 1—5, 10—18) . . . . p. 135
No 21 (bars 1—5,6—10,14—17) . . . . p. 247
No 32 (bars 1—5) . . . . Ex. 899
No 34 (bars 20—28) . . . . p. 357
No 35 (bars 1—2) . . . . Ex. 722
No 38 (bars 1—4,5—8,29—32) . . . . p. 248
No 47 (bars 1—2) . . . . Ex. 723

44 Two-Part Exercises: Kodály
No 1 (bars 1—4) . . . . Ex. 896
No 10 (bars 1—4) . . . . Ex. 889
No 11 (bars 1—8) . . . . Ex. 898
No 13 (bars 1—4,5—8) . ` . . . . p. 362
No 19 (bars 1—4) . . . . p. 251

33 Two-Part Exercises: Kodály
No 1 (bars 1—5) . . . . p. 361
No 13 (bars 1—5) . . . . Ex. 900
No 20 (bars 1—4) . . . . Ex. 902
No 26 (bars 1—3) . . . . Ex. 897
No 27 (bars 1—4) . . . . p. 364

22 Two-Part Exercises: Kodály
No 3 (bars 1—2) . . . . Ex. 726
No 4 (bars 1—3,9—11,18—20) . . . .
No 5 (bars 1—2) . . . . Ex. 726
No 15 (bars 19—22) . . . . p. 366

Tricinia: Kodály
No 3 (bars 12—20) . . . . p. 147
No 7 (bars 2—8,9—15) . . . . p. 369
No 17 (bars 8—11) . . . . p. 257
No 24 (bars 1—4) . . . . p. 371
No 25 (bars 1—4) . . . . p. 372

Epigrams: Kodály
No 4 (bars 9—12) . . . . p. 151

(d) For all countries of the world except Hungary, Albania, Bulgaria, Czechoslovakia, the Chinese People's Republic, Poland, the German Democratic Republic, Roumania, the Soviet Union and Jugoslavia (for these countries: Editio Musica Budapest):

Pentatonic Music: Kodály
Volume I, No 34. (bars 4—6) . . . . p. 23
Volume III, No 66. (bars 1—4) . . . . p. 131

(e) For all countries of the world except Hungary, Roumania, Czechoslovakia, Poland, Bulgaria, the German People's Republic, Albania, the German Federal Republic and Austria (for these countries: Editio Musica Budapest):

For Children: Bartók
Volume III, No 9. (bars 1—7) . . . . Ex. 1220
Volume III, No 17. (bars 1—14) . . . . Ex. 1474
Volume III, No 20. (bars 1—8) . . . . Ex. 1298

UNIVERSAL EDITION A.G. WIEN:

(a) For all countries of the world:

      Psalmus Hungaricus: Kodály
        (bars 16—24) . . . . Ex. 973
        (bars 345—350) . . . . Ex. 628

      Marosszék Dances: Kodály
        (bars 74—81) . . . . Ex. 649
        (bars 181—196) . . . . Ex. 1125

      Cello Sonata Op.4.: Kodály
        Movement I, (bars 1—4) . . . . Ex. 975
        Movement II, (bars 1—4) . . . . Ex. 959

(b) For all countries of the world, except for the territory of the USA (for USA and its possessions: Boosey and Hawkes INC. 30 West 57th Street, New York, N.Y. 10019):

      44 Duos: Bartók
        No 12 (bars 1—7) . . . . Ex. 563
        No 20 (bars 8—19) . . . . Ex. 1294
        No 29 (bars 1—6) . . . . Ex. 584
        No 33 (bars 6—15) . . . . Ex. 1475
        No 36 (bars 5—8) . . . . Ex. 562
        No 41 (bars 1—8) . . . . Ex. 578

      Bluebeard's Castle: Bartók
        (5 bars) . . . . Ex. 963
        (7 bars) . . . . Ex. 646
        (14 bars) . . . . Ex. 1123

      Three Rondos: Bartók
        No 1. (bars 1—8) . . . . Ex. 731
        No 1. (bars 28—35) . . . . Ex. 581
        No 2. (bars 90—97) . . . . Ex. 583
        No 3. (bars 6—13) . . . . Ex. 727

      Cantata Profana: Bartók
        (bars 115—118) . . . . Ex. 639
        (bars 146—148) . . . . Ex. 642

2nd Piano Concerto: Bartók

    Movement I (bars 184—187) . . . . Ex. 803

    Movement I (bars 214—215) . . . . Ex. 1119

    Movement II (bars 1—5) . . . . Ex. 736

Fifteen Hungarian Peasant Songs: Bartók

    No 2. (bars 9—20) . . . . Ex. 1469

    No 6. (bars 1—4) . . . . Ex. 1223

    No 8. (bars 13—24) . . . . Ex. 1381

Dance Suite: Bartók

    Movement II (8 bars) . . . . Ex. 972

    Finale (8 bars) . . . . Ex. 807

(c) For all countries except Hungary:

    Jesus and the Traders: Kodály

    (bars 1—4) . . . . Ex. 632

    (bars 21—28) . . . . Ex. 643

EDITIO MUSICA BUDAPEST:

(a) For all countries of the world:

    Valsette: Kodály

    (bars 37—44) . . . . Ex. 802

    I shouldn't have seen you: Bartók

    (bars 1—8) . . . . Ex. 1226

    Pillow Dance: Bartók

    (bars 1—17) . . . . Ex. 811

    Hungarian Pictures: Bartók

    No 2 (bars 21—28) . . . . Ex. 976

    10 Easy Piano Pieces: Bartók

    No 3 (bars 1—5) . . . . Ex. 725

(b) For Hungary:

    Peacock Variations: Kodály

      (bars 32–39) . . . . Ex. 801

      (bars 137–140) . . . . Ex. 641

      (bars 253–263) . . . . Ex. 967

      (bars 408–415, 424–431) . . . . Ex. 965

    Rhymed Song for Children: Kodály

      (bars 5–8) . . . . Ex. 957

    Treacherous Gleam: Kodály

      (bars 6–9) . . . . Ex. 793

      (bars 26–33) . . . . Ex. 635

    Whitsuntide: Kodály

      (bars 109–116) . . . . Ex. 575

    Jesus and the Traders: Kodály

      (bars 1–4) . . . . Ex. 632

      (bars 21–28) . . . . Ex. 643

    Let Us Sing Correctly: Kodály

      No 89 . . . .

    Fifteen Two-Part Exercises: Kodály

      No 13 (bars 1–5) . . . . Ex. 730

      No 14 (bars 1–4) . . . . Ex. 735

      No 14 (bars 1–4, 5–8) . . . . p. 37

(c) For Hungary, Roumania, Czechoslovakia, Poland, Bulgaria, the German People's Republic and Albania:

    see page 557

(d) For Hungary, Albania, Bulgaria, Czechoslovakia, the Chinese People's Republic, Poland, the German Democratic Republic, Roumania, the Soviet Union and Jugoslavia:

    see page 559

OXFORD UNIVERSITY PRESS, LONDON:

For all countries of the world except Hungary:

    Whitsuntide: Kodály

      (bars 109–116) . . . . Ex. 575

B. SCHOTT'S SÖHNE MUSIKVERLAG, MAINZ:

44 Duos: Bartók

No 1 (bars 1–8)	Ex. 582
No 6 (bars 17–22)	Ex. 1470
No 9 (bars 9–16)	Ex. 572
No 14 (bars 13–20)	Ex. 576
No 19 (bars 8–12)	Ex. 1224
No 30 (bars 10–17)	Ex. 1124
No 31 (bars 1–8)	Ex. 1472
No 37 (bars 1–9)	Ex. 1296

ERNST EULENBURG, LEIPZIG:

Violin Concerto in A Minor: Glazunov

Allegro (8 bars)	Ex. 958

EDITION SALABERT, PARIS:

Sonatina for Violin and Cello: Honegger

(bars 1–10)	Ex. 812
	804

Jeanne d'Arc: Honegger

Scene VIII (bars 3–10)	Ex. 806
Scene VIII (6 bars)	Ex. 1120

G. RICORDI AND C. S. P. A., MILAN:

Turandot: Puccini

Act II (9 bars)	Ex. 633
Act II (8 bars)	Ex. 640
Act II (8 bars)	Ex. 1378

F. AND B. GOODWIN LTD., LONDON:

String Quartet in G Minor: Vaughan Williams

Movement II (bars 3–8)	Ex. 650

Responsible for publishing: The Director of Editio Musica Budapest.
Responsible Editor: Lilla Fantó. Technical Redactor: Veronika Izsák.
Technical Manager: Nándor Blaskó.
Z 60001
Published in 49,35 A/5 gatherings.
Printed in Hungary by Zeneműnyomda, Budapest.
Responsible Manager: Imre Kormány.

PLANNING SUGGESTION FOR CHAPTER VI.

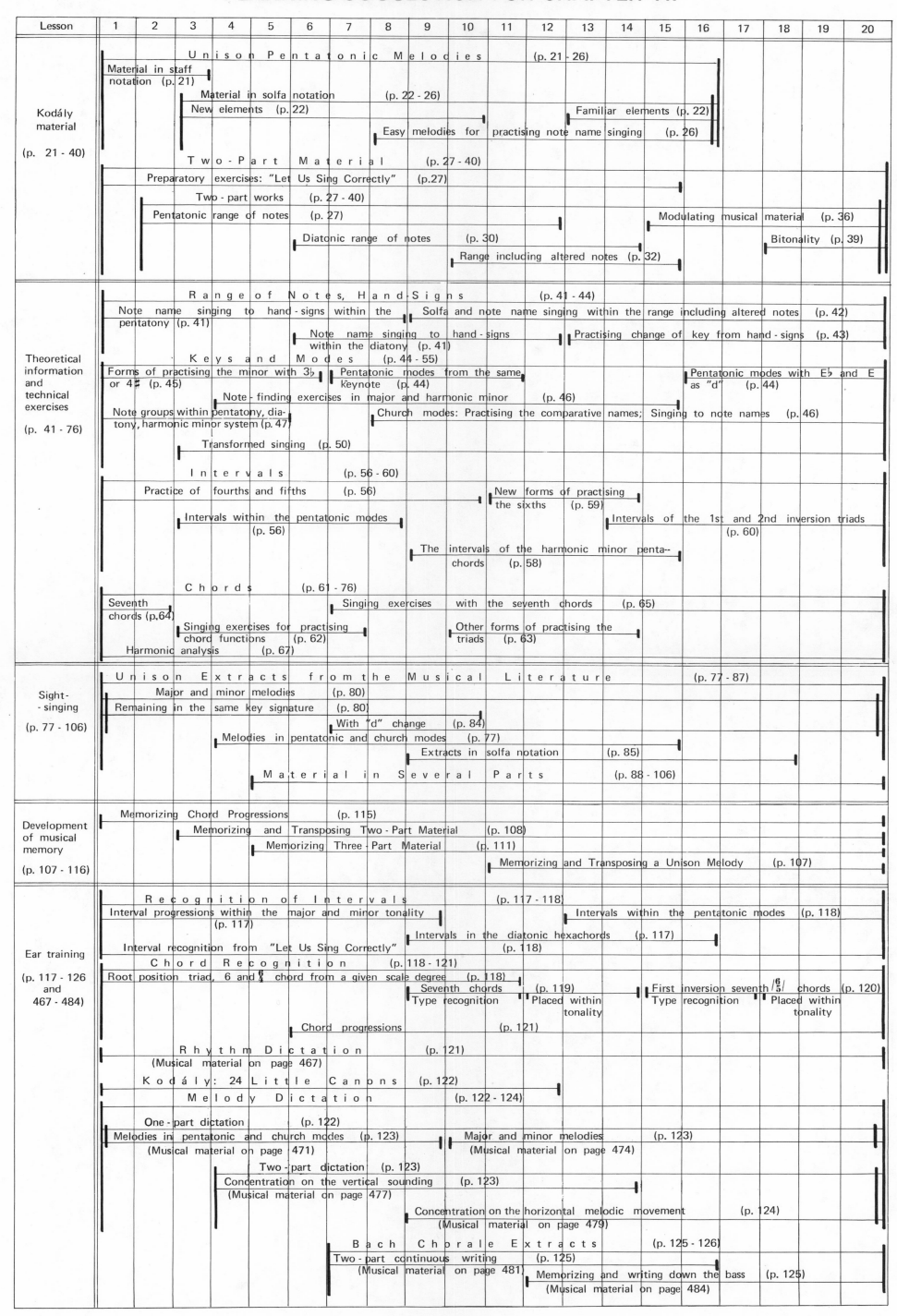

Lesson	1	2	3	4	5	6	7	8	9	10	11	12	13	14	15	16	17	18	19	20

Kodály material (p. 21 - 40)

- Unison Pentatonic Melodies (p. 21 - 26)
- Material in staff notation (p. 21)
- Material in solfa notation (p. 22 - 26)
- New elements (p. 22)
- Familiar elements (p. 22)
- Easy melodies for practising note name singing (p. 26)
- Two - Part Material (p. 27 - 40)
- Preparatory exercises: "Let Us Sing Correctly" (p.27)
- Two - part works (p. 27 - 40)
- Pentatonic range of notes (p. 27)
- Modulating musical material (p. 36)
- Diatonic range of notes (p. 30)
- Bitonality (p. 39)
- Range including altered notes (p. 32)

Theoretical information and technical exercises (p. 41 - 76)

- Range of Notes, Hand-Signs (p. 41 - 44)
- Note name singing to hand - signs within the pentatony (p. 41)
- Solfa and note name singing within the range including altered notes (p. 42)
- Note name singing to hand - signs within the diatony (p. 41)
- Practising change of key from hand - signs (p. 43)
- Keys and Modes (p. 44 - 55)
- Forms of practising the minor with 3♭ or 4♯ (p. 45)
- Pentatonic modes from the same keynote (p. 44)
- Pentatonic modes with E♭ and E as "d" (p. 44)
- Note - finding exercises in major and harmonic minor (p. 46)
- Note groups within pentatony, diatony, harmonic minor system (p. 47)
- Church modes: Practising the comparative names; Singing to note names (p. 46)
- Transformed singing (p. 50)
- Intervals (p. 56 - 60)
- Practice of fourths and fifths (p. 56)
- New forms of practising the sixths (p. 59)
- Intervals within the pentatonic modes (p. 56)
- Intervals of the 1st and 2nd inversion triads (p. 60)
- The intervals of the harmonic minor penta--chords (p. 58)
- Chords (p. 61 - 76)
- Seventh chords (p.64)
- Singing exercises with the seventh chords (p. 65)
- Singing exercises for practising chord functions (p. 62)
- Other forms of practising the triads (p. 63)
- Harmonic analysis (p. 67)

Sight-singing (p. 77 - 106)

- Unison Extracts from the Musical Literature (p. 77 - 87)
- Major and minor melodies (p. 80)
- Remaining in the same key signature (p. 80)
- With "d" change (p. 84)
- Melodies in pentatonic and church modes (p. 77)
- Extracts in solfa notation (p. 85)
- Material in Several Parts (p. 88 - 106)

Development of musical memory (p. 107 - 116)

- Memorizing Chord Progressions (p. 115)
- Memorizing and Transposing Two - Part Material (p. 108)
- Memorizing Three - Part Material (p. 111)
- Memorizing and Transposing a Unison Melody (p. 107)

Ear training (p. 117 - 126 and 467 - 484)

- Recognition of Intervals (p. 117 - 118)
- Interval progressions within the major and minor tonality (p. 117)
- Intervals within the pentatonic modes (p. 118)
- Interval recognition from "Let Us Sing Correctly"
- Intervals in the diatonic hexachords (p. 117)
- (p. 118)
- Chord Recognition (p. 118 - 121)
- Root position triad, 6 and 6/4 chord from a given scale degree (p. 118)
- Seventh chords (p. 119)
- First inversion seventh 6/5 chords (p. 120)
- Type recognition
- Placed within tonality
- Type recognition
- Placed within tonality
- Chord progressions (p. 121)
- Rhythm Dictation (p. 121)
- (Musical material on page 467)
- Kodály: 24 Little Canons (p. 122)
- Melody Dictation (p. 122 - 124)
- One - part dictation (p. 122)
- Melodies in pentatonic and church modes (p. 123)
- Major and minor melodies (p. 123)
- (Musical material on page 471)
- (Musical material on page 474)
- Two - part dictation (p. 123)
- Concentration on the vertical sounding (p. 123)
- (Musical material on page 477)
- Concentration on the horizontal melodic movement (p. 124)
- (Musical material on page 479)
- Bach Chorale Extracts (p. 125 - 126)
- Two - part continuous writing (p. 125)
- (Musical material on page 481)
- Memorizing and writing down the bass (p. 125)
- (Musical material on page 484)

PLANNING SUGGESTION FOR CHAPTER VII.

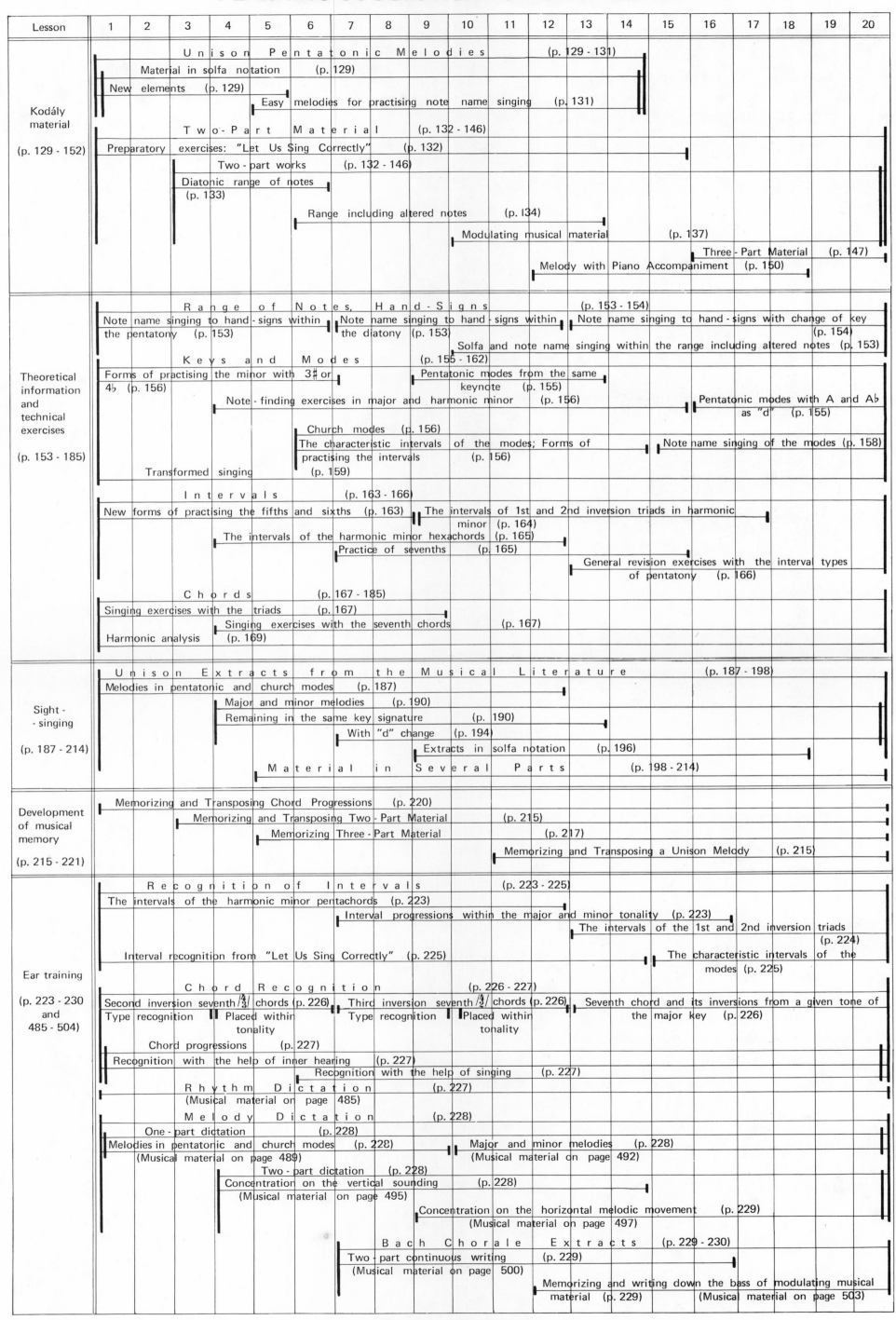

Lesson	1	2	3	4	5	6	7	8	9	10	11	12	13	14	15	16	17	18	19	20

Kodály material (p. 129 - 152)

Unison Pentatonic Melodies (p. 129 - 131)
Material in solfa notation (p. 129)
New elements (p. 129)
Easy melodies for practising note name singing (p. 131)
Two-Part Material (p. 132 - 146)
Preparatory exercises: "Let Us Sing Correctly" (p. 132)
Two-part works (p. 132 - 146)
Diatonic range of notes (p. 133)
Range including altered notes (p. 134)
Modulating musical material (p. 137)
Three-Part Material (p. 147)
Melody with Piano Accompaniment (p. 150)

Theoretical information and technical exercises (p. 153 - 185)

Range of Notes, Hand-Signs (p. 153 - 154)
Note name singing to hand-signs within the pentatony (p. 153)
Note name singing to hand-signs within the diatony (p. 153)
Note name singing to hand-signs with change of key (p. 154)
Solfa and note name singing within the range including altered notes (p. 153)
Keys and Modes (p. 155 - 162)
Forms of practising the minor with 3# or 4♭ (p. 156)
Pentatonic modes from the same keynote (p. 155)
Note-finding exercises in major and harmonic minor (p. 156)
Pentatonic modes with A and A♭ as "d" (p. 155)
Church modes (p. 156)
The characteristic intervals of the modes; Forms of practising the intervals (p. 156)
Note name singing of the modes (p. 158)
Transformed singing (p. 159)
Intervals (p. 163 - 166)
New forms of practising the fifths and sixths (p. 163)
The intervals of 1st and 2nd inversion triads in harmonic minor (p. 164)
The intervals of the harmonic minor hexachords (p. 165)
Practice of sevenths (p. 165)
General revision exercises with the interval types of pentatony (p. 166)
Chords (p. 167 - 185)
Singing exercises with the triads (p. 167)
Singing exercises with the seventh chords (p. 167)
Harmonic analysis (p. 169)

Sight-singing (p. 187 - 214)

Unison Extracts from the Musical Literature (p. 187 - 198)
Melodies in pentatonic and church modes (p. 187)
Major and minor melodies (p. 190)
Remaining in the same key signature (p. 190)
With "d" change (p. 194)
Extracts in solfa notation (p. 196)
Material in Several Parts (p. 198 - 214)

Development of musical memory (p. 215 - 221)

Memorizing and Transposing Chord Progressions (p. 220)
Memorizing and Transposing Two-Part Material (p. 215)
Memorizing Three-Part Material (p. 217)
Memorizing and Transposing a Unison Melody (p. 215)

Ear training (p. 223 - 230 and 485 - 504)

Recognition of Intervals (p. 223 - 225)
The intervals of the harmonic minor pentachords (p. 223)
Interval progressions within the major and minor tonality (p. 223)
The intervals of the 1st and 2nd inversion triads (p. 224)
Interval recognition from "Let Us Sing Correctly" (p. 225)
The characteristic intervals of the modes (p. 225)
Chord Recognition (p. 226 - 227)
Second inversion seventh $\frac{4}{3}$ chords (p. 226)
Type recognition — Placed within tonality
Third inversion seventh $\frac{4}{2}$ chords (p. 226)
Type recognition — Placed within tonality
Seventh chord and its inversions from a given tone of the major key (p. 226)
Chord progressions (p. 227)
Recognition with the help of inner hearing (p. 227)
Recognition with the help of singing (p. 227)
Rhythm Dictation (p. 227)
(Musical material on page 485)
Melody Dictation (p. 228)
One-part dictation (p. 228)
Melodies in pentatonic and church modes (p. 228)
(Musical material on page 489)
Major and minor melodies (p. 228)
(Musical material on page 492)
Two-part dictation (p. 228)
Concentration on the vertical sounding (p. 228)
(Musical material on page 495)
Concentration on the horizontal melodic movement (p. 229)
(Musical material on page 497)
Bach Chorale Extracts (p. 229 - 230)
Two-part continuous writing (p. 229)
(Musical material on page 500)
Memorizing and writing down the bass of modulating musical material (p. 229)
(Musical material on page 503)

PLANNING SUGGESTION FOR CHAPTER VIII.

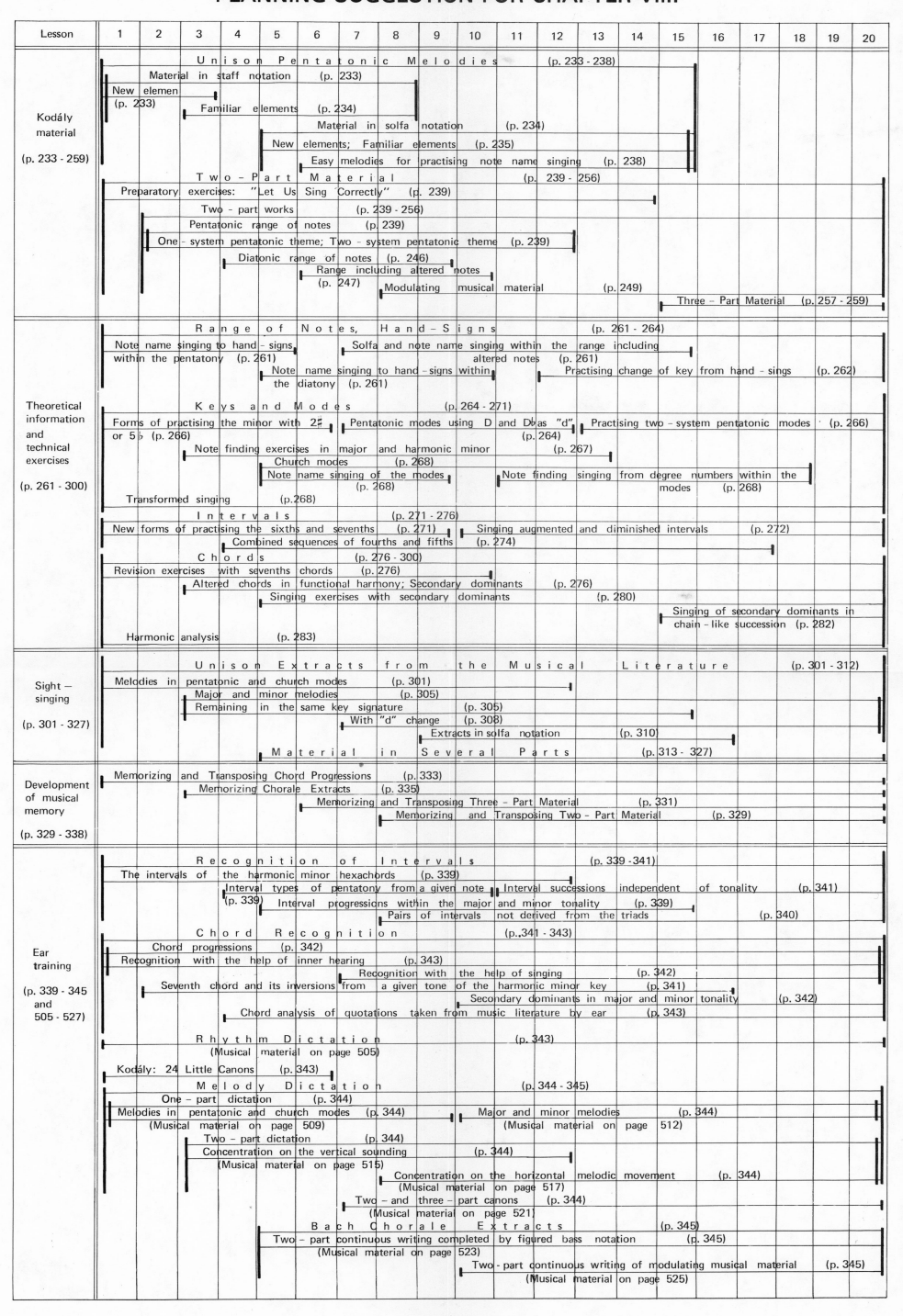